The Knowledge Entrepreneur

WITHDRAWN
UTSA LIBRARIES

Other books by Professor Colin Coulson-Thomas

(1992) *Creating the Global Company: Successful internationalisation*, McGraw-Hill, London

(1992) *Transforming the Company: Bridging the gap between management myth and corporate reality*, Kogan Page, London

(1993) *Creating Excellence in the Boardroom: A guide to shaping directorial competence and board effectiveness*, McGraw-Hill, London

(1993) *Developing Directors: Building an effective boardroom team*, McGraw-Hill, London

(1994, 1996) *Business Process Re-engineering: Myth and reality*, Kogan Page, London

(1995) *The Responsive Organisation: Re-engineering new patterns of work*, Policy Publications, Bedford

(1997, 1998) *The Future of the Organization: Achieving excellence through business transformation*, Kogan Page, London

(1999) *Developing a Corporate Learning Strategy: The key knowledge management challenge for the HR function*, Policy Publications, Bedford

(1999) *Individuals and Enterprise: Creating entrepreneurs for the new millennium through personal transformation*, Blackhall Publishing, Dublin

(2000) *The Information Entrepreneur: Changing requirements for corporate and individual success*, 3Com Active Business Unit, Winnersh

(2001) *Shaping Things to Come: Strategies for creating alternative enterprises*, Blackhall Publishing, Dublin

(2002) *Pricing for Profit: The critical success factors*, Policy Publications, Bedford

(2002) *Transforming the Company: Manage change, compete and win*, Kogan Page, London

All of these publications can be ordered from the bookshop of The Networking Firm: www.ntwkfirm.com/bookshop.

The Knowledge Entrepreneur

How your business can CREATE, MANAGE and PROFIT from intellectual capital

COLIN COULSON-THOMAS

KOGAN PAGE

London and Sterling, VA

First published in Great Britain and the United States in 2003 by Kogan Page
Limited

120 Pentonville Road   22883 Quicksilver Drive
London N1 9JN   Sterling VA 20166-2012
UK   USA
www.kogan-page.co.uk

© Colin Coulson-Thomas, 2003

The right of Colin Coulson-Thomas to be identified as the author of this work has been asserted by him in accordance with the Copyright, Designs and Patents Act 1988.

ISBN 0 7494 3946 7

British Library Cataloguing-in-Publication Data

A CIP record for this book is available from the British Library.

Library of Congress Cataloging-in-Publication Data

Coulson-Thomas, Colin.
    The knowledge entrepreneur : how your business can create, manage and profit from intellectual capital / Colin Coulson-Thomas.
        p. cm.
Includes bibliographical references and index.
    ISBN 0-7494-3946-7
    1. Knowledge management. 2. Information technology--Management. 3. Information technology--Economic aspects. 4. Intellectual capital. I. Title.
    HD30.2.C666 2003
    658.4'038--dc21

                        2003013318

Typeset by Jean Cussons Typesetting, Diss, Norfolk
Printed and bound in Great Britain by Biddles Ltd, Guildford
www.biddles.co.uk

To Yvette, Vivien and Trystan Coulson-Thomas

Contents

About the author   *xi*
Foreword   *xiii*
Acknowledgements   *xv*

1 **Entrepreneurship in the knowledge economy**   1
   Abundant and accessible information 1; Implications,
   impacts and consequences 3; Knowledge-based
   opportunities 6; The need for help 12; The knowledge
   entrepreneur 13; Aims and scope of book 18

2 **Managing knowledge and intellectual capital**   24
   Knowledge management 24; Loss of knowledge 26;
   Knowledge exploitation 31; Knowledge frameworks 35;
   Premium knowledge 38

3 **Corporate learning and knowledge creation**   43
   Knowledge creation 43; Knowledge as a flow rather
   than a stock 46; Knowledge and learning 48;
   Knowledge creation as a corporate priority 52;
   Protecting intellectual capital 65; Where knowledge
   entrepreneurs can help 66

4 **Contemporary information problems** 76
Information overload: winners and losers 76; Winning
and losing 78; The search for single solutions 80;
Taking certain approaches too far 83; Barking up the
wrong tree 87; Barriers to entry 89; Changing
organizations and emerging issues 92

5 **Requirements of different stakeholders** 97
Customers 97; Suppliers and business partners 99;
Investors 101; The contribution of boards 103; The
myth of inevitable progress 107; Supportive approaches
to management 109; Leadership for learning 112

6 **Creating enterprise cultures** 125
Becoming a player 125; Working with employers 127;
Organizing for entrepreneurship 128; Unity and
diversity 131; Ten essential freedoms 132

7 **Monitoring trends and the scope for knowledge** 147
entrepreneurship
Freedom of operation 147; Understanding issues and
implications 149; Effective issue monitoring 154;
Supporting wealth creation 157

8 **Identifying and assessing specific opportunities** 162
Establishing search criteria 162; Searching for
performance improvement opportunities 169;
Improving sales productivity 173; Job support tools
175; Benefits of using support tools 177

9 **Creating information- and knowledge-based offerings** 183
Packaging what you know 183; Building job support
tools 185; Lessons that can be learnt 188;
Differentiation 191

10 **Becoming a knowledge entrepreneur** 195
Entrepreneurial qualities 195; The knowledge
entrepreneur 198; Crossing the Rubicon 201; The
challenge of launching new products 202; Creating a
new product launch support tool 204; Advantages of a
product launch support tool 205; Using examples of
best practice 206

11 Getting started   **210**

Routes to entrepreneurship 210; Turning a hobby into a business 211; Selecting corporate partners 213; Creating a welcoming corporate environment 214; Creating communities of entrepreneurs 217; Organizing for learning and entrepreneurship 218; Public policy requirements 220

References   *229*
Further reading   *231*
Index   *235*

About the author

Professor Colin J Coulson-Thomas helps boards and entrepreneurial teams to create and exploit knowledge, differentiate their offerings and develop their businesses. He counsels individual directors and entrepreneurs and has advised over 70 boards on change and knowledge management, differentiation and corporate venturing, transformation and learning. A regular speaker at corporate events and international conferences, he has given some 300 presentations in over 20 countries.

An experienced businessman, Colin is currently Chairman of Cotoco Ltd, Adaptation Ltd and Policy Publications Ltd; Chairman of the Judges for the eBusiness Innovations Awards; and Professor of Competitiveness at the Centre for Competitiveness at Luton University. He leads the winning business research programme (see Appendix to Chapter 11) and reviews processes and practices for winning competitive bids, building customer relationships and managing change and knowledge. Colin is also a member of the Institute of Directors' Professional Standards Committee, Board of Examiners and Chartered Accreditation Board.

A Visiting Professor at the Management Development Institute, Delhi since 1997, he was Hooker Distinguished Visiting Professor at McMaster University, Canada in 1995; and Visiting Professor at East China University of Science and Technology, Shanghai in 1996. From

1994 to 1997 he was the Willmott Dixon Professor of Corporate Transformation, Dean of the Faculty of Management and Head of the Putteridge Bury campus at the University of Luton and a Senior Associate at the Judge Institute of Cambridge University.

Colin was Chairman of ASK Europe plc for nine years, a member of the Board of Moorfields Eye Hospital for 10 years and Deputy Chairman of the London Electricity Consultative Council for six years. He served two terms on the Council for Professions Supplementary to Medicine, nine years on the National Biological Standards Board, five years on the Council of the Foundation for Science and Technology and four years as Corporate Affairs Adviser to the British Institute of Management. He is a past Chairman of the Crossbencher Parliamentary Liaison Programme and a past Chairman and past President of the Focus Group.

Colin has served on the governing bodies of representative, professional, learned and voluntary institutes, societies and associations, including as chairman and president. He led the European Commission's COBRA initiative that examined business restructuring across Europe, and was the principal author and co-presenter of the 'employment and training' module of the CBI's European single market initiative.

Colin has led various change management, re-engineering and transformation projects and surveys of entrepreneurial and boardroom issues, attitudes and practice for the Institute of Directors, Chartered Management Institute, Chartered Institute of Personnel and Development, government departments and the NHS. Practical lessons derived from these surveys and his work with particular entrepreneurs and various boards are summarized in over 30 books and reports.

Colin was educated at the London School of Economics (Trevennon Exhibitioner), the London Business School, the EAESP – Fundacao Getulio Vargas (Brasilian Government Scholar), and the universities of Aston, Chicago (Deans List) and Southern California (Graduate School Distinction). He obtained first-place prizes in the final examination of three professions. He can be contacted by telephone: +44 (0) 1733 361149; fax: +44 (0) 1733 361459; www.ntwkfirm.com/colin.coulson-thomas; or e-mail: colinct@tiscali.co.uk.

Foreword

The industrial revolution has come and gone, and the developed nations of the world are now in the grip of the information revolution. Manufacturing is moving to places with cheap labour and raw materials, which leaves the developed nations unable to compete with, for example, the booming economies of the Far East. The edge which Europe and the US have in the global marketplace is less likely to be found in tangible products, but rather in the intangible assets of information, knowledge, creativity and ideas. How companies lever these assets to best effect determines how successful they will be in the future.

Having an asset, any asset, is no good unless you know how to use it. A factory full of machines is worth nothing if it is idle. The same is true of intellectual capital. Define it narrowly if you will as patents, trade marks, designs and copyright (collectively known as 'intellectual property', or IP), or define it broadly as encompassing goodwill, know-how and trade secrets as well. You may have a designer whose knowledge of your firm and products is so profound that she produces the best results time and again, faster than any external consultant. Can you put a value on that? What would it cost to replace that expertise if she suddenly left or was taken ill? Is not her unique skill-set a quantifiable asset?

To succeed you must maximise the potential of all your IP rights. A trademark is more than just a right to sue counterfeiters, but is in fact the bedrock of a brand. A patent is more than a licence to litigate, but is in fact a source of venture capital, a bargaining chip, licence revenue and a spoiler *versus* your competitor's later patents. Learn to trade in your knowledge and creativity – they will always be your strongest 'unique selling points' because no-one can be a genius quite like you.

Peter Lawrence
Director of IP Policy & Innovation
The Patent Office
July 2003

Acknowledgements

I would like to thank my colleagues at the Centre for Competitiveness at the University of Luton, Adaptation Ltd, Cotoco Ltd, Policy Publications Ltd and The Networking Firm; and also the team at Kogan Page for their encouragement and support. I am particularly appreciative of the suggestion of directors of 3Com UK that I revisit Adaptation Ltd checklists and look beyond information entrepreneurship at the broader question of creating, packaging and exploiting know-how; and of Don Fuller and the team at Cotoco Ltd for both inspiring a closer examination of how it can be used to improve workgroup productivity and transform corporate performance, and preparing the accompanying CD, which contains illustrative examples of knowledge-based job support tools the company has produced. The European Social Fund has helped to support the review process. I owe a special debt of gratitude to Susan Honeyborne and my parents Elsie and Joseph Coulson Thomas, and to Yvette, Vivien and Trystan Coulson-Thomas to whom this book is dedicated for their understanding during the many hours I spent writing it.

1

Entrepreneurship in the knowledge economy

ABUNDANT AND ACCESSIBLE INFORMATION

In recent years there has been a dramatic increase in the availability and accessibility of information. We live in the age of the Internet, the satellite dish, CD ROM discs and the Freedom of Information Act. It has become almost impossible to avoid exposure to various forms of information. We need to leave our mobile phones and portable computers at the entrance to a monastic quiet room to become 'stimulus free'.

Information and communications are all-pervasive. We see and hear them, sense their impacts and feel their vibrations. Many of us develop a love-hate relationship with the deluge of messages that never seems to leave us alone. Distractions are all around us from the moment we awake, rather like the air we breathe. People are even assailed by muffled sounds as they sleep.

Information travels along cables under land and sea, and through and around the walls of offices and homes. It is beamed through the ether – out into space and back again via satellite. Within seconds various forms of communication can reach more people than have died in most of human history. Audiences of hundreds of millions can share particular broadcast events.

Media companies and their moguls can get hold of unprecedented numbers of people 24 hours a day. We are spoilt for choice. The passive can become couch potatoes. The active can use search engines to identify quickly what is available. Popular Web sites attract millions of individual hits.

Enormous rewards accrue to those who can package their know-how or intellectual property in the form of best-selling books, recognized brands or chart-topping songs. Such superstars sell their services to the highest bidder, or take control of their own destinies by turning themselves into personality businesses and individual brands. Increasingly, they will only work for organizations that enhance their market value.

There are also adverse consequences or 'downsides'. Information is often persistent and can be very intrusive. Much of it is 'motivated' and essentially about the sender rather than the recipient. For example, marketing teams may be eager to expose us to their corporate and sales messages. People want us to visit their Web sites and react to information in ways that benefit them.

We have become targets. We are subjected to an increasing flow of information about events, activities and opportunities. Sales literature and junk mail drop through our letterboxes. Text messages accumulate on the mobile phones in our pockets. Ever more of the day is devoted to dealing with our e-mails, both welcome and unwelcome. Sometimes we feel jaded and we struggle to cope.

Additional information does not necessarily increase our understanding. As headcounts are reduced in order to save costs there are often fewer people on hand with expert knowledge to help us. Even specialists have difficulty keeping up with the latest developments. As a consequence, many of them and us feel insecure. We are confronted with options and developments we do not comprehend.

Many of the messages to which we are subjected are designed to secure a share of our wallet. However, other communications are designed for our benefit. Friends give us advice. Maybe we requested assistance on how to do something. Public bodies list and profile their services and issue warnings. Smart companies provide us with guidance and support. They help us to help ourselves.

The availability of water, grain, iron, steam and coal – or more accurately the knowledge of how to make beneficial use of them – gave rise to dramatic improvements in the quality of life. Information in its various forms reveals much about an age and is a core indicator of progress. It both denotes and enables contemporary civilization.

We should not forget that information about price levels and movements is the lifeblood of the economy. Markets cannot function without these vital indicators and signals. However, the mere availability of information can sometimes give a misleading impression. What is provided and its significance may not be understood. Comprehension, use and application usually determine its impact.

To a degree access to information has become democratized. Once, only people who belonged to particular institutions, or held certain jobs, could visit the locations at which information was stored. Many more people can now obtain the information and knowledge they need from others 'on demand' and in whatever formats make it easiest to understand and use. The CD ROM discs in a drawer may contain the files of many more periodicals than are available in the local college library.

Today much of the information that is available is equally attainable from almost any point on the globe to those who own or have the use of the relevant technologies. The owners of personal and laptop computers with a modem connection can reach a great wealth of information from home, car, aeroplane or boat via the Internet for the price of a local telephone call. Direct access is also possible while on the move via a growing range of portable palmtop and hand-held devices.

IMPLICATIONS, IMPACTS AND CONSEQUENCES

Information can now be ordered and delivered far more easily than either bread or milk. As a consequence profound social changes are occurring, and problem areas represent potential opportunities for the entrepreneurial. Those who are setting out to package and exploit information and knowledge need to be aware of the implications, impacts and consequences of their greater abundance and accessibility.

So much information is available for free that many people are increasingly reluctant to pay for it. Frequent Internet users may perceive books and reports as 'expensive'. Suppliers of information services find themselves competing with gratis alternatives.

At the same time, other people find it increasingly difficult to penetrate the sheer volume of what is available and locate precisely what they want. The original sources and quality of the many alternative Web sites may not be immediately apparent. This creates new opportunities for providers of search engines, screening facilities, bespoke research and intelligent monitoring.

The standing of many individuals whose status used to depend upon the possession of scarce information has been eroded. Having 'in one's head' knowledge that has become widely available may attract little interest. Whereas once people might have been impressed with the reciting of facts and the recall of detail they now say 'so what?'. Relational and other interpersonal skills are regarded as much more important than being knowledgeable.

In many organizations in-depth expertise has become rare. Yet, competitive advantage goes to those who move beyond the 'basic level of provision' and can quickly critique, assemble, develop and deploy whatever information and knowledge is available to do something interesting, better or different.

Simply providing greater access to information and knowledge is not enough. Smart companies understand that information and experience are usually needed to create knowledge, while expertise is generally the product of not just knowledge but also the skills and tools to apply it. Understanding how 'experts' do certain things extremely well needs to be captured in ways that allow others to improve their performance. When all competitors can recruit from the same pool of potential employees the winners will be those that use the most effective job support tools.

It sometimes seems that an inverse law is in operation. The more effort that is devoted to 'knowledge management', re-engineering processes, the creation of corporate repositories of knowledge and the establishment of call centres, the less chance there seems to be of encountering anyone who appears to know much about anything. One or two supplementary questions are often all that are needed to trigger a transfer to a 'supervisor' who may suggest looking it up on a Web site. While huge amounts of management time and consultancy effort have been devoted to making people less capable, there are many cost-effective ways of boosting their performance.

Academics and scientists who do endeavour to remain current with a particular field of knowledge face pressures to become ever more specialized as the volume of new research findings grows at exponential rates. Specialist professionals and 'techies' find it difficult to communicate with other than a small peer group. Those who are unfamiliar with the latest jargon are excluded. Such understanding gaps represent rich arenas of opportunity for knowledge entrepreneurs.

Most people giving elevator pitches to possible financiers or potential customers struggle to no avail to explain the essence of what they are about and summarize what is different about their particular approach, offerings or technology. Many high-tech businesses find it very difficult to communicate what they do. Yet the smart use of animation and graphics within support tools can quickly transform understanding.

Flexible patterns of 'location-independent' work and network models of organizations as portfolios of relationships have emerged. People no longer need to travel to distant locations to obtain the basic information they need to do their work. They can be linked together and can teleconference and telework. But in many organizations much better ways need to be found to share information, knowledge and understanding among the geographically scattered members of virtual teams that result.

Tasks and related support tools can now be sent to individual knowledge workers where once they travelled to work. Physical interaction may still be needed to stimulate creativity and build team spirit but more time can now be spent in different places. And there are cost-effective ways of providing stimulating electronic workspaces. Ultimately, the impacts upon transportation and the physical and social geography of city centres and suburbs will be profound as neighbourhoods serve different purposes and reinvent themselves.

The information revolution is also affecting education. There is a greater diversity of provision than there used to be. Distance and life-long learning are more widespread. Applications of learning technologies can tailor both content and pedagogical approach to the needs of an individual learner. So much material is often available that the emphasis can shift from the memorization of facts and the 'personal ownership' of information and knowledge to its effective use. However, in many cases understanding would benefit from an institutional ability to handle a wider range of formats than text and simple graphics.

Governments have set ambitious targets for the online delivery of public services. Many areas such as healthcare and social services could be transformed. For example, as 'evidence-based medicine' spreads, the clinical decisions of individual doctors need no longer remain dependent upon their own personal experience of cases. Support tools can capture best practice and enable them to draw upon the collective experience of their peers when making a diagnosis of an unfamiliar condition and suggesting a course of treatment.

Remote diagnosis, monitoring and support could enable more people to be treated at home. A knowledge framework such as K-frame (www.K-frame.com) can be used to assemble interactive information and guidance quickly in a variety of formats from animation and visual images to video and audio material that would allow individuals to assess their condition and identify when and where a general practitioner or other specialist intervention might be required. Regularly updated CD ROM discs or Web sites can incorporate e-mail links to suitable sources of assistance, and requests for help could be accompanied by the results of any self-assessment that has been undertaken.

KNOWLEDGE-BASED OPPORTUNITIES

Profound economic restructuring is occurring as knowledge-based sectors grow in importance. A steadily rising proportion of wealth and the value of commercial transactions is accounted for by the knowledge component of goods and services, while the relative contribution of physical resources falls. End products depend upon many different forms of intelligence, the exercise of which has to be stimulated and the results captured and shared.

Improvement and entertainment – both based upon the selection, packaging and communication of information in a variety of formats – are growth industries. Creative talents are also at work in many laboratories and workshops. Breakthroughs are occurring in a variety of scientific fields. However, to exploit developments in areas such as materials science, users need to understand how intelligent coatings and other possibilities work and might benefit them.

Emerging industries such as genetic engineering are based upon specialist arenas of knowledge. However, before the genetic code can be manipulated it must also be understood. The scale of the communications challenge if misunderstandings are to be avoided and public concerns alleviated creates further opportunities for knowledge entrepreneurs.

Technological developments and changing practices in purchasing and outsourcing, and new ways of working and learning are enabling people, companies and societies to overcome many of the traditional barriers of function, organization, distance and time. They are opening up access to relevant information, knowledge, skills and other capabilities and creating new requirements for communication and comprehension.

Examples of information- and knowledge-based businesses

There are many opportunities for establishing information- and knowledge-based businesses within the global marketplace. Large corporations, small enterprises, individuals, communities and even families can all participate. The following are but a selection of the many commercial knowledge-based offerings that have been successfully launched by enterprising individuals:

- *Personal support services for busy people.* These could range from knowledge search or research assistance and screening, reviewing, analysing and categorizing incoming e-mail, to preparing draft responses and suggesting standard replies.
- *Preparation of presentations, proposals and reports.* Support provided can range from the writing of speeches and origination of slides to formatting material and the preparation of graphics. Some people may want help in preparing content while others will be concerned that the subject matter they provide is attractively laid out and effectively displayed.
- *Online information services and electronic publishing.* The Internet can be used to distribute electronic newsletters and updates to a subscriber base. Self-publishing provides a direct route to a self-selecting audience.
- *Direct provision of packaged intellectual property.* Products as varied as music, games, animations, support tools and software can be downloaded from a Web site via the Internet.
- *Electronic publishing.* There are still many opportunities. Particular packages of information, knowledge and understanding can be licensed for internal corporate use or external dissemination to the members of a network or community. These can range from a prospects list or user base to alumni and subscribers to a trade association.
- *Customized information and research services for particular individuals and groups.* Intelligent search engines will only go so far in tracking down developments that people really want to know about. The information or knowledge sought may be relatively obscure but potentially extremely important to those concerned.
- *Various forms of back-up, stand-in and administration services for professionals and knowledge workers.* These could include permanent call forwarding and response services, periodic specialist help and the temporary provision of practice cover during illness, annual and public holidays or periods of peak workload.
- *The capture, storage in accessible form and management of different categories of knowledge that exist in a variety of formats.* A knowledge framework such as K-frame (www.K-

frame.com) could be used for this purpose. Many corporate repositories find it difficult to handle visual images, audio and video material and animations.

- *Knowledge-related counselling, mentoring and support to those seeking to become better informed and more aware of particular topics.* People also sometimes need help in understanding how different areas of knowledge relate to each other.
- *Support from an electronic tutor or counsellor.* Use can be made of mobile technologies to bring people into contact with each other as and when required. Having access to someone who is willing to act as an adviser or sounding board can be immensely valuable.
- *The provision of a personal coach who can address particular learning problems, understanding blockages or undesirable behavioural characteristics that a person might have.* A one-to-one service can be tailored and bespoke.
- *Shared learning services.* Groups of peers with similar responsibilities and problems can be brought together to form a shared learning network of people who are prepared to learn from each other. A range of support services could be provided to such groups.
- *Technical, financial and other forms of advice that can be delivered online.* A network or group could concentrate upon the needs of a particular sector or category of organization, for example small and medium-sized enterprises.
- *Help desk support and various forms of one-stop-shop service, for example covering many of the issues that a growing business or professional practice is likely to face.* Specialist assistance and back-up can increase the proportion of time that principals are able to devote to customers and clients.
- *Troubleshooting and advice on how to overcome certain obstacles and barriers.* There are many sanitized success case studies, but what people really want to know is how particular difficulties that were encountered have been overcome.
- *Personal counselling versions of such a service could focus upon blind spots that individual executives might have,* such as difficulty in understanding complex accounts, professional jargon, mathematics or scientific formulae.
- *Advice specifically relating to the acquisition, installation and application of emerging technologies.* People may want to be able to do something rather than just know about it. Thus

guidance could be given on how best to overcome the practical problems of establishing and managing virtual teams.

- *Support activities relating to exploiting the systems that support, and enable the emergence of, the information society, such as writing code for new applications.* Suppliers of different technologies might not be aware of how two or more of them could be integrated.
- *The establishment and management of a Web presence or a corporate intranet.* Many individuals and organizations need help. Services can range from the design of a Web page to transaction support and sales fulfilment.
- *Advice relating to alternative models of organization, different ways of working and new approaches to learning.* There are many purveyors of single solutions and individual building blocks when what is required is independent counsel on how the various elements of a solution can be brought together in a particular context.
- *Guidance on how offices and homes can become information and knowledge resource centres and more effective and creative working environments.* Distinct areas may be needed for quiet reflection and group work and interaction.
- *Auditing, testing and monitoring activities.* Proofreading and checking exceptions reports, customer complaints and computer code line by line are among activities that can be undertaken remotely.
- *Virtual departments to provide non-core services or capabilities in areas in which organizations may either be reluctant or find it difficult to establish internal provision.* For various reasons, which might include cost, insufficient work for a 'whole person' or recruitment problems, an organization might 'outsource' or 'buy in'.
- *Network or virtual partnerships that bring together groups of individuals who would not otherwise be able to work together because of barriers of distance and time.* Such communities can be global in scope, and collaboration could cover sales and marketing, delivery and management activities.
- *Management of the work and coordination of international project groups and teams, and other activities that are undertaken at a number of locations and/or in different time zones.* Many joint venture and collaborative projects would benefit from independent and dedicated project management.

- *Issue monitoring and management and competitor intelligence.* A degree of independence from a corporate organization can increase objectivity and result in greater sensitivity to both trends and developments and how others are likely to react to them.
- *Sales and marketing activities from consumer research to the design and implementation of various promotional campaigns.* For example, targets could be identified, their requirements assessed and appropriate messages composed and disseminated.
- *Various public relations activities.* Many of these can be undertaken by electronic means. They can be very effective at reaching tightly defined target groups whose members are widely scattered when the etiquette of the Internet is observed.
- *Opinion and other surveys.* Some of these can be undertaken online and the results quickly analysed. Live discussion and focus groups can also be organized, held and facilitated, and follow-up activities managed.
- *Lobbying campaigns can be initiated, coordinated and managed by e-mail.* Representative pressure can be stimulated, assembled and presented to both the media and political and corporate decision makers.
- *Help in bringing about change, for example overcoming resistance and challenging the status quo.* Using corporate e-mail or the Internet to appeal directly to individuals can sometimes circumvent organizational and other barriers.
- *The direct sale of goods.* Virtual stores sell products ranging from books and compact discs to fresh fish from Cornwall and cakes. Packages of processes, technologies and support services are available that cover almost every aspect of setting up an 'electronic' business.
- *Trading and brokering services.* Although among the earliest forms of business to be established, they are particularly suited to electronic operation. Individuals can trade for others or for themselves, for example investing on their own account.
- *New or alternative online markets.* Buyers and sellers can be brought together and noticeboard or auction facilities provided.
- *Various interactive games can be played online and supported remotely.* These can range from informal matches involving friends to sophisticated war games and business simulations.
- *Creation of a virtual community.* Online catalogues, bulletin boards, newsletters and discussion groups can be initiated and

supported with or without related advertising. Subscriber and advertisement fees can represent a source of income.

- *Representation.* Some individuals act as representatives of others in particular forums. They can be selected on a 'horses for courses' basis to act as the 'eyes and ears' of a sponsor and report upon what happens. During meetings and conferences they can ensure that particular points of view are put across.

The fact that similar services might be already provided by a highly motivated enthusiast for free should not preclude one or more commercial alternatives that are differentiated, meet unmet needs and offer value for money. There is often scope for entrepreneurship in arenas that have already been visited by others. One person's interest or hobby might become the inspiration of another's venture or business.

Exercise 1a: Gap analysis

Companies undertake gap analyses in order to assess their prospects and prepare future plans. Projections are made and estimates prepared of where they are likely to find themselves in relation to where they would like to be. If gaps emerge between expectations and intentions, and outcomes and achievements, the analysis leads on to a consideration of whatever actions need to be taken to bridge them.

Individual entrepreneurs and venture teams often lack carefully thought-out plans. Some find it easier to focus upon what exists than to identify missing elements. Are there holes or deficiencies in what you and your colleagues or clients are setting out to achieve? Does everyone have all that they need to fill them, or are certain building blocks missing? What cement is needed to hold the various blocks together? What new factors need to be considered or additional features put in place?

Many gaps are knowledge related. Crucial experience, skills and know-how may be missing within the team. Plugging them may require the acquisition of specialist expertise or particular support tools. Perhaps individuals with the competencies and understanding that are missing can be identified. Undertaking gap analyses for customers and targets may help identify new and additional services that could be offered to them.

THE NEED FOR HELP

There are so many possibilities that one could devote the whole of this book to the implications and consequences of the greater availability of accessible information and knowledge. Only a small proportion of the full potential has yet been harnessed. Yet already issues and problems have arisen. New disadvantaged groups have emerged, including the 'information poor' and the 'excluded' who lack the means of accessing the wealth of free digital information that is available. Social entrepreneurship is required.

Meanwhile many early heavy surfers of the Internet have become bored or neutralized. Some are overwhelmed by the sheer volume and variable quality of what is available. As recipients and users of information and knowledge seek more relevant and personalized support, successive waves of opportunity are being created for knowledge entrepreneurs.

More people now also seek 'greater control' over their relationship with the media and available resources. Some aspire to becoming participants and contributors rather than fly-on-the-wall voyeurs. They want the tools to help themselves. They would like to become producers as well as consumers of information and know-how.

We are positioned at the intersection of social, economic and technological revolutions that can give rise to personal and corporate transformation and create unprecedented opportunities for entrepreneurs. Affordable technology allows us to access the information, knowledge and support tools we require; work flexibly with others in the creation of value; and deliver the results to users around the world. It also enables us to communicate in ways that assist comprehension and enable greater understanding.

The individual citizen today can access more information than past presidents or prime ministers. However, the gap between aspiration and achievement has grown. Access to information is more widespread than an understanding of how to use it effectively. A key core and limiting competence is the ability to acquire, develop, share and exploit relevant information, knowledge and support tools.

So much information is now on tap and easily passed on that busy people struggle to keep up with the flow. Individuals are bombarded with information in a variety of formats. Mobile phones incessantly interrupt, computer screens are covered in Post-it notes, and mailboxes are invariably full of e-mails. People who worry about missing an occasional message that might benefit them, if not fundamentally change their lives, are reluctant to delete or bin individual items without quickly scanning them.

While some individuals drown in information, others are addressing the unprecedented opportunities for providing services to help them cope. Information, knowledge and relevant support tools need to be located, sifted, screened and sorted, and presented in ways that make them relatively easy to digest, understand or use. Increasingly, people are demanding tailored support packages and services that are relevant to particular requirements, issues, responsibilities, objectives or decisions.

Many people are bemused and confused, and some become passive or are rendered ineffective as a result of the quantity of information and complexity of knowledge to which they are subjected. The use to which information and knowledge are put rather than their existence determines their commercial value. Do they increase our understanding and sense of well-being? Do they enable us to create new options or allow us to take better-informed decisions? Do they make us more effective at creating and delivering value? To reap more of the latent benefits of greater access to captured information and knowledge we need support tools and knowledge entrepreneurs.

THE KNOWLEDGE ENTREPRENEUR

Many organizations have devoted great effort to capturing knowledge and building extensive corporate intranets. However, the extent to which the enormous potential of stored information and knowledge is realized, and additional revenues are generated, depends upon the energy and imagination of information and knowledge entrepreneurs, people whose calling and practice is the acquisition, development and commercial exploitation of information, knowledge and understanding.

The knowledge entrepreneur needs to understand how to:

- acquire, develop, package, share, manage and exploit information, knowledge and understanding, and related support tools;
- help and enable others to use and apply them effectively;
- communicate and share information and complex knowledge in ways that assist comprehension and increase understanding;
- create, badge, protect, manage and exploit intellectual capital and 'best practice'-based job support tools;
- identify and exploit market opportunities for distinctive information and knowledge-based products and services;
- develop and launch new information- and knowledge-based offerings and services;

- use combinations of emerging technologies to network people, organizations and relevant sources of information, knowledge and support tools together;
- handle knowledge in multiple formats, including animation, audio and video material;
- develop and use appropriate job support tools to increase individual productivity and corporate performance;
- collaborate with others, and work and learn in new ways in order to create and deliver greater value; and
- lead and manage knowledge workers, network organizations and virtual teams.

Some knowledge entrepreneurs are instinctive or born. Others possess specialist expertise or know about particular technologies. However, an overview appreciation of how particular combinations of people, know-how and technology can be brought together and beneficially managed, and understanding how to establish, launch and manage a knowledge-based business are less widespread. They need to become more common if we are to take full advantage of current opportunities to transform so many aspects of our lives.

Strategic opportunity checklist

Corporate decision makers need to ensure that the organizations for which they are responsible and their people can operate effectively in the knowledge economy. The following questions could be used to assess the significance of particular trends and developments:

▶ What are the growth, competitiveness and employment consequences of the emergence of the 'information society' and the globalization of markets for information, knowledge and understanding? What strategic and policy issues arise, and how might these be handled and addressed?

▶ In which commercial sectors are information, knowledge and understanding accounting for an increasing proportion of the value being generated for customers? Are existing players equipped to cope? What will happen to those that are not? In which of the sectors do they face exclusion?

▶ What are the consequences for individuals of the emergence of a knowledge-based economy? What help will be required by those who are less well placed to cope? What will the more fortunate need to seize the opportunities open to them?

▶ How attractive are the corporate, local and national contexts as a launch pad for intending knowledge entrepreneurs? What are the main concerns of those operating or planning knowledge-based ventures and businesses?

▶ Will new training and development initiatives be needed to develop any additional skills and competencies that might be required? What further forms of support will be required?

▶ What help will the educational system and its institutions require to encourage and develop the attitudes, qualities and competencies required by knowledge entrepreneurs? Can they handle knowledge and deliver it in a variety of formats?

▶ Could professional, learned, trade and representative institutes, associations and other bodies do more to encourage their members to become knowledge entrepreneurs? How might they be helped to become more effective as support networks? What support tools might their memberships require?

▶ What is preventing the more effective acquisition, development and sharing of information, knowledge and related support tools? What needs to be done to tackle obstacles at corporate, local, regional, national and international level?

▶ How could more value be added in terms of creating new information, knowledge and support tools as opposed to processing or using that which already exists?

▶ What could be done to improve the acquisition, development, sharing and utilization of information, knowledge and support tools within government? What new mechanisms, processes and networks are required?

▶ What help will be required to increase the sharing of information, knowledge and understanding at European and/or international levels? What new European and international networks could to be established?

▶ What lessons can be learnt from the establishment and operation of community-wide information networks? How might such developments be monitored and their implications investigated?

▶ What help do companies and public bodies require to report upon: 1) the information and knowledge they hold; 2) their learning and knowledge development activities; and/or 3) the value of their intellectual capital?

▶ What assistance will be required to ensure that information and intellectual property is appropriately and fairly recognized, valued and exploited?

▶ What can be done to encourage, develop and support knowledge entrepreneurs?

▶ Where, when and how would public policy intervention be appropriate and desirable? Is there scope for collaboration between public and private sector organizations?

▶ What will happen as a result of removing existing obstacles and barriers to the acquisition, development and sharing of information, knowledge and understanding? Will new ones be created?

▶ Are particular types of organizations, or those of a certain size, especially at risk? What needs to be done to increase their awareness of the situation and help them respond?

▶ Who should be the main targets of proposed actions, and how might they best be reached? What form should any public interventions take and what external inputs might be required?

▶ Are there particular practices, procedures or regulations that should be changed or removed? Who needs to be consulted and what help will be required?

▶ How should the actions that need to be taken be communicated and delivered? How will roles and responsibilities be allocated among the various organizations and institutions that may need to be involved? Are there gaps that will need to be filled?

▶ What action do individuals and organizations need to take to protect their intellectual property? What steps are required at national, European and international levels?

▶ What needs to be done to increase the security of private and public, and governmental and intergovernmental, networks for the communication and sharing of information, knowledge and understanding?

If there are implications for public policy there may well also be commercial opportunities for both companies and individual entrepreneurs. Government bodies at all levels may need external help in determining and introducing appropriate responses.

Resulting initiatives will also have to be made known to those who must take whatever action is required for them to be effective. Implementation teams will need to be familiar with dissemination options and issues. The members should themselves be role models in relation to the communication and sharing of information, knowledge and understanding.

Exercise 1b: Looking beneath the surface

All is not always what it seems to be. Appearances can be very deceptive. Packaging can mislead. Well-stocked knowledge repositories may be found to be inadequate in relation to particular requirements. More generally, consumers are often insecure when faced with new choices, especially if these incorporate novel elements and there are implications that they may not fully understand.

The gulf of potential misunderstanding and deception that can occur between appearance and reality, or surface and substance, can give rise to many business opportunities. Investigate trends and developments in areas in which you have a special interest or particular expertise:

- Identify the areas in which surface appearance is, or may be, most misleading in terms of understanding the reality of what lies beneath.
- In relation to developments and offerings that are relatively new, examine whether there are particular groups that are more at risk than others of being misled.
- Assess whether there are information- and knowledge-based services that could be provided that would help them to understand better the substance of what is on offer.
- Assess also whether there are diagnostic checklists or 'rules of thumb' that could be developed that would help interested parties to take better-informed decisions.
- Consider whether in certain areas there might be scope for offering advisory services, undertaking consulting projects or

publishing some form of league table or ranking to which interested parties could subscribe.

- Assess whether there might be an opportune moment to issue a report or newsletter or organize a conference or knowledge exchange event.
- Review the prospects for offering a purchasing or consumer protection service.
- Examine the areas in which there appears to be some significant deterioration in the quality of the 'substance' that is being offered.
- Consider whether people may have been disadvantaged by a change such as the replacement of a local expert by a central and remote call centre.
- Assess also whether certain groups might be disadvantaged, for example the provision that is usually offered may not be available in a particular locality.
- Where some slippage of standards has occurred consider whether there might be a market for an 'original' or 'classic' version of what is on offer that would appeal to traditionalists, and which might attract a premium price.

AIMS AND SCOPE OF BOOK

Contemporary trends and developments present both profound challenges for established companies and societies, and unprecedented opportunities for those who are aware, open, restless, ambitious and entrepreneurial. Information, 'know-how', money, technology and, as a consequence, knowledge-based jobs are potentially mobile between locations across national borders.

Appropriate job support tools can lift new entrants towards superstar levels of performance. Many call centre jobs have already moved 'offshore'. Specialist and higher-level professional roles may follow. National as well as corporate competitiveness is at stake.

The results of winning are often exciting as well as financially rewarding, while the consequences of losing can be traumatic. It is hoped this book will act as a catalyst in encouraging people and organizations to recognize, assess and respond to the many commercial opportunities being created in the knowledge society and by the emergence of global markets for information- and knowledge-based services.

The basic purpose of this book is to encourage and help people and organizations to make more money from information and knowledge by profitably packaging and selling them, creating knowledge-based offerings and ventures and using job-based support tools to transform individual and corporate performance. It poses questions that may suggest particular possibilities and stimulate entrepreneurial responses.

The book aims to provide a practical guide for intending and practising entrepreneurs, managers, consultants and professional advisers. Knowledge management has been much written and talked about, and a growing number of companies and professional firms have already taken steps to capture and share some forms of know-how. However, after this initial wave of activity and some disappointing early results the debate now needs to move on.

Many initiatives have already run out of steam. People assert the importance of know-how, capture some existing knowledge, set up a corporate intranet and then claim to have 'done' knowledge management. Recognizing the onset of the knowledge economy does not make one a knowledge entrepreneur. We need to progress and start creating, packaging and exploiting knowledge as well as capturing and managing it.

Much of the current literature puts the case for the importance of 'knowledge management'. It examines what selected companies have done to capture and share historic and current information and knowledge without exploring what might be done to use it to conceive and develop new opportunities and generate incremental income streams.

Most companies adopt a managerial rather than an entrepreneurial approach. The focus is upon managing existing knowledge rather than creating new information- and knowledge-based services, tools, ventures and businesses.

We need to step up from knowledge management to knowledge entrepreneurship. Smart companies are already exploring what needs to be done. Research findings have appeared at national, regional and international levels stimulated by research councils, the European Commission and bodies such as the International Labour Organization (ILO). Many individual entrepreneurs are also already at work. However, additional help is required.

Consultancy assignments and conference case studies focus invariably upon the requirements of particular organizations. Often these are atypical, and many of the lessons that emerge are not applicable to most companies. Many publicized examples have involved large corporations and major consulting firms that are unrepresentative of businesses in general. There is a requirement for more generally applicable guidance and revealing questions that can be posed in a wider range of enterprises.

Researchers, consultants and managers often focus upon particular aspects of implementation, according to their individual roles or professional specialism, rather than address emerging challenges and opportunities from the more holistic perspective of the venture team or boardroom. Some reinterpretation of lessons from an organizational or user point of view may be needed.

The corporate and wider public policy implications of many investigations and projects have not necessarily been uppermost in the thoughts of those undertaking the work. Much of what has been put into the public domain and is accessible via the Internet has resulted from research programmes whose primary purpose has been academic rather than commercial.

Many academic researchers and leading consulting firms prefer to operate at what is perceived as the 'leading edge' rather than at a more fundamental but prosaic level that might contribute much more to corporate competitiveness. Programme-managing a grandiose corporate intranet development might seem more glamorous and visible than designing a practical job support tool to help dealers launch a new product or increase sales force productivity. However, the latter might well do far more to boost performance and profitability.

Entrepreneurs are practical people who tend to apply 'so what' tests, passing research and other findings through filters of commercial relevance, significance and viability. A business may not be able to afford the collection or justify the storage of most areas of corporate knowledge even though this might be possible. Pragmatists and smart companies focus instead on the knowledge and support tools needed to increase performance, compete and win in areas that are critical to corporate success (Coulson-Thomas, 2002b).

Different stakeholders in a company can have overlapping and hopefully complementary perspectives on the commercial significance of corporate knowledge and the potential for knowledge entrepreneurship. The questions they should be asking will reflect their particular responsibilities, requirements and concerns.

This book is intended to encourage and support a reassessment of the prospects for knowledge entrepreneurship by various stakeholder groups that may have both shared and distinct interests in an organization. Checklists are provided of the key questions that each group needs to address. In many instances they will have common concerns and in some cases it may be desirable to establish a dialogue between such groups.

The book provides checklists for assessing both general potential and specific opportunities for developing information- and knowledge-based offerings. Different members of the management team should be able to use particular sets of questions and individual exercises within their own departments and business units. Guidance is also given on the attitudes and approaches needed to succeed.

Overall a positive view is presented, which draws upon insights revealed by research projects of the Centre for Competitiveness at the University of Luton (www.luton.ac.uk/cfc) led by the author on knowledge creation (Coulson-Thomas, 1999a) and the packaging, management and exploitation of intellectual capital (Perrin, 2000). Other studies have examined entrepreneurship (Coulson-Thomas, 1999b), marketplace innovation by challenging traditional assumptions to create new and distinctive offerings (Coulson-Thomas, 2001) and the effective management of information, knowledge and understanding (Coulson-Thomas, 2000).

The book also benefits from a decade of experience of corporate practice in such areas as corporate renewal, learning and transformation, and process and knowledge management, including periods the author has spent as the process vision holder of major national and international projects (www.ntwkfirm.com) and many years of practical experience of packaging and selling information and knowledge.

Other sources of insight have included the author's long involvement in the eBusiness Innovations Awards (www.ecommerce-awards.com), including as Chairman of the Panel of Judges since 1995. Each year the judges examine a wide range of applications of various information and communications technologies and, in the case of all shortlisted entries, meet and receive presentations from the teams involved.

Examples given in the text include knowledge application and exploitation projects undertaken by Cotoco Ltd (www.cotoco.com), a specialist supplier of knowledge-based job support tools. Applications of the company's knowledge management framework (www.K-frame.com) have won national and international awards. Those who keep their feet on the ground and think and act like entrepreneurs can quickly achieve much with modest budgets.

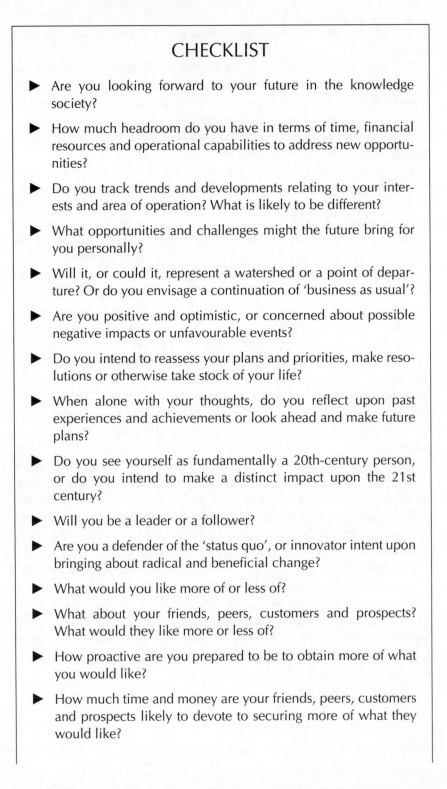

CHECKLIST

▶ Are you looking forward to your future in the knowledge society?

▶ How much headroom do you have in terms of time, financial resources and operational capabilities to address new opportunities?

▶ Do you track trends and developments relating to your interests and area of operation? What is likely to be different?

▶ What opportunities and challenges might the future bring for you personally?

▶ Will it, or could it, represent a watershed or a point of departure? Or do you envisage a continuation of 'business as usual'?

▶ Are you positive and optimistic, or concerned about possible negative impacts or unfavourable events?

▶ Do you intend to reassess your plans and priorities, make resolutions or otherwise take stock of your life?

▶ When alone with your thoughts, do you reflect upon past experiences and achievements or look ahead and make future plans?

▶ Do you see yourself as fundamentally a 20th-century person, or do you intend to make a distinct impact upon the 21st century?

▶ Will you be a leader or a follower?

▶ Are you a defender of the 'status quo', or innovator intent upon bringing about radical and beneficial change?

▶ What would you like more of or less of?

▶ What about your friends, peers, customers and prospects? What would they like more or less of?

▶ How proactive are you prepared to be to obtain more of what you would like?

▶ How much time and money are your friends, peers, customers and prospects likely to devote to securing more of what they would like?

▶ How might additional information, further knowledge and new support tools benefit them?

▶ What could you do to help them?

▶ Are they willing to cover the full costs of developing and supplying whatever you feel you could provide with enough of a margin to compensate you for the risks involved?

2

Managing knowledge and intellectual capital

KNOWLEDGE MANAGEMENT

In recent years there has been a significant increase of interest in knowledge management. More companies have appointed chief knowledge officers. However, attention often focuses upon particular stages of the creation, capture, deployment, sharing, use, development and valuation of the knowledge cycle rather than the whole process. Knowledge entrepreneurs need to confront the reality of the situation within many organizations, namely that certain aspects have been largely overlooked.

In many companies there are issues to address. For a start, colleagues may not agree on a definition of what knowledge management is or should be. Given a diversity of assumptions, approaches and interpretations it is important to retain an overview of the situation and be sensitive to vested interests when discussing the allocation of roles and responsibilities.

Knowledge can exist and be expressed in many forms, for example: facts, attitudes, opinions, issues, values, theories, reasons, processes, policies, priorities, rules, cases, approaches, models, tools, methodologies, relationships, risks and probabilities. Diverse combinations of these are also possible. Responses and initiatives in a particular situation and context may require the assembly and deployment of various types of knowledge.

Many different formats are also possible. Data, visual images and sounds can all be expressed and captured in physical and electronic forms. The various categories of knowledge needed for a particular purpose may exist in different formats and be located in a multiplicity of sources. They may also be accessible through alternative services and various people, in a number of ways and places, and at varying times.

The greatest contribution that many knowledge entrepreneurs within companies can make is to work with particular groups and teams to identify the information, knowledge, skills and tools they need to 'do a better job' and become more effective. The challenge is to select what is most relevant and represents best practice and package this in the form of job support tools that assist comprehension and increase individual productivity and team performance in areas such as winning business and building more intimate customer relationships that are the keys to competitive success. The aspects to concentrate upon are the critical success factors for managing change, competing and winning (Coulson-Thomas, 2002b).

Particular communities of knowledge worker may vary in their perceptions of what constitutes or represents 'knowledge'. Thus professionals tend to value practical know-how that can be used in client relationships, and stress the sensitivity, awareness and familiarity that often come from experience. Academics on the other hand may focus upon theoretical understanding, and value acceptable additions to what a peer group regards as being known about a particular topic.

Within some subject areas, different 'schools of thought' may offer conflicting interpretations, categorizations or definitions of knowledge. Much might be made of boundaries between categories, such as the distinction between 'pure' and 'applied' research that can appear distinctly fuzzy to 'outsiders'. Very often, crucial areas of the knowledge that people may actually need to work upon priority tasks is found to 'fall between the cracks' at the interface of two or more 'neighbouring' disciplines or occupational groups.

For many professionals information and knowledge are instrumental. They are a means to an end. However, for an IT specialist, maintaining particular data stores and flows may become ends in themselves, just as managing a repository of knowledge is for a librarian. Custodians of data and information have a particular perspective, but they also need to be sensitive to the requirements of users.

Some sources of knowledge may be, or might appear to be, more reliable or authoritative than others. People may disagree on which is best. The cost of information can reflect factors such as reputation, exclusivity and supply and demand. The time taken to respond may also vary. Choices and trade-offs need to be made.

A knowledge map can provide an overview of the relationships between different areas and types of knowledge. Overlays can be used for particular purposes, for example to distinguish between internal and external sources or indicate the ownership of intellectual property or restrictions on access. A holistic perspective might enable gaps in knowledge and areas of relative deficiency to be identified.

Exercise 2a: Volcano analysis

Few jewels are located because they sparkle in the sunlight on the surface of the earth. Most are buried in earth and mud, and we have to dig them out. Entrepreneurs often need to look behind the facades of contemporary life in order to uncover underlying root causes, buried opportunities and overlooked potential. They must avoid being distracted by appearances, and may have to penetrate beneath the surface in order to seek out latent forces that might be hidden or blocked.

Think of the intellectual power and imagination that could be lurking within either you or your colleagues. Is there a fire at your core, an inner person waiting to burst out? Are there outlets for your passions and energies, or are the vents blocked? Is there a desire to innovate, explore and discover? Is pressure for change building up? Will it be enough to overcome inhibitions, obstacles and barriers, and enable you to break out? Could an explosion occur? Or are you all ash and gas? Are you an active or an extinct volcano?

LOSS OF KNOWLEDGE

Another important aspect of corporate reality is that knowledge can be lost or stolen as well as obtained or created. Companies that take steps to protect themselves against motivated and organized theft are sometimes oblivious to how much is forgotten, misplaced or destroyed as a result of technological and organizational change, management decisions and staff turnover.

Sometimes the loss of knowledge is deliberate, but often it is hidden or the unintended consequence of a contemporary management approach. Despite the attention given to 'knowledge management', many fads and instinctive responses systematically lay waste or eliminate access to valuable areas of corporate knowledge (Coulson-Thomas, 1997).

Some companies reorganize with irritating frequency. Corporate restructuring can disrupt established practices, flows and relationships that support and enable the sharing of information, knowledge and experience. Customers may find themselves dealing with 'new faces', people who are unaware of their particular requirements and 'special arrangements'. The mutual trust and respect that once led to shared learning might be lost.

People may feel threatened by the prospect of change. They may keep their heads down and retreat into their shells. The insecure may become protective and unwilling to share. Over time, former 'team players' may become emotionally and intellectually isolated. Innovation and the creation of new knowledge may be put on the back burner.

In the case of resignations and redundancies a person's knowledge may walk out of the door one last time never to return. Some 'headcount reduction' or 'downsizing' programmes actually target older employees who have the greatest experience. Little or no effort is made to capture it before it is lost. A company may not even be aware of who its 'superstars' are in certain roles, a necessary first step to capturing their distinctive ways of doing things in the form of methodologies, routines or tools that might benefit others.

Certain companies have unconsciously erased whole areas of past corporate memory. The younger professionals who remain may have a much smaller 'caseload of experience' to draw upon than former colleagues who once acted as their mentors and guides. As a consequence they may become less competent or even flounder.

Re-engineering can lead to 'dumbsizing'. Some companies have adopted 'me-too' re-engineering exercises that have eliminated significant areas of specialist expertise. They have lost the flexibility to route cases differently according to their merits and questions raised. Many have seriously compromised their ability to tailor responses to the requirements of individual customers. Over a period of time workflow systems with their prescribed responses can both de-skill and lead to lower job satisfaction.

The drive for multi-skilling can result in people knowing a little about a lot of things at the expense of in-depth expertise in particular areas. Anchor lines to the foundations of knowledge needed to handle detailed enquiries and important differentiators from a customer perspective may be lost. Companies have lost touch with those who could help when they could have been put on to flexible support contracts with a brief to remain current in certain areas, perhaps working from home, attending conferences and networking with knowledgeable peers at the cutting edge.

Some organizations have become populated with energetic individuals whose understanding has become glib and superficial. Their mercurial 'progress' around and up the corporate structure is ever more dependent upon the support of a diminishing band of ageing colleagues and 'back-room' specialists with a greater depth of expertise who can 'rescue' them whenever they encounter questions they cannot answer.

When specialist units are shut down to 'save overheads', many 'high-flyers' can find themselves adrift, or floundering in a quicksand of uncertainty and insecurity. When they themselves are 'let go' they have little to fall back on in the way of marketable expertise. Others who already have bravado and 'front' may be looking instead for an ability to add value.

Many individuals have built successful careers as independent consultants as a result of being 'plateaued' or 'blocked' long enough for them to become experts in a niche area. As a consequence of not progressing and broadening their experience they have accumulated sufficient specialist expertise that people in other companies are prepared to pay for. After becoming redundant they find themselves in demand while former senior management colleagues prop up bars in golf clubs and try in vain to secure non-executive directorships.

The fashionable practice of outsourcing and 'a focus upon core competencies' can result in the loss of future strategic options. Areas of knowledge of critical importance to a corporation's future may be 'given away' or overlooked. With the benefit of hindsight, many wrong choices have been made.

Prudent companies take steps to capture and update valuable expertise that is sold or divested in case it might be required again or there are other opportunities to exploit it. There may be possibilities for licensing it for use in other locations or sectors that do not compete with the activities of an initial purchaser. Packaging know-how in the form of methodologies or job support tools may increase its market value and generate other sales prospects.

Situations and circumstances can change. Many management teams find they have lost the capability to act and take advantage of opportunities because of contracting out areas of activity and capability that have suddenly become important. Many companies have missed promising chances to exploit new windows of opportunity as a result of 'putting all their eggs in the wrong basket'. As a consequence of a desire to focus they forgo the possibility of changing direction.

In order to achieve cost savings some organizations contract out distinct areas of activity or infrastructure to a variety of organizations on differing timescales. The new partners may have expertise relating to a particular building block of overall capability. However the company undertaking the outsourcing may lose the discretion to redeploy individual elements flexibly. Also 'knowledge of the big picture' and of how different factors interact may be lost. There may no longer be an integrated whole to transform unless compensation is paid to unscramble past arrangements.

Regular upgrades of technology can pose a threat to corporate knowledge. Electronically held information may be overlooked or lost because it cannot be accessed on newer systems. The 'latest versions' of software that are installed may not handle files produced using an earlier generation. Programming and support knowledge soon atrophies when it is not used and individual members of staff change jobs or move on to new employers. COBOL looked set to become an 'extinct language' until the 'discovery' of the millennium time bomb issue sent many corporations scurrying to track down their 'early retirees'.

Many companies suffer from a combination of these factors, each of which has its own negative consequences. People are often subjected to an excess of initiatives that lead to self-contained islands of knowledge that are not integrated. The collective impact of many individual responses to short-term pressures can have serious longer-term implications, ranging from a significant drop in morale to the loss of strategic business development options. Once trust, commitment and context-specific experience is lost it may be very difficult to replace.

What is particularly worrying is the inability of many companies to anticipate and track emerging and future problem areas. For example, directors do not think through the consequences of an ageing workforce. Thus who will monitor the operations of the first generation of nuclear reactors when the engineers with an understanding 'in their heads' of the individual idiosyncrasies of particular power plants retire? What is being done to capture their expertise and prepare support manuals?

Certain large companies with proud and historic names resemble hollow shells. They are shadows of their former selves. In others, time clocks are counting down to a future implosion when a critical mass of required in-depth understanding is no longer available. Their only hope is that retiring or de-layered employees make senior managers aware of the risks before they depart and are willing to retain some form of continuing association and cooperate with knowledge entrepreneurs who can capture their expertise and communicate it to others.

Exercise 2b: Establishing the fundamentals of success

Knowledge entrepreneurs should focus upon those areas that are likely to have the greatest impact upon corporate performance, such as the critical success factors for winning more business. The following steps could be taken to identify what needs to be done in a particular situation:

- Draw up a list of what you and/or your colleagues consider to be the most significant qualities, competencies and capabilities of your organization.
- Distinguish the items that you feel represent the essence of the business, and also those you consider most differentiate its offerings and activities from those of its competitors.
- Identify and list the key factors – which may be a small proportion of the whole – that contribute the greatest proportion of the value delivered to customers.
- Ask customers and prospects about the considerations that have the greatest impact upon them and most concern them when they evaluate and select potential suppliers.
- Draw up a further list of the factors that are regarded as most significant from a customer perspective when purchases and decisions to continue or terminate a commercial relationship are made.
- Compare the lists and evaluate any differences between your assessments and those of your colleagues, customers and business partners. Pay particular attention to any evaluations undertaken from a customer viewpoint.
- Assess whether the differentiating factors and those that influence purchase decisions represent relative strengths of your organization.
- Consider whether enough effort is devoted to the areas of greatest importance from a customer perspective, and whether there are particular qualities, competencies or capabilities that need to be built.

- Review also whether there are particular factors, for example capabilities that might be lost, that could have a significant adverse impact upon the business.
- Undertake a comparative exercise for major competitors to identify relative strengths and weaknesses.
- Ensure that the results of your analysis are shared and incorporated into the design of support tools provided to customer-facing staff and the members of direct and indirect sales channels.

KNOWLEDGE EXPLOITATION

Not all knowledge is lost. However, another arena of omission is the failure to exploit knowledge that has been retained and captured. The sale of specialized expertise or the licensing of intellectual capital such as particular approaches or tools and techniques can contribute additional income streams. However, the report *Managing Intellectual Capital to Grow Shareholder Value* suggests that most of the 51 companies surveyed fail to manage properly and fully utilize the 20 categories of intellectual capital examined (Perrin, 2000).

The term 'intellectual capital' encompasses all forms of corporate knowledge that can be converted into profit, including know-how and processes, patents and copyrights, as well as the skills and experience of employees and relationships with customers and suppliers. The study reveals that some companies, or the 'leaders', are much more active in managing it and successful than others, particularly 'laggards' who derive the least benefit from their know-how.

'Leaders' already generate significantly more income from intellectual capital than 'laggards'. They also expect the contribution of know-how to product or service value to rise either substantially or significantly over the next five years, while the 'laggards' expect it to increase only slightly, remain the same or decline. The 'leaders' understand key management of intellectual property issues, while the 'laggards' fail to make 'know-how' an important driver of shareholder value.

'Leaders' are much more motivated than 'laggards' to exploit their intellectual capital. Developing new income streams, enhancing profits and growing existing revenues are given a higher priority, and they recognize that intellectual capital can be used to create additional opportunities and attack and penetrate new markets. 'Leaders' are also more likely to measure their performance at managing and exploiting 'know-how'.

Customer information, design rights and R&D know-how are currently the three most significant income generators. Both 'leaders' and 'laggards' anticipate that all 20 categories of know-how examined in the report (Perrin, 2000) will become increasingly important. The 'leaders' expect over 30 per cent revenue growth from five categories of intellectual capital: namely licences, brands, market intelligence, Web sites and the Internet, and management methodologies. However, the majority of companies fail to manage properly most types of intellectual property.

The greatest growth in revenue earnings is expected to result from exploitation of Web sites and the Internet, management methodologies, customer information, brands, distribution networks, licences, market intelligence and management tools and techniques. The least growth is expected to result from copyrights, goodwill, patents, royalties, design rights, proprietary technologies, software and R&D know-how, areas that some companies have hitherto been most successful at managing.

A wide range of executives can contribute to the more effective management of intellectual capital. The three most active groups are chief executives, marketing directors and financial directors. About a third of the annual reports and accounts of the companies surveyed contain some informal reference or a passing mention of the contribution of know-how, but fewer than 10 per cent of the balance sheets show a value for intellectual capital. Most of the companies fail to report intellectual property developments to the board.

More boards should undertake formal reviews of corporate approaches to the management of intellectual capital, and formulate proactive strategies for harvesting more value from it. Incentives should be put in place to encourage this. The focus should be upon areas where knowledge management activities can have most impact upon the critical success factors for achieving key corporate objectives.

The *Managing Intellectual Capital* research report (Perrin, 2000) and *The Information Entrepreneur* guide (Coulson-Thomas, 2000) suggest some key areas that should be addressed. Boards need to determine the significance of know-how as a source of customer and shareholder value within their sectors of operation and ensure its contribution is both assessed and tracked. The sharing of information, knowledge and understanding and use of knowledge-based support tools should be measured.

Sufficient resources also need to be devoted to thinking, learning and the acquisition, creation, management and exploitation of information, knowledge, understanding and job support tools. Intellectual capital has to be identified, packaged, badged and protected. Intellectual property should be valued and periodically revalued and appropriately treated in the annual report and accounts.

'Leaders' are far more determined than 'laggards' to exploit corporate know-how, and much more effective at monitoring intellectual capital performance and revenue contribution. They are also more likely to identify know-how as a primary driver of shareholder value; focus on the roles different management functions should play in creating and exploiting intellectual property; and address the relevant people, culture, process and IT factors.

Investors' checklist

Investors interested in the future value of their investment portfolio should take account of the potential for exploiting information, knowledge and understanding when buying and selling shares. In relation to individual companies they should pay particular attention to the following questions when examining annual reports and accounts, and related issues could also be raised at an annual general meeting:

▶ Is the company operating in a sector in which information, knowledge and understanding account for a significant and/or increasing proportion of the value being generated for customers?

▶ Does the board of the company understand the extent to which future prospects depend upon how effective it is at accessing, developing, sharing and exploiting information, knowledge and understanding?

▶ To what extent is the company a consumer or a producer of information, knowledge and understanding? What is the value of knowledge that it has bought in as compared with that created in-house? Is the proportion rising or falling?

▶ Is the company making a distinctive contribution to what is generally known or practised? What would the world lose if it ceased to exist?

▶ Is there an explicit knowledge creation and exploitation policy and strategy? Have specific goals and objectives relating to the acquisition, development, sharing and exploitation of information, knowledge and understanding been set?

▶ Who among the membership of the board have specific responsibility for the acquisition, development, sharing and exploitation of information, knowledge and understanding? Is progress in these areas monitored and reported?

▶ Within its particular field of operation or market sector is the company a 'leader' or a 'follower' in relation to innovation and 'best practice'? Does it explore, discover and pioneer new approaches, offerings and ways of working?

▶ Does the company have a reputation for innovation and knowledge creation and exploitation? How effective is it at attracting, recruiting and retaining creative, imaginative and entrepreneurial people? Are they equipped with appropriate job support tools?

▶ Is the company aware of how major competitors, potential new market entrants and leaders in other sectors acquire, develop, share and exploit information, knowledge and understanding? Does it monitor their experience and learn from them?

▶ Does the company attract, encourage and successfully manage approaches from potential business partners with ideas for exploiting its know-how, creating new offerings and establishing new knowledge-based ventures?

▶ What arrangements are in place to encourage and support the entrepreneurial interests and endeavours of employees? Are they encouraged to come forward with commercial ideas and proposals?

▶ Is the company a member of relevant learning consortia and partnerships? Is it plugged into critical information and knowledge flows, or excluded from them?

▶ Are the 'knowledge content' and competitiveness of the company's goods and services rising or falling in comparison with the offerings of other suppliers? Is it climbing up or sliding down the value chain?

▶ Does the company possess the critical mass of know-how it needs to remain a player within its market or become a global leader within its sector?

▶ Is the company able to attract and retain the 'brightest and the best' customers, or are key accounts and demanding users being lost to competitor organizations?

▶ Does the company put a financial value upon its knowledge? Does it report on the extent to which it is adding to its intellectual capital?

▶ Is there a central repository of knowledge and intellectual capital? Is this managed? Are there knowledge assets that are not being sufficiently exploited?

▶ What measures or indicators does the company employ to assess the extent of: innovation and learning that is occurring at individual, group and corporate levels; and knowledge creation, capture, sharing and exploitation?

▶ In relation to creating and exploiting information, knowledge and understanding, is the company relying upon its past heritage and living for today or is it still vital and vibrant and actively preparing for tomorrow? Does it intend to shape the future?

Overall, does the company have what it takes to survive and thrive in the information age? In particular, are the motivations, processes and technologies in place to support the acquisition, development, sharing and exploitation of information, knowledge and understanding?

KNOWLEDGE FRAMEWORKS

Only just over 11 per cent of respondents to the *Managing Intellectual Capital* survey (Perrin, 2000) thought creating asset registers and similar tools is either important or very important. However, approaching 47 per cent considered better ways of archiving and accessing knowledge to be either important or very important.

Ideally people need not only relevant knowledge but also practical help in applying it and using it to achieve their objectives. Many more companies would benefit from a knowledge management framework that can handle knowledge in a variety of formats and enable people quickly to capture, access, present, understand and exploit pertinent know-how and employ appropriate support tools.

Because there are many different forms of intellectual capital, people responsible for keeping records and protecting knowledge assets increasingly need knowledge management frameworks and repositories that can handle a diversity of formats. The various categories of know-how range from electronic databases, printed documents and slides through designs and other visual images, to audio and video material and animation.

K-frame (www.K-frame.com) allows intellectual capital from text and spreadsheets to multimedia and information off the Internet to be captured and stored within a single portable framework. Fuzzy searches can be undertaken, including of audio and video content. The search function can cope with spelling mistakes and even look for words in audio files and voice-overs. Knowledge creation tools and report and presentation generators can be included. Knowledge entrepreneurs can use K-frame to exploit the many opportunities that exist to increase productivity and performance.

Such a knowledge management framework can also support other activities that various members of the board are involved with, such as the production of corporate credentials or annual reports. Thus multimedia content could be issued to interested parties by means of a CD ROM disc. Laptop computer-based sales support applications developed for companies like call centre technology supplier Eyretel incorporate a pricing engine and proposal generator.

Applications should ensure people have access to relevant and critical information, captured knowledge, educational and training modules, and application tools – as and when required – in a single and easy-to-use framework. People may need to learn rapidly, and automation of the more routine aspects of their roles frees up time for differentiation, tailoring and the creation of extra value.

Compatibility with the Internet and mobile technologies is increasingly important. By making its use the easiest possible route to accomplish a task, and building in suitable tools and checks in the process, the right knowledge framework can help people achieve a highly systematic approach to getting things right first time every time and deliver consistently high-quality outputs.

Knowledge workers can use a knowledge framework to gather all relevant documentation, tools and process information together in a single resource. People find it easier to locate what they require. If people only have to look in one place, and there are fast search tools, they will find what they need rapidly. If a wide variety of media are used (even visual and audio content that can be packaged and searched), it also allows the user to learn faster.

Intranets do offer some of this capability. However, often there is so much material on them that people experience difficulties locating what they need. Often it is hard to get the ideal solution included within the services that are provided. Technology should be an enabler rather than a constraint. A framework such as K-frame offers a job-focused portal that can gather together a wide variety of material, including integrating intranet-based resources.

Exercise 2c: Balance between action and reaction

Timing is often the critical determinant of successful knowledge entrepreneurship. The moment may or may not be right for a particular innovation. Sometimes it is wise to take the initiative. 'First movers' may establish a large enough market share to secure a disproportionate share of rewards. On other occasions it pays to be cautious and to monitor the activities of others and learn from their mistakes. Later entrants can avoid blind alleys into which the reckless and impatient have blundered.

The costs of establishing a new knowledge-based service can often be considerable. It may be wise to wait until an external prospect has recognized the need, relevance and value of what is under consideration. Responding to a customer requirement may result in one or more users funding the development of what is required.

Knowing when to act or react is a key entrepreneurial competence. Either action or reaction, or a combination of both could be appropriate in a particular context according to the circumstances. A balance also has to be struck and maintained, between initiation and response:

- Consider the market context and the situation you are in from both an individual and a corporate perspective.
- Draw up a list of the critical factors that will determine whether or not you and any organizations you are involved with will succeed or fail.

- For each of these factors indicate the extent to which it would be advisable to adopt an active or a reactive approach or strategy taking the costs and risks of each into account.
- In each case, consider how active or reactive you and the organization with which you are involved are on a selected scale from very active at one end to very reactive at the other.
- Draw up two lists, one for yourself and one for the relevant organization with which you are involved, ranking the factors in order of divergence between the current situation and what is considered desirable.
- Starting with the factor for which the gulf between an actual and a desired state is the largest, assess what needs to be done to close the gaps that have been identified.
- Review also how active or reactive other players are in the same marketplace or another field with which you are familiar.
- Consider whether there are specific products and services that could be offered to help other people and organizations become more active and less reactive.

PREMIUM KNOWLEDGE

Whether or not a knowledge framework will transform an organization's fortunes will depend upon how it is utilized and for what purpose. Will it be used to develop new offerings, create additional options or launch additional ventures?

Copying, me-too approaches, benchmarking and accessing and sharing common knowledge are not usually the route to market leadership. Entrepreneurs question, challenge, explore and discover. They use the 'know-how' of their superstars and creative spirits to craft distinctive offerings that provide customers with new alternatives and genuine choice (Coulson-Thomas, 2001). They regard their knowledge, processes and ways of working as a source of competitive differentiation.

Higher prices and greater profitability can depend upon the creation of additional value through distinctive and bespoke offerings (Coulson-Thomas, 2002a). In our confusing and chaotic world consumers are assailed from all directions with a multitude of similar but conflicting messages. Being noticed is crucial for a business that needs to attract new customers. Differentiation and tailoring to individual requirements can also enable the avoidance of commodity product traps and generate the higher margins needed to fund future developments.

Advances in manufacturing, process and information technologies give us the potential to reflect our individuality. However, despite multifarious possibilities we find very often when we strip away advertising claims that various suppliers offer essentially the same product. Thus all cars within each price bracket seem to have the same aerodynamic shape. We buy software packages that furnish us with the same capabilities as everyone else when bespoke development would enable us to be different and might create additional intellectual capital.

People should strive to provide customers with additional options, genuine choices and better alternatives than those that are currently available. Boards should seek alternatives to bland consensus and middle ways. They should champion reflection, debate and challenge; and instil a desire to innovate and an urge to discover.

Some people may need to be helped to distinguish fundamentals from fads, substance from surface and reality from illusion. Checklists that knowledge entrepreneurs can use to do this and question contemporary assumptions, and exercises for formulating new marketplace offerings are available (Coulson-Thomas, 2001). People can be equipped to challenge the relative importance of action and reaction, complexity and simplicity, activity and reflection and change and continuity (Coulson-Thomas, 2001). Shifting the balance between them can produce genuine alternatives.

We need to keep information technology in perspective and avoid panaceas and single solutions. The top three management issues for participants in the managing intellectual capital survey are people rather than technology related, namely recruiting 'good quality' staff, developing a culture of innovation and providing board leadership (Perrin, 2000). The 'leaders' outscored the 'laggards' in all three areas.

Over 70 per cent of 'leader' companies felt that improving staff training and learning was either important or very important for building or enhancing intellectual capital compared with less than 60 per cent of the 'laggards' (Perrin, 2000). Passive learning needs to be replaced with creativity, active problem solving and innovation. People may need to be provided with support tools to help them learn.

Organizations need to be transformed into flexible and responsive networks for creating and exploiting relevant and premium knowledge; and stimulating, enabling and supporting information and knowledge entrepreneurship (Coulson-Thomas, 2002b). The elements required to do this are known, and what those who succeed do differently from those whose change initiatives and transformation programmes falter and fail has also been identified (Coulson-Thomas, 2002b).

The tangible consequences of knowledge creation and exploitation include improved employee and customer satisfaction, an enhanced image and an increased share valuation. Those responsible for training and development should consider whether their current activities are contributing to uniformity and resulting in a standard attitudes, knowledge and skills set or stimulating diversity and knowledge creation.

Training teams could be tasked with becoming separate and profitable businesses. Individuals could become 'customers' with personal learning accounts. Targets and measures should reflect these changes. Input indicators such as 'bums on seats' should be replaced by verifiable outcomes. For example, what proportion of turnover do new products and services account for? What value is ascribed to recently packaged intellectual capital?

In many companies the emphasis should switch from standard competencies and providing people with a common experience to self-directed learning and creating learning environments, such as a corporate university, that can respond to the interests and aspirations of individual members of staff and encourage innovation and knowledge creation (Coulson-Thomas, 1999a). Staff can be seconded for specified periods to work upon strategic knowledge creation and exploitation projects. Think tank environments can be conducive to 'blue skies' thinking, and the open-minded, systematic and imaginative consideration of alternatives.

Working and learning environments must offer greater variety, maybe peace and solitude for one task and interaction and stimulation for the next. Knowledge entrepreneurs in search of 'big ideas' may need to forsake anaemic offices, avoid the distraction of mobile phones and seek out quiet areas such as patches of grass along riverbanks or on cliffs where they can sit, dream, meditate and think.

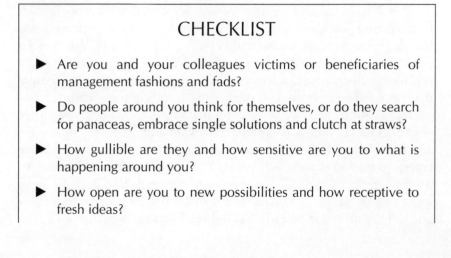

CHECKLIST

▶ Are you and your colleagues victims or beneficiaries of management fashions and fads?

▶ Do people around you think for themselves, or do they search for panaceas, embrace single solutions and clutch at straws?

▶ How gullible are they and how sensitive are you to what is happening around you?

▶ How open are you to new possibilities and how receptive to fresh ideas?

▶ Do you think through your own positions on important issues, or do you follow the crowd?

▶ Do you monitor issues and trends in the business environment?

▶ Can you already identify what is likely to be in the next wave of popular preoccupations?

▶ Do you know what your peers, customers, suppliers and business partners are expecting, anticipating or intending?

▶ What could or should you do to secure advantages and help others to gain from future bandwagons?

▶ Are there processes or services that could be put in place to protect people from the harmful consequences of certain fads and fashions?

▶ What could be offered to increase awareness and enable people to derive greater benefit from them?

▶ Is potentially valuable know-how being overlooked, forgotten or lost?

▶ What could and should be done to protect, safeguard, retain or exploit potentially useful information and knowledge as staff, technologies and priorities change?

▶ Do you understand what represents premium knowledge in relation to what you and others are seeking to achieve?

▶ Are you and your colleagues able to handle information and knowledge in a variety of formats?

▶ Could either you or your colleagues start a new trend? If not, do you know those who could? How might you associate with them?

▶ What opportunities might there be to assemble and disseminate information and knowledge relating to a new movement or development?

▶ Are there exploitation rights you could secure before take-off occurs?

▶ Who around you gives you honest and independent advice on fashions, fads and fundamentals?

> ▶ How open are you when you give feedback and comment on contemporary issues and trends?
>
> ▶ How often do you and your colleagues challenge assumptions and question fundamentals?

3

Corporate learning and knowledge creation

KNOWLEDGE CREATION

The most valuable knowledge is current, relevant, vital and accessible. In many companies existing knowledge, which may or may not be relevant to current priorities and future intentions, is being shared but the new knowledge needed to deliver greater customer and shareholder value is not being created (Coulson-Thomas, 1997, 1999a). Contemporary approaches to knowledge management focus excessively upon sharing an existing stock of knowledge and pay inadequate attention to the determination and development of new knowledge required for achieving priority objectives.

Far too many people access and use corporate know-how without reviewing it, updating it and replenishing the supply. People copy responses to similar requirements, problems and situations rather than think for themselves, or if they do try something different they fail to record what it was and what happened as a result for the benefit of colleagues.

Many companies have difficulty identifying the net contributors to know-how who are so vital to the future prospects of knowledge-based

businesses. Within any community of knowledge workers and professionals there are usually a small number of high performers and a long
tail of those who do just enough to be retained but who do not go the
extra mile to innovate and suggest changes to processes, practices and
procedures.

The 'superstars' at creating new knowledge are not necessarily the
silver-tongued or the best presenters, or those who work the longest
hours. Sometimes they find themselves the victims of de-layering, headcount reductions and ageism. As was pointed out in the last chapter,
restructuring and de-layering can result in the loss of valuable knowledge (Coulson-Thomas, 2000).

When reviewing processes related to knowledge entrepreneurship
(see Appendix to this chapter) board members need to ask themselves
some fundamental questions. What proportion of people are actively
creating, packaging and exploiting know-how? Are the various forms
of knowledge – from designs, Web sites, patents and copyrights to
processes, skills and customer and supplier relationships – that exist
being fairly valued, fully exploited and converted into profit and ulti-
mate shareholder wealth? Is the expertise of 'superstars' being captured
in the form of job support tools that can improve the performance of
their colleagues?

In fast-moving and competitive contexts knowledge creation can
determine continuing relevance. Moving up the value chain may
depend upon new forms of differentiation and additional ways of
adding value.

More bespoke responses to the requirements of individual customers
might require new attitudes, skills and tools as well as redesigned
processes and either additional investments in supporting technology or
its more effective use. Efficiency and cost-cutting drives need to be
complemented by efforts to generate higher margins, for example from
improved exploitation of intellectual capital.

The proportion of final value delivered to customers that is repre-
sented by 'know-how' continues to increase. This trend may accelerate
as emphasis switches from re-engineering and retrenchment to value
creation and the generation of incremental revenues (Coulson-Thomas,
1997). Consequently, people will need to become more effective at
creating, packaging, sharing, applying and generally managing and
exploiting information, knowledge and understanding (Coulson-
Thomas, 2000).

There has been a recent growth of interest in knowledge management: the creation, capture, deployment, sharing, use, development,
valuation and exploitation of knowledge. A knowledge entrepreneur

needs to confront the realities of the situation within most organizations, rather than become carried away by the rhetoric of 'knowledge management'. Books may have been bought and conferences attended, but what has happened as a result?

Knowledge management should be an end-to-end process from identifying knowledge requirements and gaps, though knowledge creation and the sharing and packaging of knowledge to its application to doing new things and delivering additional income streams. However, surveys of corporate practice undertaken by the Centre for Competitiveness (see Appendix to Chapter 11) suggest many knowledge management initiatives are focused almost exclusively upon the middle or sharing section of the process. The missing dimensions of knowledge creation, knowledge management and knowledge exploitation need to be addressed.

Exercise 3a: Work experience analysis

If organizations are to establish more open and trusting relationships with their people and inspire them to develop new knowledge and intellectual capital, they need to understand how various aspects of corporate life can have a positive or negative impact upon employee satisfaction and creativity. Steps may need to be taken to encourage helpful factors and address inhibitors, obstacles and barriers in the working environment.

The work experience as a whole should be conducive to knowledge creation and exploitation. In relation to your organization, what aspects of corporate culture, processes or practices and the general working environment increase or decrease the degree of satisfaction and enjoyment that you (or your colleagues) derive from your working life? Think about or discuss with colleagues the helpful factors that you would like more of, and also consider any irritants, inhibitors and frustrations that you would like less of.

List the resulting 'helps' and 'hinders' separately in order of priority. What changes need to be introduced to increase the 'positives' and reduce the 'negatives'? Can the existing working environment be improved to provide what is needed or is a fundamental transformation required? Would a number of different working and learning spaces be preferable, each of which could be used for particular purposes?

KNOWLEDGE AS A FLOW RATHER THAN A STOCK

Early approaches to knowledge management tended to view knowledge as a stock. Emphasis was placed upon knowledge capture and storage. However, knowledge accumulated from the past might or might not be relevant to future opportunities. What may be of greater importance in dynamic, fluid and uncertain contexts is the flow of information that allows knowledge to be kept up to date, and new knowledge that is relevant to emerging customer requirements and future plans to be created: hence the importance of learning at individual, group, corporate and supply chain levels.

Shared learning is especially important. In many companies, there are few if any learning economies of scale. People and groups keep to themselves and do not share what they have learnt with each other. They are unsupported by knowledge-based job support tools. When each person, and each partner within a supply chain or other relationship, hoards knowledge, the performance of the whole is limited. This is why niche suppliers or boutique consultants that stay current can flourish while much larger firms flounder.

Information- and knowledge-sharing agreements form the heart of many collaborative arrangements and network models of organization. People may be encouraged to join them to participate in shared learning opportunities. For members of a community to take full advantage of each other's data searches, understanding and support tools, principles and rules need to be established covering how information and knowledge is to be categorized, captured and accessed.

A balance has to be struck between the interests of a group and those of its individual members. Thus despite complex interdependencies some means may need to be found of giving recognition and financial rewards to those who create new intellectual capital. The group's interests also need to be protected against third parties. The development and operation of an appropriate framework is a service that a central coordinator or core team can provide.

If the effective sharing of existing knowledge, collective learning and the creation of new knowledge is to occur, appropriate policies, processes and supporting systems and knowledge frameworks need to be in place. Choices need to be made according to the likely costs, perceived advantages and what is known about those involved. Thus flows of updating information could be provided to certain people, but a cheaper option would be to let them know where periodic updates might be found and leave it up to each person to decide when to access such sources according to personal inclination. Some individuals like to keep abreast of a range of topics while others might prefer to search as and when appropriate.

More companies are following pioneers such as Skandia and exploring ways of valuing their knowledge. A distinction needs to be drawn between knowledge as a stock or resource and the ongoing activity of learning. Merely collecting and storing information can become an obsession, and a dangerous one when what has been assembled within a repository can quickly become out of date. The size of the store may give an unjustified feeling of confidence.

Knowing what one does not know and would like to know is as important as – if not more important than – knowing what one does know. It can act as a spur to learning. But however worthy and stimulating learning might be it should not become an end in itself. Learning takes time and in a corporate context has to be paid for, if only in terms of the opportunity cost of what could have been done with the time of those concerned. Those interested in the 'pursuit of knowledge' as a vocation should join a university. The entrepreneur learns in order to improve, innovate or deliver more value.

Exercise 3b: Freedom analysis

Corporate environments often constrict and constrain people rather than inspire and liberate them. The following steps could be taken to identify what may need to be done to make working environments more creative and inspiring:

- Examine work processes and working environments with which you are familiar, and/or for which you are responsible, and consider how much freedom people have to work in ways, and at times and places, of their choice.
- Assess the extent to which they are free to negotiate the objectives of their work and determine how they will undertake tasks and projects for which they assume responsibility.
- Consider how much time and emotional 'space' they have for blue skies thinking and other creative activities.
- Review objectives, priorities, measures, methods of assessment, and approaches to management in relation to whether sufficient emphasis is placed upon innovation and knowledge and value creation.

- Evaluate whether there is an appropriate balance between reflection and action, and between preparing for tomorrow and delivering today's priorities.
- Consider how tolerant the organization concerned is towards diversity in working practices and relationships.
- Consider also the extent to which individuals are able themselves to determine and select the people, processes, systems and support tools they require.
- Review whether working facilities and environments are conducive to reflection and thought, and also enable creative interaction and the sharing and exploitation of information, knowledge and understanding.
- Ask the people concerned to identify and articulate changes that would allow and enable them to be more productive and creative.
- Seek some quantification of the likely impacts of both their proposals and suggestions, and the other possible actions you have already identified.
- In particular, assess the likely value of any additional knowledge that might be created and the extent to which this and existing knowledge might be better exploited.
- Estimate the costs of the various possibilities for beneficial changes that have emerged, and rank them in order of potential for being the greatest and most cost-effective contribution to innovation and value and knowledge creation.
- Consider whether any of the possibilities that have been identified might form the basis of approaches, methodologies, tools or services that could be either licensed or offered to other organizations.

KNOWLEDGE AND LEARNING

In many companies there is a wealth of knowledge. Knowledge can exist in abundance but, as BT, General Motors, IBM and Sears Roebuck have all discovered, that accumulated yesterday may not be relevant to today's issues. There is a danger that newly appointed chief knowledge officers might concentrate upon the management of a current stock of knowledge at the expense of focusing upon supporting the learning that would ensure its development, continuing relevance and greater value.

'Commodity knowledge' that is generally available may be of little benefit unless it is deployed creatively. Its worth depends upon its application to activities that themselves add value or its use in novel ways. Challenging orthodoxy and making new links and connections can enable entrepreneurs to create additional offerings (Coulson-Thomas, 2001). An organization may need to be alert, capable and competent, rather than clever and knowledgeable. Perhaps corporations should recruit 'capability champions' rather than 'knowledge managers'.

Many corporate approaches to restructuring, downsizing and outsourcing cut out capabilities that are not directly related to immediate priorities. As we saw in the last chapter this can result in the loss of the intellectual resources and the capacity to operate in tomorrow's markets. As the workloads of survivors increase, people may be put under so much pressure that they no longer have time to think.

When economic prospects are uncertain, people feel insecure and success appears transient, the best guarantees of continuing relevance and future earnings growth are loyalty and trust, commitment to learning and a willingness to change. These are all areas that have been undermined by many corporate change programmes.

Many managers find it hard to distinguish between reflection and daydreaming. They are 'action oriented' and 'results driven'. They want fewer inputs and more outputs. Investigating alternatives, assessing implications and evaluating consequences take time. This may also be unwelcome to impatient knowledge entrepreneurs. In a 'deal' culture people want quick returns. Toil and sweat are for previous generations.

Almost instantaneous responses from databases have resulted in a 'low tolerance' of delay. After a couple of clicks people may feel they have 'done the job'. A lack of relevant 'hits' encourages them to 'get on with it'. Such an outcome may be preferred to the discovery of data that have to be reanalysed. Eager souls warn of the dangers of 'analysis paralysis'.

Often the sheer volume of information that is collected, and the ease and speed with which even more might be obtained, makes it imperative that sufficient time is allocated to its assessment and interpretation. Great insights and discoveries do not often 'jump out of the page'. An interative process of interaction with the information may be needed, and this creates opportunities for individual knowledge entrepreneurs.

Learning and knowledge creation should not be assumed. The support of knowledge entrepreneurs may be required and they might need to be actively encouraged (Coulson-Thomas, 1997). In the case of a corporate organization:

- The corporate mission, ethos and culture should value the creation, sharing and exploitation of information, knowledge and understanding. It may also help to make them explicit.
- People who perform well should also be encouraged to identify and capture the essence of their success and seek help in expressing and disseminating this in the form of job support tools that can be used by colleagues.
- Clear development, reward and status progressions could be provided for those who learn, create knowledge and generate intellectual capital, rather like the different levels of academic title or the distinctions between consultants, senior consultants and managing or principal consultants.
- Job titles may need to be replaced by opportunities to grow by moving through a succession of roles, and memberships of new venture teams, project groups and task forces that provide new experiences and contribute to the development of sought-after capabilities and competences.
- The equivalent of research grants and venture capital funds could be provided to individuals and teams to help with the creation and exploitation respectively of new areas of knowledge and understanding. Special think tank or incubator unit environments could also be provided.
- Specific learning opportunities and environments may need to be created, and relevant learning processes and supporting learning technologies put in place and an appropriate knowledge framework developed or acquired.
- Learning and transformation partners may be needed to identify and overcome barriers to learning, and advise on appropriate learning approaches, technologies and support tools.
- Learning across functional, project group, business unit and organizational boundaries should be encouraged. It can be a crucial source of advantage in competitive markets.
- Learning within and along supply and value chains should also be supported. It may represent a vast frontier of opportunity for collaboration and shared learning.

Many companies need to develop new approaches to learning and knowledge creation to cope with the complex interdependencies of the world in which they operate. It may be necessary to monitor and track the learning that is occurring among the various members of an extended network of customers, suppliers and business partners in order to assess whether or not there are gaps, and the extent to which particular individuals and organizations are contributing to a shared repository of information, knowledge and job support tools or living off it.

Although learning may be occurring within individual teams, action may be required if what is learnt is to be shared across different groups. Many large companies appear to possess few if any learning advantages over much smaller competitors. Because learning is not shared between project groups and across unit boundaries, they fail to exploit potential learning economies of scale. Business units, project groups and venture teams absorb the costs of reallocated group overheads without reaping one of the major possible corresponding advantages.

The right support tools can enable people in modest enterprises to outperform their peers in much bigger entities who are not so well equipped. Scale has emerged as an obstacle to the rapid dissemination of new developments in many companies. For example, on learning of a technology upgrade a small business may simply go out and buy it. Within days it may be in use.

A major corporation within the same field might not be so lucky. The weight of responsibility can make senior managers cautious. Staff may need to draft an application to the board to fund a worldwide migration plan to upgrade several thousand machines. In the event of a budget being secured, the start date of a 'corporate programme' might then be dependent upon the selection of an acceptable project manager and securing appropriate consultancy support by competitive tender.

Many large companies have been outsmarted by tiny businesses that simply spent more time thinking up better alternatives and were then able to incorporate the results more quickly into their activities. Others have endeavoured to cope with more nimble competitors by putting a combination of incentives, approaches, processes, systems and tools in place to exploit the potential for group as well as individual learning.

Exercise 3c: Learning as a business opportunity

In many organizations, education, training and development are viewed as a cost rather than an area of business opportunity in their own right. Take your own organization or another to which you have access, and consider the following questions:

- Do people view training and development activities as a cost or an investment in the creation of new skills and knowledge?

- What proportion of the training and development budget is devoted to critically important areas such as winning business, creating internal entrepreneurs or building strategic account relationships?
- Additionally, what proportion is devoted to supply and value chain requirements or joint initiatives with other organizations?
- Could particular courses or even complete programmes be externally validated and lead to the award of a formal qualification?
- Would employees, staff in customer, supplier and partner organizations and other third parties be prepared to pay to obtain such qualifications?
- Are there specific customer, user or business partner education needs that could be addressed?
- Would there be an external market for information, knowledge, tools, techniques and methodologies created by colleagues, if they were appropriately packaged and imaginatively sold?
- How many people have the desire and necessary qualities to become effective knowledge entrepreneurs?
- In relation to the culture and senior management attitudes, what are the prospects for information and knowledge entrepreneurship?
- Are there other specific education, training and development activities that if packaged might have the potential to become businesses in their own right?
- Could certain of the company's facilities and activities be opened up to external parties and/or developed jointly or in association with them?

KNOWLEDGE CREATION AS A CORPORATE PRIORITY

Many companies devote excessive attention to cost cutting rather than innovation and revenue building. Emphasis is placed upon endeavours that are clearly visible at the expense of other areas that might appear less tangible. In general, more effort needs to be devoted to activities that generate customer and shareholder value, in particular critical success factors for competing and winning (Coulson-Thomas, 2002b), including beneficial customer, supply chain and shared learning relationships.

In the knowledge society learning needs to be a top priority. Increasingly, the basis of competitive advantage is the willingness and ability to learn. People should wake up and log on with the intention of learning as well as working. Learning can be a critical determinant of an organization's future prospects: 'Quality thinking about tomorrow may be more important than thinking quality today. Companies need to establish intellectual leadership in targeted areas of opportunity' (Coulson-Thomas, 1997).

In some companies internal understanding of learning approaches, processes and technologies is relatively limited. Learning partners and 'learning catalysts' should be appointed with specific responsibilities for assessing and improving the quality of individual, group and organizational learning.

The combination of learning, creativity and knowledge entrepreneurship can lead to additional intellectual property, new job support tools, incremental revenues and higher share prices. The benefits of learning that is captured and shared can often be applied outside of the context in which it has arisen. However, many companies do not even consciously consider what their employees and business partners may have learnt. A critical deficiency in many companies is a lack of appreciation and self-awareness of learning potential at individual, team and corporate levels.

We do not all necessarily learn in the same way. People should be helped to become aware of how they might best learn, and enabled to adopt approaches to learning and working that match their requirements and preferences:

The challenge is to support and facilitate the learning of individuals, groups and organizations by means of an appropriate and tailored combination of content, process and delivery mechanisms that matches the situation, circumstances and context and both enables people to harness more of their potential and allows them to learn at the time and place, and in a mode, that best suits their preferences and natural aptitudes for learning.

(Coulson-Thomas, 1997)

Current training programmes, development preoccupations and learning priorities can be a significant determinant of future attitudes, skills and knowledge. More boards should assess whether training and development inputs result in new knowledge, job support tool and intellectual capital outputs. All too often data-warehousing software is bought to help capture existing knowledge and corporate intranets are established to make it available but insufficient effort is devoted to learning and creating new knowledge.

In many companies training and development activities deserve closer scrutiny. Could business development and the processes of value and knowledge creation be better supported? Could particular training activities be made a revenue centre, a separate business or simply outsourced?

A two-year examination of corporate learning plans and priorities has addressed such questions. The investigation included corporate visits and 69 structured interviews with individuals responsible for the training and development of some 460,000 people. The results with case studies, checklists and key action points are summarized in the report *Developing a Corporate Learning Strategy* (Coulson-Thomas, 1999a).

The findings are sobering. Many courses have passed their 'sell by' date, while essential requirements and critical corporate priorities are largely ignored. Millions have been spent on fashionable concepts such as empowerment and general 'teamwork' training, yet only one of the organizations surveyed is equipping its people to be more successful at bringing in new business (Coulson-Thomas, 1999a). People receive standard courses regardless of their individual interests and needs.

While value is increasingly delivered by supply chains rather than individual companies, the organizations examined focus overwhelmingly upon the internal training of employed staff. External development needs of customers, contractors, suppliers, value chain partners, virtual team members and business associates are being ignored.

Overall, little effort is devoted to business development and relationship building, e-business, or knowledge creation and entrepreneurship. Overwhelmingly the emphasis is upon squeezing and cutting costs, rather than income generation. Training and development are not perceived as a source of incremental revenues. Nor are they used as a means of building relationships with key decision makers in strategic customers, suppliers and business partners.

The education, learning, training and updating markets represent exciting business opportunities. The *Developing a Corporate Learning Strategy* report (Coulson-Thomas, 1999a) identifies no fewer than 25 different categories of learning support services that could be offered. Intellectual capital from simple tools to advanced techniques can also be licensed or sold. There is enormous potential for knowledge entrepreneurship. Yet, despite these opportunities, most trainers are not directly supporting the creation, sharing and application of knowledge and understanding.

Managing current stocks of information, knowledge or understanding might or might not be relevant to individual aspirations, customer requirements or corporate objectives. But new insights, discoveries and breakthroughs, the dynamics of the creation and application of pertinent knowledge, are often the keys to leadership in competitive markets, particularly when knowledge sought or created relates to critical success factors for competitive advantage (Coulson-Thomas, 2002b).

Education, training and development expenditures are still widely regarded as costs rather than vital investments in the creation of knowledge, support tools, intellectual capital and benefits for customers. Switching the emphasis from cost cutting to innovation, business building and value creation would result in both enhanced corporate performance and greater personal fulfilment (Coulson-Thomas, 1999b).

The *Developing a Corporate Learning Strategy* report (Coulson-Thomas, 1999a) suggests a way ahead. Boards and managers should actively champion enterprise and learning. Knowledge development should be explicitly rewarded.

Pioneers do not play 'me too' or 'catch-up' according to yesterday's assumptions and principles. They are energetic creators, imaginative innovators and restless explorers (Coulson-Thomas, 1999b). They devise and set up new games with different rules (Coulson-Thomas, 2001). When tailoring responses, differentiating and generating novel alternatives the ability to learn quickly and effectively is a source of both value and competitive advantage. The most successful enterprises will evolve into communities of knowledge entrepreneurs (Coulson-Thomas, 2000).

Learning processes can be created, improved or re-engineered, and learning support tools developed or acquired. Learning should also be built into work processes. Standard training offerings should be abandoned in favour of specific and tailored interventions to support learning and knowledge entrepreneurship.

Knowledge creation should start with what an organization is setting out to do. Next, roles and responsibilities, processes, and ways of working and learning to achieve the desired objectives have to be designed and agreed. Role model behaviours and, importantly, the knowledge, experience and skills likely to be required can then be determined, along with any additional tools, techniques and methodologies that may be needed (Coulson-Thomas, 1999a). Centres of excellence, or panels of experts, could review certain areas within a company's 'body of knowledge' to keep them up to date.

Establishing a corporate university, learning or enterprise centre

Some companies establish distinct units or separate entities with a specific mandate for knowledge creation and/or exploitation. Thus a corporate university might be expected to encourage discussion and investigation and engage in activities that lead to new knowledge and greater understanding. An enterprise centre could be given a brief to support new knowledge-based ventures.

At the planning and start-up phases there are a number of issues to address if a new centre is to become effective and remain relevant, particularly if some form of external validation or recognition is sought. The questions below can be used as a 'health check' diagnostic to identify areas of deficiency that need to be addressed. They could also act as a questionnaire for evaluation and comparative purposes, for example to assess the attributes and qualities of potential learning partners.

There are a number of areas that need to be examined when either: 1) establishing a corporate educational capability; or 2) carrying out some form of health check of an existing institution. The areas indicated below are designed to be suggestive rather than exhaustive. Individual areas should be followed up in more or less detail depending upon how confident people are about the relevance and quality of what is being observed.

Background

▶ What is the corporate learning unit or centre called?

▶ Who owns it?

▶ Where is it located?

▶ When was it established?

▶ How is it funded, and for what periods of time?

▶ Who are the key stakeholders and major customers?

▶ Have the particular interests of the various parties been clearly defined?

▶ Is there regular and two-way communication between the unit or centre and the various individuals and groups that have an interest in it?

The corporate context

▶ To whom does the head of the unit or centre, or its director, report?

▶ How supportive is the organization as a whole of what the centre is seeking to achieve?

▶ How committed are corporate top management?

▶ Are the role and purpose of the centre understood by key decision makers?

▶ Are mechanisms in place to monitor developments in the corporate context and business environment, assess their implications and determine what needs to be done in response?

Role and purpose

▶ Has the unit or centre been given a clear mission and purpose?

▶ What is this?

▶ How does it relate to knowledge creation and exploitation?

▶ Does the unit or centre have an agreed and shared vision, and clear goals and measurable objectives?

▶ What are its plans and priorities?

▶ How rigorous is the planning process?

▶ Is there an agreed code of values?

▶ Are the vision, values and goals compatible with those of the wider corporate context?

▶ Does the culture of the unit or centre encourage innovation, creativity and the development and exploitation of knowledge and expertise?

Constitution

▶ What is the formal status of the unit or centre?

▶ Who runs it and is accountable for its performance?

▶ To whom or what body is this person accountable?

▶ To what extent is the unit or centre a distinct and independent entity?

▶ Does it have a separate constitution?

▶ Does it have its own committee or board?

▶ Who sets its budget?

▶ Does it manage its own financial affairs?

▶ Is the entity able to determine its own academic policy?

▶ What freedom of operation does it have and in what areas?

▶ Does it own or have a stake in the intellectual property its people create?

Resources

▶ What is the size of the unit or centre in terms of budget or turnover?

▶ Does it have a specific venture capital fund?

▶ Do one or more external parties contribute a proportion of this fund?

▶ How many full-time, or full-time equivalent, members of staff are employed?

▶ What investment has been made in learning infrastructure, facilities and resources?

▶ Is the working environment conducive to reflection and creativity?

▶ What arrangements are in place to support the creation, sharing and exploitation of information, knowledge and understanding?

▶ Do these cover the creation, protection and exploitation of intellectual property?

▶ Is there a remit and related capability to design and produce job support tools?

▶ Do staff, students and course participants have effective access to the facilities and resources they need?

▶ Does a knowledge framework that is able to handle information and knowledge in a variety of formats support their activities?

▶ How many people participate in the entity's various programmes each year?

▶ What proportion of these are producers rather than consumers of knowledge?

▶ Are the available resources and knowledge framework adequate in relation to the goals and objectives that have been set?

▶ Is the staff-student or guide-learner ratio rising or falling?

▶ How is the use of facilities and resources monitored?

▶ What is the value of the entity's intellectual capital?

▶ How much income has been generated as a result of its exploitation?

▶ What steps are being taken to secure additional resources?

Staffing arrangements

▶ How adequate are staffing arrangements in relation to customer requirements and what the unit or centre is seeking to achieve?

▶ Does it attract the brightest and best?

▶ How do people hear about the unit or centre?

▶ How are staff selected, appointed, promoted and rewarded?

▶ Are satisfactory induction, involvement and development arrangements in place?

▶ Is role model conduct defined?

▶ How are staff activity, performance and development assessed and monitored?

▶ Do members of staff regularly receive student and other feedback?

▶ What proportion of staff is currently active in the development of new approaches, tools and techniques?

▶ Who among them has a distinctive competence?

▶ How many members of staff are active in bidding for external research or learning contracts?

▶ How many of them have entrepreneurial experience and/or experience specifically relating to the creation and exploitation of knowledge?

▶ What arrangements are in place to deal with underperformance?

▶ Are adequate counselling and support provided?

▶ Does this extend to 'associates' and other external providers of teaching inputs and learning, assessment and enterprise support services?

▶ Do contractual arrangements with staff and associates adequately protect intellectual quality?

▶ Are these fair to all the parties involved?

Academic quality

▶ Does the unit or centre have an agreed statement of academic quality?

▶ Is there an agreed teaching and learning strategy?

▶ Is this, and the statement of quality, explicit and observed?

▶ What arrangements and processes are in place to monitor and assure quality?

▶ Do these cover remote locations and the activities of collaborative partners?

▶ How are consistency and adequacy maintained across a variety of different locations?

▶ To what extent is there external and independent validation?

▶ What, if any, quality standards are held, and how relevant are these to learning outcomes and the creation of new knowledge and ventures?

▶ How is customer and staff feedback obtained?

▶ Are the unit or centre's processes and practices regularly reviewed?

▶ Are quality improvement projects and initiatives in place?

▶ How is the need for these identified, agreed and communi-cated?

▶ Are resources directed at the areas where improvements are most needed?

Enterprise support

▶ Does the unit or centre support the development of new knowledge-based enterprises?

▶ Is there an agreed enterprise support policy and agreed arrangements for deciding which ventures to support?

▶ Are these explicit and observed, and are any conflicts of interest declared and recorded?

▶ What arrangements and processes are in place to monitor and assure fair dealing and investment quality?

▶ Are members of staff in other locations and partner organiza-tions eligible for support?

▶ How is consistency maintained across a variety of different locations and diversity of ventures?

▶ Is there an external and independent input into decisions relating to which ventures to support?

▶ Are investments subject to separate and independent audit?

▶ How is feedback obtained from the individuals and teams that are supported?

▶ Are investment policy and performance regularly reviewed?

▶ Are processes in place to ensure that lessons of success and failure are captured and shared?

Programmes

▶ What is special or distinctive about the entity's programmes or offerings?

▶ How do proposals for new programmes arise, and from whom do they originate?

▶ Are ideas and initiatives drawn from a wide variety of sources?

▶ Are they based upon investigation, analysis, monitoring and research?

▶ How are such proposals, and any future changes, scrutinized and approved?

▶ How is implementation monitored and reviewed?

▶ Are programmes regularly updated in the light of review findings and customer feedback?

▶ What arrangements are in place to examine complaints and appeals?

▶ What is done to look after the interests of customers when programmes are discontinued?

Customers

▶ Who uses the services of the unit or centre?

▶ What other groups could be considered as potential users?

▶ What proportion of eligible and target groups participate in its activities?

▶ Are there particular obstacles and barriers to further participation?

▶ Are the description and promotion of programmes adequate?

▶ Is a clear indication given of learning outcomes?

▶ What value is the unit or centre adding?

▶ Does this include the design and development of new job support tools?

▶ Is new knowledge and intellectual capital captured, protected and valued?

▶ If so, what is the value of intellectual capital that has been created?

▶ Are customers able to influence the relevance and quality of what is delivered?

▶ How sensitive and responsive to customer concerns and requirements is the unit or centre?

▶ Do members of staff take responsibility for individual customers?

▶ What arrangements are in place to monitor student activity and the activities and affairs of supported ventures?

Learning assessment

▶ How is student and learner performance assessed?

▶ How are learning assessment criteria established and monitored?

▶ Do they adequately reflect learning objectives and outcomes?

▶ Do they specifically cover knowledge creation and exploitation?

▶ Are external and independent assessors and examiners involved?

▶ How well supported and effective are they?

▶ Are students and learners given clear feedback about their performance?

▶ Are adequate arrangements in place to monitor the progress of distance learning students?

▶ Are learning assessment processes and procedures regularly monitored and reviewed?

Collaborative arrangements

▶ What collaborative arrangements are in place with other organizations?

▶ How are these established, reviewed and monitored?

▶ How are relationships with collaborators, suppliers and business partners managed?

▶ Are the roles and responsibilities of the various parties agreed and clear?

▶ What is done to learn from customers, collaborators and other external organizations?

▶ Does the unit or centre have learning partners?

▶ Does it belong to relevant shared learning networks?

▶ How are the relevance and quality of potential partners and collaborators assessed and monitored?

▶ What feedback is provided to and from collaborators, including on collaborator contribution and performance?

▶ How are disputes between collaborators and disagreements involving them handled?

▶ How are collaborative arrangements ended, and what steps are taken to protect the interests of the various parties involved when termination occurs?

▶ In particular, how is confidentiality assured and intellectual property protected?

Performance assessment

▶ How is the performance of the unit or centre, and the value it adds, measured and reported upon?

▶ Are learning and knowledge creation and exploitation outcomes measured and related to associated costs?

▶ Is process performance, and particularly that of learning and knowledge creation and exploitation processes, assessed?

▶ How is staff and customer satisfaction assessed?

▶ Is the development of staff competence and centre capability assessed?

▶ How are individual contributions and particular relationships assessed?

▶ Are the creation and exploitation of new knowledge and intellectual capital measured?

▶ Is the sharing of information, knowledge and experience assessed?

▶ Is sufficient attention devoted to quality issues and measures or learning outcomes?

▶ How is the distinctive contribution that the unit or centre makes to knowledge, practice and entrepreneurship assessed?

▶ Are reporting arrangements and practices adequate in relation to what is, or ought to be, reported?

PROTECTING INTELLECTUAL CAPITAL

Intellectual capital needs to be protected as well as created (Coulson-Thomas, 1997). Companies that are world-class inevitably find themselves 'targets' of the 'learning' of competitors. The openness and intellectual resources at the command of the contemporary corporation make it especially vulnerable. With its global network of relationships and a variety of external electronic links it is particularly at risk of being intellectually asset stripped. Each additional connection and data flow can provide hackers and thieves with another route in.

Organizations that are being restructured, re-engineered or otherwise in a state of transition are also at risk. During the process of change or transformation expertise may be lost and also new opportunities for abuse created. Activities that are dropped because they do not appear to 'add value' may have offered 'space' for reflection and learning, or provided useful 'checks and balances'. People sometimes rue instant responses.

Conflicts of interest abound in contemporary organizations. A team that is alert to an attractive opportunity for a management buyout may 'go slow' and underperform in the hope that a board might lose interest in the area in question. They may also keep quiet about the true value of intellectual capital and delay further contract negotiations and business development initiatives until such times as they secure a personal equity stake.

Some people are devious and malevolent. They join virtual teams and network organizations in order to obtain access to knowledge that they may then seek to turn into proprietary intellectual capital. Effectively they take advantage and live off others. Arrangements may need to be put in place to protect the intellectual capital of net contributors from freeloaders and parasitic adventurers.

Companies with long histories, proud names and impressive facades can become hollow shells. Their intellectual capital may have 'walked out of the door' as their brightest and best left to establish their own businesses, perhaps staging a management buyout assisted by external capital. The unscrupulous will conceal the potential of an opportunity until they are in a position to exploit it themselves rather than on behalf of their employer.

Some companies lose the ability to embrace future generations of technology and end up serving more successful competitors as subcontractors of commodity products. Only plateaued 'time servers', the consumers rather than producers of intellectual capital, may remain: 'Too many companies drain the well of inspiration and creativity dry, and wake up one day to find there is not much in the way of intellectual capital and capacity left. Mature boards recognize that ever more creative uses of a finite resource need to be balanced by the break-throughs that create new sources of supply' (Coulson-Thomas, 1997).

A moving target is more difficult to catch up and hit than a stationary one. Attempts can be made to ring-fence an existing stock of information, but its value in a dynamic market context is likely to fall over time, especially when priorities change. Continuing relevance and competitiveness may depend upon a flow of information, intelligence, expertise and insight of relevance to contemporary issues and concerns. The necessary processes, relationships and network connections to do this need to be put in place.

WHERE KNOWLEDGE ENTREPRENEURS CAN HELP

Many companies adopt a custodial rather than an entrepreneurial view of knowledge management. The priority issue is access to particular forms of knowledge, especially data that are held electronically or information stored in defined places, rather than application and exploitation. In some instances, the practice of knowledge management is tantamount to an exercise in 'data warehousing' or 'data mining'.

Availability of knowledge and its effective use are different issues. An improved capability to undertake online and World Wide Web searches may not be matched by greater understanding of how to assess what is relevant or utilize what has been located. Understanding and appropriate application are sometimes inversely related to the volume of information collected. Where this is a general problem knowledge entrepreneurs may be able to help by providing appropriate evaluation services.

It helps to know what you know and don't know. Many corporations lack any form of categorization of the full extent of available and relevant knowledge, or an overview of who is responsible for it and the relationships between various information flows, repositories or knowledge sets. Opportunities for shared learning and relative deficiencies are hence difficult to locate, as are corporate policies in areas such as retention and updating. Important areas may miss the net.

Knowledge entrepreneurs can help companies to construct knowledge maps and formulate knowledge creation, management and exploitation policies. A degree of independence and objectivity may be required to do this. Many people exaggerate the value of internal knowledge while being unaware of relevant external sources. Thus managers may only have contacts with business and management schools when more relevant areas of knowledge might be located elsewhere within the same universities.

Some companies are oblivious to rich fields of knowledge of direct relevance to critical corporate issues and do little to encourage a diversity of subject backgrounds. All managers may be sent on the same management programme when other areas might be more appropriate. For example, insights from the study of alliances, international relations and diplomacy could be very relevant to negotiation of global collaboration arrangements. It is helpful to consider the factors that strengthen and undermine cooperative activity.

A company should establish processes for learning from alliances, partnerships and other collaborative relationships. These can be valuable and may prove a significant determinant of the strategic benefit that is derived from joint venture arrangements.

Many companies remain introverted and departmental. People may have little awareness of what is happening next door. Academics sometimes search their own subject's repositories for an area of knowledge that may have been developed more extensively and earlier in other departments in a different faculty. Increasingly, universities are recruiting knowledge entrepreneurs with a brief to exploit knowledge that runs across all organizational units.

Ideas often take far too long to penetrate departmental barriers. Good examples are 'organic' and systems approaches for learning and coping with an uncertain and at times chaotic environment. Ideas in these areas were introduced into many corporations by business school academics and management consultants who 'packaged' them as concepts for corporate consumption. However, systems thinking and writing was widespread among academics in subjects such as politics and international relations a generation earlier, and two generations before in the case of engineering, while three generations before many biologists were similarly active.

Knowledge entrepreneurs need to have a nose for know-how that might have an application in a different context. Understanding where to look other than in the 'usual places' and the ability to sense that a particular area of knowledge may be relevant are important skills.

Intelligent search engines may still need to be complemented by restless, intuitive and imaginative individuals. In essence, knowledge entrepreneurs are aware and creative individuals who ask first-principles questions about who might require what combination of information, knowledge and support tools where, when and in which formats.

CHECKLIST

▶ Do you think before you act, or do you 'shoot first and ask questions later'?

▶ Are you driven by the needs of others or what you would like to do?

▶ Are those around you impressed by activity for its own sake?

▶ How important is it to be seen to be busy within the context in which you work?

▶ Is assessment based upon inputs of energy or time, or tangible outcomes such as particular objectives achieved?

▶ What proportion of your colleagues' time is spent thinking about tomorrow, as opposed to dealing with today's problems?

▶ Are there 'quiet areas' that can be used for thinking and reflection, and shared spaces for discussion and debate?

▶ Is anyone tracking the sources of the most valuable ideas to help determine how best to stimulate imagination and creativity?

▶ Do people regularly review and reflect upon what they have learnt?

▶ What proportion of your time is spent upon creative thinking? Do you know how to think imaginatively?

▶ Are those around you being helped to be innovative and more inspired and inventive in their thinking?

▶ When you have the time and 'space', do you think about trivial issues or reflect upon matters of great consequence?

▶ Do you have a 'thought agenda' of problems that you would love to tackle and solve and/or issues that you would like to clarify and resolve?

▶ If you were granted a sabbatical to consider a 'big idea', what would it be?

▶ How open and tolerant towards different patterns of working and learning are the people and culture in the context within which you operate?

▶ When processes are reviewed, improved or re-engineered are the various possibilities for new ways of working and learning taken into account?

▶ Are opportunities identified and taken to introduce more effective job support tools?

▶ How flexible are the approaches that have been adopted? Do they allow easy and rapid access to relevant skills as and when they are required?

▶ Do they enable effective learners and net contributors to knowledge and understanding to be identified and rewarded?

▶ What pattern of work would enable you to work, learn and think more effectively?

▶ Are patterns of work and approaches to learning tailored to people, tasks and priorities?

▶ Do they reflect both individual and corporate values?

▶ Is work to be done defined, negotiated and agreed in output terms?

▶ What learning, knowledge and intellectual capital outputs are expected, targeted, monitored and managed?

▶ Are appropriate learning tools and environments made available and properly used?

▶ Do learning partners and counsellors provide effective support?

▶ Do you know how you learn? What is your preferred pattern, style or approach?

▶ Have you agreed learning and development objectives? Do you regularly review what you have learnt?

▶ Are there particular shared learning networks that you should join?

▶ Where would your organization appear on learning league tables in comparison with its main competitors?

▶ What should be done to improve its ranking?

▶ How might learning be built into the culture, soul and DNA of the organization?

Appendix to Chapter 3: People, process and organization checklist

Process vision

Does the overall process vision of the organization and its people embrace the acquisition, development, sharing and exploitation of information, knowledge and understanding and the provision of appropriate support tools? Who is responsible for this vision? Does the individual's role specifically embrace knowledge entrepreneurship?

Is the vision translated into actual processes with the necessary people, organization and supporting systems, procedures and tools and a knowledge framework in place to operate them effectively? The following questions could be used to identify areas of deficiency:

▶ What processes are in place specifically to support the acquisition, development sharing and exploitation of information, knowledge and understanding?

▶ Is relevant information and knowledge captured and shared at each stage of these processes? Can this be done in a variety of formats?

▶ Are feedback loops, and opportunities for the review, refinement, sharing and exploitation of information, knowledge and support tools built into the operating processes of the organization?

Process ownership and status

Is each of the relevant processes owned, approved and operational? In particular:

▶ Does each process have an owner who is accountable for end-to-end performance?

▶ Are the process roles and responsibilities clear to the process owners, and in relation to other processes?

▶ In the case of processes that are still under development, when are they due to 'go live'? Who is responsible for final sign-off?

▶ Has the overall business process vision holder approved the processes?

▶ Are the process owners involved in periodic and regular reviews?

Process documentation

Is each process adequately documented? In particular:

▶ Have appropriate diagrams been produced? Do these clarify supporting knowledge and tool requirements? Have all significant areas been covered?

▶ Does the documentation capture the essence of what is special about the organization and its activities and offerings?

▶ Is the documentation stored in an accessible form? Is it considered part of the intellectual capital of the organization?

▶ Are exploitation opportunities reviewed, for example licensing the processes to other organizations?

▶ Are the diagrams for the documented areas up to date? Are arrangements in place to capture any changes?

▶ Are links with other related processes, for example providing triggers or receiving outputs, clear and understood?

▶ Where appropriate, is supporting process documentation available in a compatible format and on a central repository?

▶ Does the process documentation include sufficient explanatory notes to guide users?

▶ Could the documentation be used for induction and training purposes? Might this be a source of external income?

▶ If appropriate, is relevant information available on a corporate intranet? If not, are other arrangements made to provide help desk support to the operators of these processes?

Process management

Are arrangements in place for the proper management of each process? In particular:

▶ Have process performance objectives been set for process outputs, efficiency and improvements? Have appropriate measures been established? Are these reported and monitored?

▶ Are people operating the processes provided with the job support tools and other enablers they will require to achieve desired performance improvements?

▶ Have points within the processes been identified at which operational and/or management reports could and/or should be generated?

▶ Have the process owners specified the reports required to monitor and manage the processes? Have arrangements been made for these to be generated?

▶ Do the reports cover the extent to which the acquisition, development, sharing and exploitation of information, knowledge and understanding, and the proper use of support tools are occurring?

Process operation and support

Is each of the processes properly supported? In particular:

▶ Is an appropriate form of organization in place? Is this documented?

▶ Do the people concerned have job or role descriptions? Do these cover the acquisition, development, sharing and exploitation of information, knowledge and understanding?

▶ Are adequate systems, procedures and job support tools in place? Do these include appropriate approaches, tools and technologies for supporting the acquisition, development, sharing and exploitation of information, knowledge and understanding?

▶ Have the supporting systems, procedures and tools been properly tested and documented? Is adequate back-up and technical support provided?

▶ Have the people operating the processes been adequately trained? What specific tests of competency have they passed? Is further development required?

▶ Does the competency framework of the organization specifically embrace competencies relating to the acquisition, development, sharing and exploitation of information, knowledge and understanding, and the use of job support tools?

▶ Have appropriate arrangements been negotiated with shared learning and knowledge creation and exploitation support partners?

▶ Are people operating the processes aware of their roles and responsibilities and supporting systems, procedures, tools and partnerships?

▶ In the case of new and re-engineered processes has a knowledge transfer plan been prepared to ensure that the process teams (and the business unit/area concerned) will be sufficiently confident and competent to operate the processes at the 'go live' date?

▶ What changes to support arrangements will be required thereafter to ensure effective operation? Are the necessary steps being taken to ensure that these are in place, documented and monitored?

▶ What is being done to capture and exploit knowledge specifically relating to the support of the processes concerned?

▶ Could this knowledge and any of the tools be used to support the people and processes of other organizations?

Process review and revision

Are arrangements for process review and revision in place? In particular:

▶ At what intervals are the processes and job support tools reviewed to ensure they continue to reflect process designs and current objectives and priorities?

▶ Who undertakes these reviews?

▶ Are the knowledge creation and exploitation aspects adequately addressed?

▶ When systems developments, activity changes and other projects that may have process implications are undertaken, are the risks to process integrity assessed?

▶ If changes are to be made, who examines their consequences?

▶ Are the implications for knowledge creation and exploitation adequately assessed?

Process control

Are arrangements for process control in place? In particular:

▶ Are controls in place to prevent unapproved changes from occurring?

▶ Are there controls to ensure overall process considerations are taken into account when individual changes are made?

▶ Who is responsible for ensuring that proposed changes and updates to the processes are compatible with overall 'end-to-end' or total process requirements?

▶ Do controls adequately address knowledge creation and exploitation considerations?

▶ Are changes and updates approved by the business process vision holder?

Process context

Where do the processes fit within the overall corporate organization? In particular:

▶ In relation to new processes, who is to run the business units/areas concerned when the processes 'go live'?

▶ Who will form the unit/area management teams?

▶ Have these teams been given a clear direction, and clear goals and priorities? Do these cover the acquisition, development, sharing and exploitation of information, knowledge and understanding, and the use of relevant job support tools?

▶ Have the roles and responsibilities of unit managers and other team members been agreed? Are these clear in relation to boundaries and interfaces with other groups?

▶ What are the key lateral relationships with other business units/areas? Are appropriate liaison relationships in place?

▶ Will training and development be needed to equip the business unit/area teams, and their individual members, to operate effectively?

▶ Will this cover the creation and exploitation of knowledge and the use of appropriate job support tools? How important is this for the teams concerned?

▶ Are the members of the business unit/area teams themselves role models in relation to the acquisition, development, sharing and exploitation of information, knowledge and understanding, and use of relevant support tools?

Process accountability

How do the processes (or units of which they are a part) relate to the business entity as a whole? In particular:

▶ Where do they fit into the entity management process and its annual calendar of meetings? Do these cover the processes' or units' key activities?

▶ What contribution are they expected to make to knowledge creation and exploitation within the entity as a whole?

▶ Is there an effective link with relevant committee/meeting owners, and are the units aware of relevant agenda items, terms of reference, inputs/outputs, reports, etc?

4

Contemporary information problems

INFORMATION OVERLOAD: WINNERS AND LOSERS

The market environments within which people and organizations operate have experienced profound and continuing changes. Many of these relate to the acquisition, development, sharing and exploitation of information, knowledge and understanding. They are creating both problems, as people struggle to cope, and opportunities for those who would like to make money by helping them.

Individual entrepreneurs and corporate managers vary greatly in the extent to which they are aware of what is happening around them and taking appropriate action. People who focus upon what others need to do to respond and achieve their objectives are more likely to succeed.

Individuals at most levels and in many roles require assistance. The 'others' who might need help could range from stressed-out senior executives seeking some means of screening their flow of 'inputs' to relatively homogeneous groups of workers whose performance might massively benefit from best practice know-how that is captured and accessible via practical job support tools.

The collection, processing and communication of information and knowledge are core activities of contemporary organizations. Indeed they are the rationale and *raison d'être* of many of them and the focus of competition. Know-how accounts for a steadily growing proportion of corporate added value and operating costs. Once the possession of communications technology is assumed, winning requires more than the ability to reach a target, or making material available and providing access. If they are to have an impact, complex messages need to be quickly understood as well as rapidly disseminated.

Increases in publicly available knowledge and widely distributed information can lower barriers to entry. Elsewhere, however, the additional know-how required for effective operation due to technological and scientific advance, or the introduction of complex regulations, has raised them. Some markets have opened up, while in others there has been a shake-out of marginal players.

Existing market participants may find ways of retaining the ownership and control of specialist expertise. Professional bodies, licensing authorities and administrative bottlenecks can also restrict the flow of new entrants. As some restrictive practices are removed people work hard on various pretexts to create other barriers, including the need to 'protect' the public.

Individuals and businesses face a dilemma. Participation in networks and joining a partnership may depend upon the possession of scarce – if not unique – expertise while at the same time they are expected to share what they know. Give away too much while working collaboratively and they may no longer be perceived as special.

Overall, some have benefited from the wider availability of knowledge ranging from the basic to the more advanced, while others have been disadvantaged by it. Both 'winners' and 'losers' are potential customers for knowledge entrepreneurs who set out to help people to seize opportunities and/or cope with challenges.

Exercise 4a: Likes and dislikes

Objective and impartial analysis of a situation may be the right thing from a corporate perspective. However, intending entrepreneurs who desire to take control of their lives should form a personal view of what they like and dislike about the alternatives open to them. They should pause, look and think before they jump.

People should not aim for theoretical solutions. Each person needs to determine the best course of action from his or her own individual perspective. The chosen option should be based upon what someone most enjoys doing and, as a consequence, does well or would really like to do and thus would be motivated to succeed at.

What do you most like or dislike about the current situation you are in? What is missing, including in relation to information, knowledge and understanding? What could you do without? What would you like in its place?

Whom do you most like or dislike among those around you? Which of them would you associate with if you were free to choose your own colleagues? Which of them would you avoid? Who among them contributes new knowledge, or could produce additional know-how that would be desirable?

WINNING AND LOSING

Many people experience a mild schizophrenia. They have gained in some areas and lost in others. As a consequence, they are both 'winners' and 'losers' at the same time. The ready availability of information has made some aspects of life easier, while its greater volume has made others more difficult.

Many organizations are in the same position. They simultaneously face both a feast and a famine. Being able to know more about individual customers creates additional cross-selling opportunities. On the other hand, more hours are spent analysing data and reading the rising tide of e-mails about the many possibilities. Process and systems changes may also be required before a potential benefit can become a reality.

Different individuals may also vary in their reactions to similar situations. Thus some might welcome wider choice while others are worried by it. Up to a point some people will place themselves in the former category, but beyond such a threshold of tolerance may become overloaded or confused.

Past investments in information technologies have created the ability to generate an embarrassing wealth of information on just about every aspect of corporate operation. Having 'spent the money', many managers want to use the potential they have created and visibly demonstrate their contribution by producing additional reports. However, corporate decision makers often find it difficult to obtain the specific information they require as and when they need it. From their perspective no one seems able to respond to the most basic of queries.

Customers can find themselves in the same position. If they ask more than one supplementary question a hapless call centre operator refers them to a supervisor. Often they wonder why it is that a supplier that was eager to take their money, and displays various kite marks on its notepaper, finds it so difficult to address an obvious question from a user perspective.

There are also those embarrassing moments when dramatic developments take people by surprise. Something happens that no one has foreseen and it is impossible to obtain a response. No one is confident enough to venture an opinion. Subsequently, when a post-mortem is undertaken, warning signs may be found in many quarters, but by then it might be too late.

Many operators have so much information to process that assessing, summarizing, understanding and disseminating what is relevant takes more time than is available to react and seize a window of opportunity. This is an issue as much for emergency, security and other public services as it is for businesses. Mechanisms are in place for processing data and information but not for understanding them or assessing their significance.

Such situations represent potential opportunities for knowledge entrepreneurs. By way of cost justification whatever is charged for their solutions should be compared with the consequences of inaction.

Dealing with increasing volumes of information and knowledge can be very costly and time consuming. Maybe an independent review could be offered with the aim of eliminating all reports that do not really have 'end customers' and putting screens in place to cut out marginal information flows and highlight the more significant items. Maybe the latter could be presented with a commentary and suggested next steps.

The contemporary corporation is a network of relationships with various external parties, including customers, suppliers and business partners. Innovation, collaboration and the introduction of new ways of operating may depend upon people with a broader perspective who can provide relevant answers at an acceptable cost.

The need for additional support is not good news for companies that compete on speed of response and/or need to cut costs as their margins are eroded. Moreover, they may have to do this while fewer people struggle to cope with generally heavier workloads. On the other hand, working with knowledge entrepreneurs might enable them to offer the additional services that would justify a premium price (Coulson-Thomas, 2002a).

Many organizations would benefit by letting knowledge entrepreneurs loose on their internal operations and relationships with customers and business partners. They should be encouraged, developed and supported. Increasing the cost-effectiveness of accessing, developing and sharing information, knowledge and understanding can be a vital and major source of competitive advantage, while their more effective exploitation may generate additional income streams.

Exercise 4b: Impact and reaction analysis

Various new challenges and opportunities are approaching, and many of these concern information or knowledge. As with rain clouds or a shower of meteorites, you know – either because you can see or you have been told – that they are imminent. But you may not be sure about what their effects are going to be or how you will react. Forewarned is forearmed. You need to think through *their* potential impacts and *your* possible reactions.

What is coming your way? What are the consequences likely to be for you personally and those around you? How might you gain from or take advantage of what may happen? What new information or knowledge will be required?

How are you likely to react? Are there other options? What information or knowledge would improve your ability to cope? Are there impacts that you could deflect or avoid? How might you benefit from helping others to handle what is likely to occur or react to it?

THE SEARCH FOR SINGLE SOLUTIONS

Deficiencies in the management practices of many organizations have implications for knowledge entrepreneurs. While some directors and managers may be aware of changes in the business environment, their responses are often ineffective or make matters worse. In particular, the steps they take to become more effective at acquiring, developing, sharing and exploiting know-how create new problems.

Senior decision makers are regularly subjected to sales literature promoting particular management techniques or technologies. Yet the 'solutions' offered are rarely, if ever, sufficient in themselves to address the generic problem their advocates profess to tackle. At best, even if they are beneficial, their adoption gives a purchaser the same capability as other firms supplied by the same or equivalent providers.

A standard approach that might be acceptable for hidden and 'non-core' support activities can condemn a business to obscurity when applied to a critical success factor. Innovators who fundamentally change how business is done usually do so by bringing together a novel combination of the different elements they require to stand out and deliver additional value.

What aspiring leaders need is help in bringing the various pieces of the jigsaw together to make a new picture. This is not easy to find. The sales staff of individual suppliers may have a basic understanding of the main items within their own product ranges. However, they are often clueless as to how these might relate to or link up with those supplied by competitors. Integration with the offerings of other vendors is left to systems integrators or specialist consultants.

The fashionable focus upon 'core competencies' can compound the problem of limited and selective vision. People become introverted and unaware of what is happening elsewhere. Companies concentrate upon their heartland products at the expense of sensitivity to the potential for innovation and creative combination.

As companies slim down they often lose whatever time may have been spent thinking about uses and applications and links and connections. They concentrate upon knowledge relating to their particular technology, and its past and current use colours their perception of its relevance. Their vision becomes limited by existing experience. As a consequence, they may not be aware of the full range of opportunities and alternative options that might be open to more imaginative spirits.

Accumulating more information on past usage and using data-mining tools to analyse it may not help. Previous applications might not relate to current concerns or future plans. Hence any findings that are presented may or may not be relevant. Instead, 'blue skies' thinking may be required, a skill that should be possessed by imaginative knowledge entrepreneurs.

Creative companies proactively look for alternative ways in which different elements can be brought together (Coulson-Thomas, 2001). Their processes and supporting systems are geared up to monitor challenges facing customers, flag up exceptions and model alternatives. Effort is devoted to identifying people who ask thought-provoking questions. Rather than concentrating exclusively upon the analysis of what already exists they search for gaps and speculate about what might be.

In many companies people are alert to some pieces of the jigsaw puzzle but not to others that may be needed to complete a different picture. Because they lack awareness of what they do not know they fail to introduce new variables into the equation and creatively combine different technologies and management approaches.

Most suppliers only sell particular pieces of the jigsaw puzzle. Hence objective advice concerning how different combinations of components might be brought together is sometimes hard to come by. Whole teams may be employed selling A and B as self-contained products when what is really required is someone who knows how A, B and perhaps C could be combined to achieve a desired purpose.

To make matters worse existing suppliers may have a vested interest in discouraging users from considering alternatives. Because such vendors only push services and 'solutions' based upon the methodologies or technologies they sell, corporate users need independent and objective advice about how additional elements might be incorporated. This creates opportunities for knowledge entrepreneurs with a broader perspective who focus upon what colleagues or clients are endeavouring to achieve.

Exercise 4c: Confronting reality

More information and knowledge does not automatically lead to greater understanding. Many people have had enough of illusion. Rather than juggle with the superficial and 'play games' they would like to address the fundamentals of their lives. There could be opportunities for others to help them to do so:

- Identify some areas in which illusion is widespread.
- List those in which the illusion relates to available knowledge and understanding.
- Rank these according to the extent to which there appears to be some evident or latent dissatisfaction with the status quo.
- Distinguish between those who either benefit from or prefer illusion, and those who are frustrated by it.
- Within the latter group assess how many of them may need to be helped to move beyond illusion in order to identify and work upon reality.

- Consider how important confronting reality is to those you have identified.
- Assess how much they might be prepared to pay for relevant knowledge-based services such as professional counselling and advice.
- In the light of what is required and how much could be charged, develop concepts for products and services that would help people to improve their understanding and confront reality.
- Consider who might be able to help you to develop and deliver them.
- Consider also what forms of reality are being sought, and whether there are opportunities to introduce specific offerings for those who would like to demonstrate a rejection of illusion.

TAKING CERTAIN APPROACHES TOO FAR

Not only are single solutions adopted but some approaches that might work up to a point are taken too far. They cease to be beneficial and become counter-productive. Diminishing returns may quickly set in. Further advances in one area may be obtained at the expense of additional problems elsewhere. Overall adaptability in an uncertain and turbulent environment may be compromised rather than enhanced.

In themselves many management approaches are neutral. How they are applied and for what purpose determine whether they help or harm. Many applications of process management represent an example. When 'team players' and 'generalists' replace isolated 'specialists' the ability to handle complex cases may be lost. A more balanced approach might be to complement multi-skilled and multi-functional process teams with individual professionals or centres of competence in order to bring greater expertise to bear upon certain tasks and problems. The right job support tools can also raise the performance of generalists.

While multi-skilling may offer certain advantages, such as flexibility during holiday periods, these may come at a cost. Particular expertise may be lost after centres of distinctive excellence are broken up. Trade-offs and likely implications should be addressed ahead of intended moves. Thus specialists could be retained or hired to handle exceptions or relevant support tools developed. Knowledge entrepreneurs could operate under contract to tackle exceptions and difficult questions.

Customers today increasingly demand bespoke responses. The consequences of establishing, prescribing and supporting particular paths through an organization in the interests of order and predictability can be similar to the results of replacing the flexibility of the human brain with the programmed responses of a robot. Imaginative routeing, sensitive tailoring, the accommodation of individual requirements, creative questioning and organic development may all become more difficult to achieve.

Some companies lack balance by insisting upon common approaches regardless of local circumstances. They impose a 'general solution' upon a diversity of contexts, rather than adopt a succession of bespoke responses to meet the differing requirements of each situation. A common language may help different parts of an organization to communicate with each other, and people may find it easier to switch between roles, but tailored activities might better satisfy individual customers.

Greater staff mobility is sometimes obtained at a cost. Relationships are disrupted. Individuals may not be in a particular position long enough to obtain an adequate understanding of an issue, or be able to judge to whom to refer for sound advice or a specialist opinion. They may not fully appreciate the nuances of a situation or the significance of certain developments or comments.

Such situations represent opportunities for entrepreneurs to provide supporting counsel, relevant tools and much needed continuity. In-house staff can concentrate upon their management roles confident in the knowledge that arrangements have been made to provide specialist back-up as and when required.

Of course, external individuals providing specialist knowledge and back-up services – including former employees – need to be kept up to date. Arrangements made for this could include access to technical information, attendance at internal briefing meetings, the regular updating of support tools, and opportunities to visit laboratories and workshops.

Specialist expertise that is subject, technology or application specific may be eroded overnight by technical or political developments. People who employ and retain subject experts need to be on their guard. The most expensive individual today could become the least valuable tomorrow. Besides, even when an authority or superstar's knowledge is current an organization may lack the means of capturing it and sharing it with colleagues, for example through the use of job support tools.

Certain approaches may become fashionable and common throughout an industry or sector, in which case doing something different may help to differentiate a company from its competitors. This should be borne in mind when contracting out services in order to 'share' support costs. It may be worth paying a premium in order to be distinctive where it is likely to register with customers.

Some companies that were once intellectual leaders within their fields have regressed to the level of a typical supplier as a result of adopting a 'me-too' approach to corporate restructuring. In the name of re-engineering senior managers have taken a knife to their organizations. They have cut out people with experience and expert knowledge whose value has only been understood after they have gone. Following the herd can lead to the loss of specialized expertise and erode what is most distinctive and special about an organization.

Supporting people with packaged know-how and encouraging them to refer to it can seem reasonable when transactions are similar and there are regulatory requirements to observe and commercial risks to avoid. However, again disadvantages can arise if an approach is taken too far, particularly as more bespoke responses are required. Monitoring may be reduced or even cease in the mistaken belief that checks now occur within the process. Operators may also come to distrust their own judgement.

If too much is prescribed or automated, people can become deskilled. They may simply 'go automatic' or 'follow the flow', rather than think creatively about each situation, case, task or opportunity. There are entrepreneurial opportunities for those who understand the downside of overdependence upon the 'system'.

Many organizations need help in ensuring that provision of what is already known does not inhibit innovation and the creation of new knowledge. Where differentiation and tailored responses are required, providing approved answers and suggested solutions might not be the best solution. It may be better to offer configuration tools, learning environments and workspaces that people can use to craft unique solutions.

Exercise 4d: Obstacles and barriers analysis

Obstacles and barriers to individual achievement and corporate performance need to be flushed out so that they can be brought to ground. Both individuals and organizations should undertake the following steps to assess what is required:

● Rank your organization's or clients' corporate objectives in order of priority.

- For each objective, identify the major obstacles, constraints, pitfalls and barriers that are standing in the way of its achievement.
- Group the various factors that are inhibiting or preventing progress and attainment according to features they have in common.
- Rank the factors, and any groupings that emerge, in order of perceived significance, ie the extent to which progress would be speeded up and performance improved if each of them were removed.
- Make explicit and attempt to quantify the benefits of removing particular obstacles, constraints, pitfalls and barriers.
- Examine the factors and groupings that are thought to be most significant for common root and contributory causes, and sort these into a ranking of perceived significance.
- Starting with the most significant causal factor, and working down the priority list, assess what needs to be done to address each of them, ie reduce, remove or ameliorate their impacts.
- In each case, assess how new or better information, knowledge or job support tools might help.
- Continue until a point is reached at which including a further set of actions might begin to spread the available effort and resource too thinly and hence prejudice the tackling of more important factors.
- List specific actions arising out of what needs to be done, and allocate roles and responsibilities for undertaking them.
- Identify and scope any dependencies and incremental resource or competence requirements, and prepare a business case for any expenditures and investments that may be required, utilizing the estimates already made of the likely results of removing the obstacle(s) or barrier(s) concerned.
- Systematically undertake the actions that have been identified to tackle the various factors that are standing in the way of achievement, success and fulfilment.
- Consider whether other people and organizations may be experiencing the same obstacles, constraints, pitfalls and barriers.
- If so, assess the extent to which the actions that have been identified and the experiences that are obtained in tackling them could be packaged to form the basis of a product or service that could be offered elsewhere in the marketplace.

BARKING UP THE WRONG TREE

While adopting management approaches that disrupt relationships and stress their people, some organizations overlook latent opportunities or ignore areas of obvious potential. Thus they re-engineer just about every business process except those for winning business. Inaction is justified on the grounds that bidding is a lottery or success is outside of the corporation's control because external parties are involved. Yet critical success factors for effective bidding have been identified (Kennedy and O'Connor, 1997) and can be built into sales productivity support tools.

Subjecting processes and practices for winning business to independent review and capturing and sharing the lessons of success and failure after procurement decisions are announced can significantly improve win rates. Some managers appear more concerned with ensuring re-engineering projects are self-contained and easily managed than transforming critical areas of corporate performance. Rationalization rather than inspiration appears to be the aim.

Many senior people are risk averse and inherently lazy. They avoid difficult challenges and entrepreneurial approaches in favour of straightforward tasks where results are more predictable. And they employ consultants to do the work. This at least is good news for knowledge entrepreneurs who do not shy away from difficulty. They should focus upon the areas of greatest potential for making an impact.

Another arena of missed opportunity arises because while internal processes are re-engineered those that embrace the supply chain and business partners are often ignored. If an organization only delivers say 20 per cent of the value consumed by an end customer then, from that user's perspective however effective internal re-engineering might be, it may only address a fifth of the total opportunity. Entrepreneurs can help collaborating parties to put in place the coordination and knowledge-sharing arrangements needed for effective value chain re-engineering.

Most re-engineering teams also appear to overlook direction setting, management and support processes. These can be of greater significance than the business processes they focus upon. For example, while they may recognize the benefits of becoming a 'learning organization' few boards initiate the identification and re-engineering of their companies' learning processes. Ultimately, an enterprise that learns more effectively than its competitors will be more successful. The ability to acquire, develop, share and exploit know-how should be regarded as a core competence.

A lack of ambition constrains many organizations. While paying lip service to the need for transformational change, they persist in using approaches that at best deliver incremental impacts. They analyse and document current processes and then seek to improve them.

A more radical approach starts with a blank sheet of paper and 'blue skies' thinking. People examine trends and developments in the business environment in order to open their minds to the various ways in which people, processes, systems, information and knowledge might be brought together. By enabling them to discover alternative approaches, additional elements and different skill sets, knowledge entrepreneurs can help to create a better alternative. For example, the performance of people in existing roles might be transformed by the provision of best practice-based job support tools.

Many re-engineering methodologies are excessively prescriptive and mechanical. Innovators usually find that patterns do not simply jump out of existing data. Of course some people do experience a sudden insight. More often, however, patience and persistence are required. Progress results from people asking the right questions and posing them in ways that help them to search for new information, novel links, different patterns or additional relationships.

Some organizations have already lost interest in 're-engineering'. Long before they could grasp how to implement it properly they started looking for another 'big idea' to adopt. 'Knowledge management' is a more recent contender for the management fashion crown. Yet process thinking can be usefully applied to the creation and exploitation of knowledge. For example, people could identify obstacles and barriers to knowledge sharing and corporate learning.

Many organizations move on to the next panacea or fad before the results of previous enthusiasms have come through. They do not settle long enough to have a beneficial impact. They become impatient or bored. Yet the development and sharing of new knowledge, and the creation, packaging and management of intellectual capital do not happen spontaneously of their own accord. Certain enablers from systems and procedures to attitudes and motivations may need to be in place. For example, people may need the tools to handle knowledge in a variety of different formats.

The lack of balance found in many approaches to management, the naïve faith in single solutions and the tendency to miss many of the areas of greatest opportunity create unprecedented opportunities for new knowledge-based services. To avoid introversion and obtain more objective advice there may be advantages in looking to new entrants into the marketplace rather than existing players who may find it more difficult to break away from past practices.

BARRIERS TO ENTRY

Many people are so preoccupied with their current operations they become oblivious to what is happening around them. Reference has already been made to deficiencies in contemporary approaches to management and the increasing demand from customers for more bespoke responses and personalized offerings. Let us turn now to some other developments that have implications for knowledge entrepreneurs.

Barriers to entry are changing. In many sectors scale and history are becoming less important than current relevance and future ambitions. Quite small companies, even sole practitioners, can afford the technology to make direct contact with potential customers around the world and deliver well-produced proposals and reports. The Internet and business advisory services can be used to assemble an international network of contacts and collaborating partners.

In some sectors, for example where brands are important, new entrants may be at a disadvantage. Customers may not wish to be seen with an unknown label. Image and reputation may reflect the size of an advertising budget and time an organization has had to build up a loyal following. In other arenas people are willing to switch suppliers to get a better deal or more relevant service. Maybe technological advance has rewritten the rules and the resulting game is new for all players.

A start-up company that employs a better Web designer than a bigger and longer-established one may have a more impressive and responsive 'front end'. The larger company with established procedures may be cumbersome and inflexible in comparison. Changes that involve writing off past investments and goodwill may be resisted. There might be termination payments to be paid when people are laid off. Penalties may be incurred when unexpired leases are terminated.

One advantage of size is the opportunity to collect information about the requirements and habits of a larger customer base. There should be more cases and greater user experience to analyse. This may allow statistical findings to be expressed with greater confidence. However, not all companies take full advantage of such opportunities and a committed smaller operator may learn more from fewer examples.

For many perhaps the biggest remaining barrier to entry is the change of attitude and perspective that is needed to understand what is happening and respond accordingly. Entrepreneurial organizations take the initiative. They put the necessary arrangements, people, processes and technologies in place to acquire, develop and share the know-how needed to become an effective player in new arenas of opportunity.

Military observers are familiar with the consequences of mechanically implementing a game plan, as opposed to a more thinking execution, that while focused upon end objectives is also sensitive to sudden opportunities and the conditions of the moment. Military planners devote considerable resources, and many of their most capable people, to the acquisition and analysis of intelligence and the timely provision to those in the front line of the particular information that they need to be effective in their roles and to overcome whatever problems they face.

Uncertainty can act as a barrier, and the marketplace of many corporations is as competitive, changing and confused as battlefield conditions. Hence corporate teams may seek to operate as an efficient machine rather than as a sensitive, learning and adaptive organism. This can be counter-productive. While linear improvements in certain areas may have been achieved as a result, there are many examples of a steady decline of overall capability and the capacity to renew and remain relevant and vital.

Managers' checklist

Managers need to ensure that the effective acquisition, development, sharing and exploitation of information, knowledge and understanding occur within the areas for which they are responsible, and that their people are supported with appropriate knowledge-based tools. The following questions need to be addressed:

▶ Does the organization operate in a sector in which information, knowledge and understanding are accounting for an increasing proportion of the value that is being generated for customers and end users? What are the implications of current and future trends for your role and responsibilities?

▶ Are you a good example or 'role model' to your team? Do you hoard information or do you share it with your colleagues? Do you actively champion and encourage the acquisition, development, sharing and exploitation of information, knowledge and understanding within your team?

▶ Do you encourage the members of your team to regularly record and periodically review what they have learnt? Are they learning from failures as well as successes?

▶ Is the expertise of 'superstars' and external authorities being captured in the form of job support tools that can be used by other members of your team to improve their performance? Are these tools periodically reviewed and updated?

▶ What has your unit contributed to the knowledge base of the organization of which it is a part? What is the value of the intellectual capital it has created? Could it do more?

▶ Do you take appropriate steps both to protect and to exploit the knowledge assets for which you are responsible?

▶ When external consultants are used, or members of your team engage in collaborative activities with colleagues in other units and organizations, what steps do you take to ensure that effective knowledge transfer occurs?

▶ What could or should your team do to reduce its dependence upon external sources of information, knowledge and understanding in sensitive areas, where future flows are uncertain or acquisition costs are high?

▶ Are there regular opportunities, such as particular events, for your people to share what they have learnt?

▶ Is your team plugged in to external sources of information and knowledge? Do members participate in relevant information- and knowledge-sharing networks?

▶ What do you do to motivate your colleagues to become net contributors to the knowledge base of the organization? Do you encourage reflection, enquiry, discovery, questioning and debate? Are suitable environments and facilities provided for this purpose?

▶ Do you know which members of your team are adding to the corporate well of knowledge and which are drawing from it? What are you doing to retain the services of the former group, and to encourage the latter to become net contributors?

▶ Could the more routine and repetitive work of people who are handling existing information and knowledge be automated to enable them to be switched to more creative and value-adding roles? What process changes are needed and what supporting technologies and tools would help?

▶ What are you doing to sustain the employability of the various members of your team? Do you encourage and enable them to assume personal responsibility for remaining up to date?

▶ Do you benchmark the competence and practice of your team, and what it knows, against equivalent groups in other organizations? How entrepreneurial, imaginative and innovative is it in relation to the generation of know-how and exploitation of knowledge assets?

▶ Does your group possess information, knowledge and understanding that are not being fully utilized? Could this be packaged in such a way as to be of value to other groups within the organization, or to generate incremental income from external parties?

▶ Do you foster an atmosphere and culture of trust within the group, and encourage responsible risk taking?

▶ Would you encourage or discourage someone within your team who expressed an interest in establishing his or her own business? Could your unit, or another part of the organization, become a collaborating business 'partner'?

▶ What mentoring, counselling or other support do you provide to latent and aspiring entrepreneurs? Could or should your group become an incubator unit for information- and knowledge-based ventures and enterprises?

CHANGING ORGANIZATIONS AND EMERGING ISSUES

Many organizations are undergoing a process of transformation. Increasingly, they are no longer defined in terms of people who are employed and working in buildings that are rented or owned. Instead, their parameters and capability are defined by the nature of the networks that support the various patterns of communication and interaction that are occurring, and the shared rules and principles that govern these relationships.

New skills, competencies, networks, support facilities and services are required. Markets are being established within organizations, creating internal as well as external opportunities for entrepreneurs. The nature of the senior management and board agenda is changing. Different issues such as the protection of intellectual property and the integrity of the network increasingly demand pride of place.

Investigations undertaken by the author (Coulson-Thomas, 1997) suggest that many people within commercial and public sector organizations are not clear about the distinction between information and knowledge. The two are often confused. There may well be information about available knowledge, but information itself is usually only one input into the process of producing new knowledge and understanding. Knowledge creation generally requires reflection, imagination, discovery, research and testing in addition to access to relevant data or situations in which it can be collected, generated and assessed or tested.

Knowledge *per se* is often overvalued. Some people and many organizations appear to accumulate knowledge largely for its own sake. Knowledge *of* something can be less valuable than understanding how to *do* something. Organizations generally need relevant information, knowledge and understanding. One without the other two is often insufficient. Similarly, expertise usually requires skills and tools as well as relevant knowledge.

Certain information, for example of price changes, can be of critical importance. However, in other contexts too much irrelevant information may be acquired, communicated and disseminated. It is also often treated as a commodity rather than as a resource, tool or enabler of knowledge and understanding. The development, capturing and application of expertise – for example, within appropriate support tools – may be the issue that should be addressed rather than merely adding to an existing inventory of information.

The information explosion is not the only issue that should be on management and boardroom agendas. Organizations face other challenges, from internationalization to more demanding customers. Some of these, for example the threat of terrorism or defence against hackers, might appear more pressing but an organization that does not establish for itself a value-creating role in the information and knowledge society may lack a rationale for continued existence.

We have seen that the impacts of the information revolution are many and varied. As a consequence it may not be easy to categorize them as either challenges or opportunities, or to assess and prioritize them. However, it is often found that an improved approach to accessing, communicating and sharing information can have a beneficial impact on almost every area of corporate operation. The pay-offs from knowledge entrepreneurship, both short-term and long-term, can sometimes be considerable.

Again balance is required. Too much emphasis is often placed upon 'hard' issues such as structures and systems at the expense of due consideration of other areas, for example the roles, competencies, attitudes, feelings or values of people and the quality of relationships between them.

Despite the attention given to 'balanced scorecards', measurement still tends to be focused upon indicators of corporate operation that are relatively easy to quantify, such as money or stock, while the 'softer' areas just mentioned, and less tangible considerations such as 'relevance', are overlooked. Areas to focus upon are the critical success factors for managing change, competing and winning (Coulson-Thomas, 2002b).

Many management teams fail to focus upon the areas of greatest opportunity when they use contemporary management approaches and emerging technologies. Thus in some companies just about every process is re-engineered except that for winning business. If this has happened with 're-engineering', why should it not happen again? As already pointed out, excessive emphasis is often placed upon single solutions, and there are worrying signs that 'knowledge management' could become yet another fad.

Too often new approaches are adopted and applied without adaptation to local circumstances. An imported methodology is uncritically applied and implementation is insufficiently tailored to the distinct requirements of the particular culture, situation and context. Often a general solution is not appropriate without significant modification and the addition of missing change elements.

Most research and guidance concerns the individual elements, or building blocks, of potential solutions and responses rather than how an appropriate and relevant combination of them might be brought together for a particular purpose. Knowledge entrepreneurs can help people to identify areas of deficiency and assemble what they need to succeed.

Many management teams are preoccupied almost exclusively with internal restructuring and cost cutting. While internal effectiveness is highly desirable and short-term pressures may be intense they should also consider business development requirements. More attention should be devoted to creating customer value, generating new opportunities, building longer-term relationships and securing competitive advantage.

We will return to these issues in later chapters. Effective directors and many successful entrepreneurs have a 'helicopter' or holistic perspective. They have the ability to recognize, assess, synthesize and appreciate a situation as a whole. They do not become unduly fixated with particular areas and activities at the expense of understanding the whole.

The resolution of many boardroom issues involves the integration of disparate elements. Hence a number of different people – including knowledge entrepreneurs – may be involved in the analysis and implementation of what is required. They may have to be imbued with a sense of urgency and made aware of how much is at stake and the consequences of failure. The survival of a company and the livelihoods of its people may depend upon effective responses to the many questions posed in the various checklists of this book.

CHECKLIST

▶ Do you really understand all the areas in which you claim to have specialist knowledge?

▶ Is your professional standing based in whole or in part upon illusion?

▶ Do you knowingly communicate information and knowledge that does little to increase the understanding of others?

▶ Are you reluctant to reveal the essence of your expertise and share it with colleagues in the form of job support tools that they could use to improve their performance?

▶ Do you like being perceived as an 'expert', an 'authority' or 'someone who knows'?

▶ How much of what you feel is important to you is actually a mirage or self-deception?

▶ How dependent are you upon the trappings of office, and the opinions and attentions of others?

▶ Are you attracted or repelled by sinecures, and grand-sounding but essentially meaningless titles and roles?

▶ Do you rationalize events and experiences in order to make them easier to handle, or do you confront challenges and wrestle with issues?

▶ Are you susceptible to hype or resistant to it? Do you fall for flattery?

▶ Why do you and those around you sustain certain illusions rather than address reality? Is there a collective conspiracy to avoid confronting the truth?

▶ Are you in the business of creating and sustaining illusions? Do your customers and your clients request, require or need them?

▶ What would be lost if your current role disappeared? Who in the external world would notice or care?

▶ If you could start again with a clean sheet what would you do differently? What would you like more of and less of?

▶ What options do you have for a change of direction? What is holding you back?

▶ What are the major barriers between where you are and where you would like to be?

▶ How many of these relate to you personally, and how many of them would apply to anyone setting out with similar objectives?

▶ Who or what is holding you back from confronting reality? What do you need to shed in order to get airborne?

▶ Are you constrained by past commitments and obligations? Could these be renegotiated?

▶ Do the assumptions and expectations of others inhibit you?

▶ How many of the barriers that you have identified are real, and how many of them are rationalizations or exist only in your own imagination?

▶ Should you set out to tackle them, or could they be circumvented?

▶ How much discretion and freedom of manoeuvre do you really have?

▶ Can you identify the gatekeepers or guardians that block your way?

▶ Whose support could you enlist in planning your escape?

▶ Who stands to gain or lose should you manage to break free? Might some of the potential beneficiaries become useful allies?

▶ If you succeed how might you package what you will have learnt in the form of services that could be offered to others with a desire to 'get real'?

▶ When would be a good moment to act?

5

Requirements of different stakeholders

We have seen in previous chapters that the greater availability and accessibility of information and knowledge are creating challenges and opportunities for both individuals and corporate management teams. Their combined impact brings into question the very nature of today's organizations and how they operate. To understand what this revolution means for the various groups with an interest in a company we need to examine the requirements of different stakeholders.

CUSTOMERS

Customers are interested in what current and potential suppliers can do for them. Increasingly, they both desire and demand tailored products and services, and the freedom to purchase and consume when, where and with whom they please. In short, they have become more conscious of 'buyer power', and they like to feel in control.

As suppliers respond, customers become more accustomed to having the means and the clout to specify exactly what they would like and when. Because of their convenience, many people are attracted by delivery mechanisms that begin with 'tele', from teleshopping and tele-banking to teleworking and telemedicine. This creates opportunities for knowledge entrepreneurs to provide support and relationship-building tools that present options and quickly calculate the consequences of different choices.

Consumers like to feel that they are known, understood and valued. Those dealing with them – from sales representatives to call centre staff – can be supported by a variety of systems for presenting on a screen whatever is known about each customer that calls. The analysis of patterns of past transactions may make it possible to anticipate require-ments and suggest alternatives.

Suppliers can also initiate more proactive relationships with customers, to the extent that this finds favour with them. Maybe they could be provided with self-assessment or diagnostic tools that might help them to clarify their requirements, better understand how these might be addressed, try out different possibilities and identify areas in which they might need specialist guidance. Such tools could be down-loaded or distributed to them on a CD ROM.

Like those who are endeavouring to supply them, purchasers find it ever more difficult, and sometimes impossible, to keep up with the growing range of possibilities open to them. Beyond a point, people struggle to assess the many alternatives, permutations and combina-tions that are available. Hence interactions, relationships and transac-tions between customers and suppliers may need to be supported by individuals, tools and environments that ensure that the creation and delivery of value to each individual takes account of the full spectrum of feasible options.

Another challenge for those buying many goods, services and tech-nologies is to ensure that what is acquired remains current for the likely duration of a requirement. Development or migration paths need to be communicated and understood as well as developed. The necessary support tools and arrangements need to be in place to ensure this happens. Updates provide an opportunity for continuing contact, sharing the experiences of users, and introducing upgrade possibilities.

Too many buying processes focus almost exclusively upon the initial purchase of a product, package, solution or assignment. More attention needs to be given to ongoing relationships to ensure a continuing flow of relevant benefits over time. A European survey has revealed that the 'development of purchaser-supplier partnerships' is a key issue for purchasing professionals (FitzGerald, 2000). Providing those involved with relevant knowledge and tools represents a considerable opportunity.

Where individual suppliers are not willing or able to provide what is necessary, purchasers will need to make sure that complementary support arrangements are in place. Understanding, service and support gaps create additional openings for knowledge entrepreneurs. It may be possible to change how business is undertaken within existing markets, and create new ones.

Exercise 5a: 'More of' and 'less of' analysis

Many aspiring entrepreneurs are not fully aware of the various factors that hold them back. The constraints might be either external or internal and self-imposed. Working through the different facets of your life and identifying certain aspects you would like more of and others you would prefer less of might help you to understand yourself better and move forward.

Inhibitors, deficiencies, obstacles and barriers can then be ranked in terms of the strength of your preference for either more or less. The relative positions of the various items listed could give you a clearer insight into the sort of person you are in relation to the cultural context and corporate environment in which you work. When considering alternative roles, lifestyles and ways of working and learning, you could compare the profiles of each option with your current requirements.

In relation to your current activities, roles and lifestyle, select the aspects you would prefer to have either more of or less of. Which of the 'negatives' would you most like to be rid of? Similarly, which of the 'positives' would you most like to have more of?

Prioritize your 'more of' and 'less of' requirements. Is there a pattern? Are any of the 'more ofs' and 'less ofs' related? For example, are they opposite sides of the same coin? Does the profile that emerges match your current situation, or are you 'a square peg in a round hole'? As a next step, consider what you and those around you need to do to create circumstances and conditions that are more conducive to entrepreneurship.

SUPPLIERS AND BUSINESS PARTNERS

In many sectors the sharing of information, knowledge and support tools across a supply chain is becoming increasingly important.

Collaborating networks of organizations rather than individual enterprises generate the value experienced by end customers. Those involved in such arrangements must learn how to work together and build collaborative relationships that serve their individual and shared needs.

To be competitive a collaborating network must ensure that distributed workgroups are supported with the people, processes, technologies and tools needed to ensure that full and collective account is taken of relevant know-how. Many knowledge entrepreneurs with ambitions in this area would benefit from a systematic and proven approach to using whatever technologies are current and relevant to re-engineering a supply chain (Bartram, 1996).

Smart companies link up their information systems with those of their customers to lock them in and build closer – if not partnering – relationships (Hurcomb, 1998). Facilities provided could help users to monitor stock levels and consumption patterns, and order items for delivery at the times and locations at which they are required. Creative thinking might reveal many ways in which direct links and regular contacts could be used to offer additional services that would help to justify a price premium and generate extra revenues.

Smart suppliers endeavour to anticipate the requirements of customers and help them to solve emerging problems. Thus as well as accepting and fulfilling electronic orders a company could offer to monitor activities according to pre-established control limits. Cross-selling opportunities might also be identified. HMSO was one of the first organizations to manage the budgets of those ordering electronically.

Tools can also allow customers to design their own products. They need no longer be constrained by the interest and imagination of sales staff. Rules can be built in to ensure outcomes are technically feasible, avoid commercial risks and do not contravene the requirements of a regulator. Designer furniture and fabrics can be ordered for the home, and many purchasers specify the make-up of individual batches of paints, dyes, coatings and chemicals and order them electronically.

Suppliers also need to be responsive to the individual aspirations and requirements of those who work for them. In recent years a major challenge for corporate managers has been to secure flexible access, as and when required, to people with relevant knowledge and expertise. Work–life balance has also become a more significant issue for many people.

A wide variety of patterns of work and contractual relationships can been used. Increasingly, the arrangements adopted are tailored to the requirements of particular individuals with high-level skills that are in demand. Negotiating, managing and supporting such a diversity of relationships can be complex and costly.

Even when a source of relevant skills has been secured, the expertise in question must remain current. Even world-class experts find it ever more difficult to keep up to date with the latest developments in their fields: hence the need for both flexible access to people with relevant professional competence and the supporting information sources, knowledge-based tools and learning environments they need to deploy their skills and experience effectively in changing circumstances and particular contexts.

The individuals who are most successful at refreshing their expertise have what it takes to become knowledge entrepreneurs. They join or establish the support networks they require. They demand or create the tools they need. They are open to new ideas and avid collectors of know-how and people relevant to their aims and ambitions. They bring together the elements required to address opportunities.

INVESTORS

Smart investors back business teams that can succinctly explain what they do, the value they can add and what is distinctive about them. They shun those who struggle during elevator pitches to put themselves across. Many of those seeking finance would greatly benefit from help and practical support tools when communicating their technologies and offerings.

Shrewd shareholders also monitor how effectively companies they invest in derive meaning, opportunities, customer value and intellectual capital from various forms of information and knowledge, and access, develop, share and exploit know-how. In essence this is what corporate knowledge entrepreneurship is all about.

Enhancing understanding should be a core activity of modern corporations. Securing the skills, and developing or acquiring the tools to do this should be a primary concern of their managements and boards.

Too much emphasis has been devoted to living off existing know-how, one-off decisions, 'quick fixes', and other devices for keeping existing organizations afloat. Far too little attention has been paid to: relationships and shared learning; future flows of information, knowledge and understanding; and the attitudes, processes, tools and technologies that might enable a company to learn more effectively than its competitors and set out on voyages of discovery.

Organizations that inhibit or restrict access to the information, knowledge, tools and relationships that people need to generate value and deliver it to their customers do not deserve to survive. Their people might be able to operate more productively on their own or with other support. The extent to which companies enable their staff and business partners to excel at acquiring, developing, sharing and exploiting know-how determines their future relevance and value.

Intelligent and information-rich individuals with intelligent and information-rich homes want to work for – and with – intelligent and information-rich organizations. Employing or commissioning bodies must add value over and above that which people could achieve by themselves with the information, knowledge and other resources at their command. The excess must compensate for any loss of freedom involved.

Companies need to be able to attract, develop and encourage knowledge entrepreneurs. Their activities can result in the generation of new income streams as well as greater success with existing activities. The creation of internal markets and determining distinct roles and levels of competence for knowledge entrepreneurs make it easier for their particular and crucial contribution to be both recognized and rewarded.

Increasingly, value arises out of collaborative activities. A particular company may 'own' only a proportion of the resources involved. Hence investors may find it difficult to judge corporate capacities and capabilities. Performance depends upon 'intangibles' such as the ability to establish trust, maintain relationships and acquire, build and share relevant knowledge, rather than the tangible assets reported upon in the annual report and accounts.

Similarly, the annual general meeting format is increasingly unable to meet investor requirements for an opportunity to question members of the board and senior management team. Opportunities exist for knowledge entrepreneurs to introduce new services that address these needs. Canny shareholders should ask for a demonstration of the sales and other support tools used to communicate with important groups such as customers and prospects and build more intimate relationships with them.

A company itself has interests that a board must balance against those of other stakeholders. There may come a point at which allocating an excessive share of benefits to today's stakeholders in terms of additional dividends, lower prices or extra features at the same cost, or higher salaries and fees might compromise a company's ability to generate and allocate future value.

Exercise 5b: Breakout analysis

Many people are trapped behind prison bars of their own creation. Some are constrained by cynicism or past failures. Others are lazy emotionally, intellectually and entrepreneurially. They are simply too complacent, and may need to think in terms of 'breaking out of jail' in order to confront the realities of their plight.

If your current situation represents a prison in which you are incarcerated, what are the main factors that keep you confined? Which are the weakest bars and which are the strongest? Which ones should you cut first? Do you have what it takes to break out? What tools would you most like to receive hidden in a loaf of bread? How astute are your jailers? Could you talk your way past them? Who on the outside might help?

THE CONTRIBUTION OF BOARDS

In many organizations there are serious shortcomings. Insufficient attention is devoted to the acquisition, development, sharing and application of information, knowledge and understanding. Often senior managers are simply not aware of how dependent performance is upon information flows, support tools, knowledge transfer, the exchange and sharing of relevant understanding, and knowledge entrepreneurship.

The responsibility for this sad state of affairs generally lies with boards and inadequate corporate direction. Many board members have not thought through the distinction between direction and management, the principal sources of board effectiveness, and the various areas of knowledge that a competent director and board ought to have, even though these have been known for a decade (Coulson-Thomas, 1993a, 1993b). This 'blind spot' can have fatal consequences for an enterprise.

The effectiveness of a board is a critical success factor for continuing relevance in the knowledge society:

If a company had a heart or a soul it would be found in the board-room. Intelligence and strength might be discovered in greater measure elsewhere within the corporate organization, but whether or not the company will live and grow, or wither and die, will depend upon the purpose established by the board. It will depend upon the values, the sense of will to generate customer satisfaction, and the drive to achieve excellence and quality that emanates from the board.

(Coulson-Thomas, 1993a)

At the heart of many companies lies an emotional and intellectual vacuum. There is an absence of both purpose and direction. There is insecurity rather than confidence. Far too few boards assess, let alone improve, their own effectiveness, or put in place the direction setting, management, learning and knowledge entrepreneurship processes that would enable them to escape from the dense forests of confusion and uncertainty in which they are both lost and trapped.

Various problem areas suggest that substantially higher levels of remuneration in recent years have not noticeably raised the quality of senior management and direction. Certain long-standing deficiencies (Coulson-Thomas, 1997) remain.

Board attention and many corporate policies, systems and procedures are still biased towards physical assets and tangible activities. Thus considerable effort may be devoted to protecting and maintaining physical assets, keeping records of them up to date and ensuring they are properly depreciated, appropriately described and valued in annual accounts, and physically verified by the auditors at the year end; while intellectual assets are overlooked or inadequately managed (Perrin, 2000).

Many physical assets such as buildings, plant and machinery remain in fixed locations. However, knowledge, understanding and expertise that are critical to the future of businesses 'walk out of the door' each evening in the heads of key employees. Often very little is done to capture, value and protect this know-how.

Today's superstars may already be negotiating to join competitors. If workgroups that are dependent upon them are to remain effective, best practice may need to be incorporated into job support tools and kept up to date. In many companies this is an urgent requirement.

Excessive emphasis is also placed upon 'hard' issues such as structures and systems at the expense of 'softer' consideration such as the roles, competencies, attitudes, feelings and values of people, and the quality of relationships between them. Organization diagrams and systems flow charts appear tangible. They can be modelled, stored, updated and communicated electronically. In comparison, qualities such as intuition and sensitivity that may result from experience can be more difficult to identify and share. These differentiators and determinants of success may not be found in the corporate database.

Knowledge entrepreneurs need to understand how to access and capitalize upon the special attributes of reflective, thinking and feeling people. The qualities that make some individuals more effective than others can often be captured, and devices such as 'traffic lighting' may be used to instil similar attitudes and encourage or enforce equivalent behaviours in others.

Corporate reporting systems and the performance indicators used by many boards focus upon data that are easy to collect rather than the areas that are intrinsically of greatest importance. For example, few companies systematically assess, monitor and reward learning or the creation of new intellectual capital. Knowledge management and measurement systems (Perrin, 2000) may be needed for this purpose.

Many management teams either become distracted from or overlook the areas of greatest opportunity. They sometimes appear to opt for pain rather than gain. Thus internal business sub-processes rather than supply chains or learning processes are re-engineered. Methodologies used do not even raise questions concerning new ways of working and learning, even though these can be introduced during re-engineering and may significantly improve performance (Coulson-Thomas, 1995). Existing departments are restructured while new venture teams are conspicuously absent.

In themselves, many of the methodologies, tools and techniques that companies use are neutral. Where and how they are used, and for what purpose, determine their significance and whether they help or harm (Coulson-Thomas, 1994). Knowledge entrepreneurs should ensure employers and clients gain the maximum of benefit and leverage from their activities, and use relevant and beneficial approaches.

The knowledge that is collected and the purposes to which it is put are very revealing of corporate priorities. Within many companies knowledge of particular tools needs to be complemented with a better understanding of where the opportunity to achieve the greatest impact lies. For example, there is usually considerable scope for improving corporate processes and practices for winning bids in competitive situations (Kennedy and O'Connor, 1997) and building strategic customer relationships (Hurcomb, 1998).

Knowledge can be misused as well as misunderstood and misapplied. Many companies appear locked into descending spirals towards 'commodity product' status (Coulson-Thomas, 1997). Their management teams need to complement cost control and measures to improve internal effectiveness with imagination, inspiration and the use of relevant 'know-how' for generating greater value and external opportunities if they are to 'break out' and initiate ascending spirals of competitive advantage.

It is natural for people to want to play to their strengths and to be biased towards what they know. They tend to stress the value of technologies they are familiar with. They prefer to use management approaches they understand. They are also self-interested and often self-serving. They advocate services they supply. Guidance from a knowledge entrepreneur can correct such biases.

Many boards debate which individual approach to adopt, rather than how elements of a number of distinct but potentially complementary approaches might be brought together to address the various facets of a particular problem or opportunity. Although single solutions rarely work, few directors consider how aspects of different ways of dealing with situations might be combined. Hence many corporate change and transformation programmes are incomplete (Coulson-Thomas, 2002b).

Research and guidance sometimes compound the deficiency just described. Books and conferences generally address selected aspects of reality, either those that interest their authors or speakers respectively, or those that concern the particular topic, discipline or profession concerned. Again, the preoccupation is often with individual building blocks of potential solutions rather than how they might be combined.

Some boards address these problems by introducing 'multi-skilling', or restructuring around more self-contained and self-governing workgroups. However, 'multi-disciplinary' teams also tend to be concerned with subsets of what is required rather than the whole. Knowledge entrepreneurs should adopt a more holistic perspective.

Even when they have been successful elsewhere imported approaches may also require adaptation to be effective in different circumstances. Many boards pay insufficient attention to tailoring policies and practices to the distinct requirements of particular cultures, situations and contexts.

The capturing, categorization and sharing of know-how can exacerbate this problem when only certain aspects or common elements are selected and stored. An appreciation of what is, or was, different, but actually very effective, in a particular application may be lost. The outcome can be 'commodity knowledge' and the mechanical and insensitive application of a standard and unsuitable approach.

The role of a knowledge entrepreneur at a senior level within organizations can be complex and demanding. Board policies and priorities may need to be questioned. People at many levels and corporate processes and practices might have to be challenged to ensure that the acquisition, development, sharing and use of information, knowledge and support tools are focused upon the creation of value for customers and the achievement of corporate goals and objectives.

THE MYTH OF INEVITABLE PROGRESS

Boards want to feel they are adding value. Managers feel under pressure to report progress. People generally assume, often erroneously, that information collection, knowledge assembly and learning are cumulative activities. They hope some kind of ratchet effect is in operation, with the value of the whole growing as more is added.

Many individuals exude a faith in progress reminiscent of confident Victorians. In relation to the building, sharing and application of information, knowledge and understanding they appear oblivious to the prospect of loss and regression occurring. Yet corporate approaches and policies can lead to the loss of both knowledge and experience. Although the rhetoric of 'continuous improvement' may be used, many corporate priorities, cultures and working environments do not encourage the steady accumulation of know-how and expertise (Coulson-Thomas, 1999a).

Promotion and reward decisions favour visible activity and change rather than quiet reflection and continuity. Thinking is for wimps. At review meetings people are asked about what they have 'done'. They are pressed on the new initiatives they have launched and the impacts these have had within the organization. Sharing information and understanding with others and adding to a corporate knowledge base do not capture attention to the same extent.

Superiors are impatient for 'results'. With increasing demands being placed upon them many managers have little time for individual reflection. They avoid going out on a limb and do not try alternatives in case others might doubt whether they are 'team players'. Instead they 'play the game'. They end up accommodating and compromising rather than questioning and challenging.

Mouthing slogans and following fashions may be required to 'fit in'. Yet fads come and go. When a new corporate initiative arrives previous preoccupations may be unceremoniously dumped. People focus on immediate concerns. They perceive that appearing to be current is more important than being relevant or correct.

Findings and suggestions may carry more weight simply because they are 'new'. To be seen with 'old' papers might be taken as evidence that someone is not 'moving on'. People do not want to give the impression of being behind the times. Although there may be other and more promising lines of enquiry they 'go with the flow'.

Discovery can often seem uncertain and chaotic. A catholic approach to information collection, creative methods and the demands of innovation may conflict with 'tidy desk' policies. Considering further options may conflict with calls for 'quick wins'.

People might also have limited filing space, and they may be subject to regular reorganizations and relocation. New office technologies may not be able to handle previous formats. They may feel they have little option but to ditch past papers, notes, articles and reports. This may make it difficult for them to retrace past steps and for colleagues to revisit or retrieve forgone options.

Within many contexts the progressive development of knowledge and understanding is neither inevitable nor necessarily linear. It may occur in fits and starts, only to be followed by periods of stagnation or regression. Graphs and charts that depict projections of ever improving performance may be suspect and are likely to disappoint.

As conditions and circumstances change people should review earlier assumptions. If corporate responses are to match rapidly evolving customer requirements continuous and shared learning must occur. If a periodic cycle of refinement and review does not occur the naïve may be riding for a fall (Coulson-Thomas, 1997). 'Going around in circles' may actually be desirable when the outcome is a positive spiral of knowledge and competence development.

Many boards put insufficient stress upon individual, shared and corporate learning. Improved learning practices, processes, partnerships and support tools are not given the priority they deserve. Limited and short-term improvements in time or cost are achieved at the expense of longer-term knowledge accumulation. Knowledge entrepreneurs will have to work hard to make the exponential growth of know-how and competitiveness a reality.

Exercise 5c: Time analysis

The desire of many people to save time, or use it more effectively, provides diverse potential opportunities for astute entrepreneurs. The following steps could be taken to identify the most promising of these:

- Undertake an analysis of how those whom you encounter, or work with, spend their time.
- Examine also the impacts that significant social, economic and technical trends are likely to have upon this allocation of time.
- List the uses of time that people would like to spend less on and those activities that they would like to spend more time undertaking.

- Distinguish the activities that are most time consuming, lie on a critical path or result in a disproportionate share of benefits derived or value consumed by end users. In these areas there is likely to be the greatest opportunity to make an impact.
- Assess how many other people might be in a similar situation, could have the same aspirations or would share the priorities that have been identified.
- Consider what services would save valuable time or enable a greater proportion of effort to be devoted to more important or fulfilling activities.
- Consider also how many people might be interested in each of these services and how much they would be prepared to pay for them.
- Examine the practicalities of providing each of the services that have been identified, including the costs of developing and marketing them.
- Where prima-facie commercial opportunities appear to exist, prioritize these in terms of factors such as the risks involved and initial investments required that are considered most important when determining whether or not to proceed.
- Prepare a business case for the opportunities that appear to pass whatever initial tests have been applied.

SUPPORTIVE APPROACHES TO MANAGEMENT

Some approaches to management are more supportive of knowledge creation and exploitation than others (Perrin, 2000). Many groups lack self-awareness in this area. They are uncertain of where they stand in relation to factors that inhibit or promote effective knowledge entrepreneurship. For the observant there are usually many clues.

Some of the factors that condition the selection, development, sharing and use of knowledge may not be immediately apparent. Restructuring initiatives, systems projects, technology investments and support tools can all reflect collective assumptions about how people and organizations develop, learn and change. For example, 'scientific' views of management may posit and expect rational behaviour.

Scientific enquiry often benefits from self-discipline and systematic methods. However, in the knowledge economy mechanical approaches based upon rational models are often less conducive to creative entrepreneurship than more holistic, sensitive and 'people-centred' alternatives.

Understanding the implicit principles and implied policies behind successful practices can represent important areas of knowledge and understanding. Making them explicit and building them into support tools can often raise general performance.

The 'rational' techniques employed within many corporate applications of total quality management (TQM) and business process re-engineering (BPR) during their 'golden years' of popularity have caused widespread frustration. Their purpose has been to work people harder or reduce headcounts, rather than to create intellectual capital or generate new income streams (Coulson-Thomas, 1997). Ratios have been improved at the expense of future earnings.

Companies have failed to develop the competencies and capabilities needed to sustain positive spirals of growth and development. Processes are documented and re-routed, and organization charts are changed to reflect the most recent corporate restructuring, but insufficient attention is devoted to 'behavioural' factors. Changing a corporation's architecture may have a negative impact upon people's attitudes, feelings and values.

If a company aspires to create future opportunities, building a community of people who are open minded and freethinking may be a more sensible strategy than the adoption of a complete framework such as TQM that may act as a protective cocoon or result in an excess of order and procedure that might inhibit creativity.

In recent years companies have repeated mistakes made during the last economic downturn (Coulson-Thomas, 2002b). This cannot continue. In many contexts costs have already been cut to the bone. Future increases in performance demand different approaches, particularly the use and application of information, knowledge and support tools to create greater value and additional income streams.

Greater priority needs to be placed upon qualities associated with effective knowledge entrepreneurship such as analysis, reflection, thinking and learning. Rather than subject people to general restructuring and widespread re-engineering, people should be equipped to work more effectively than competitors on key activities such as winning new business, launching new ventures and creating and exploiting know-how.

Particular attention must be devoted to superstars. Their insights and practices need to be captured and shared. People under pressure may clam up. The insecure may hoard rather than share what they know. Failures may be 'hidden under the carpet'. When only successes are communicated and celebrated, and disappointments are concealed or forgotten, opportunities to learn from mistakes are missed.

Focusing upon the accumulation, sharing and creative exploitation of information, knowledge and understanding can put previous concerns into perspective. Past preoccupations may no longer seem important. Priorities shift to more positive and supportive approaches that encourage people to flag up problem areas as quickly as possible so that they might be addressed, and appropriate lessons learnt and shared.

Corporate organization should be regarded as a means to an end rather than an end in itself: 'Organizations should exist to develop and harness the potential and capabilities of both individuals and teams, and to apply collective knowledge, capability and commitment to those activities that deliver value to customers and achieve business objectives' (Coulson-Thomas, 1997).

To achieve their purposes, organizations need to forge new relationships with their people. Many of the most talented individuals leave their existing employers to set up their own businesses rather than negotiate collaborative arrangements with them to create new offerings, ventures and choices that would benefit both parties. The combination of individual drive and initiative and institutional support can be a powerful one and lead to a better future for all concerned.

For synergy to be achieved individuals and organizations need to be open about and share their respective visions, goals, values, strategy and objectives. If full commitment is to be secured, outcomes sought should be mutually beneficial. People need to be able to work and learn in ways that best enable them to harness their potential. They should be allowed and helped to do so.

An organization should be a positive enabler rather than a negative constraint. Its structure, patterns of work, approaches to learning, and the processes and technologies provided should depend upon who is involved, the objectives of those involved and the nature of the activities on which those people are engaged.

If the skills, capabilities and support tools required are to be assembled, all the parties involved must be open about what they and others know and do not know. People also need to be self-aware in relation to how effectively they work and learn in different situations, both individually and in teams. If deficiencies, dependencies and risks are not identified they cannot be addressed.

Key areas of knowledge and understanding required are those relating to what constitutes value from a customer perspective, and what the focus of an organization should be in relation to value creation; and the range of working, learning, connectivity and support options that are available, and how these might best be combined to achieve priority objectives when particular people are involved.

LEADERSHIP FOR LEARNING

The boards of corporate organizations should act as positive role models. They should both become and visibly behave as 'learning boards', as well as ensuring that learning occurs elsewhere among the people, and within the activities, for which they are accountable. The members should periodically assess their own effectiveness, both individually and collectively, at acquiring, sharing and applying relevant information, knowledge and understanding.

Gatherings of a board should be learning events. At the end of meetings directors should review what they have learnt, both individually and collectively, as a result of their deliberations. Between sessions they should record insights, findings, thoughts and possible questions in a 'learning log'. They should also commit to share any new knowledge of relevance to colleagues.

A vital question at reviews of both board and corporate performance should be the extent to which relevant knowledge and capability are being either developed and deployed or lost and depleted: 'Boards should anticipate, support and enable. They should stress the fun of shared learning, and of future discovery and creation, rather than dwell on the pain of past restructuring' (Coulson-Thomas, 1997).

Smart and courageous boards reject comprehensive frameworks such as quality, or an unhealthy dependence upon an existing stock of knowledge. They rely instead upon attracting or developing whatever knowledge, capability and competencies are relevant to the opportunities they define and the markets their imaginations create.

As well as looking ahead, boards are responsible for ensuring that effective arrangements are in place to preserve the assets of an organization. While paying considerable attention to physical and financial assets, many boards are less active and appear relatively naïve so far as safeguarding, valuing and exploiting intellectual capital are concerned (Perrin, 2000).

Efforts to conserve and protect should not be allowed to stifle the freedom of enquiry and debate that is essential for innovation and knowledge creation and exploitation. Coping with unknown futures requires communities of people who can sense, feel and look at things in new ways. Many innovations would not have occurred if their pioneers had been limited to a standard approach, or constrained by 'commodity knowledge' that caused them to view the world and its problems in the same way as their contemporaries.

Assessments of corporate performance by boards should be holistic, realistic and pragmatic. They should encompass all those activities that are necessary to win new business, deliver continuing and relevant value to customers and remain at the cutting edge. Learning should be an individual, workgroup and corporate vocation.

Learning should also be built into the processes used to review corporate performance. Requirements can change and may vary between contexts. Many measures, including those relating to the creation and exploitation of knowledge, are arbitrary, and governed by custom and practice and what is measurable, rather than reflecting importance to the customer: 'Measurement should be a lodestar not a shrine. It should enable and guide, rather than constrain or block' (Coulson-Thomas, 1997).

Boards need to assess the extent to which a corporate culture, a prevailing philosophy of management, and current practices are conducive to knowledge entrepreneurship. They should look out for clues. The extent to which workgroups use support tools, communications are horizontal and upwards, learning is occurring, and know-how is accumulated and effectively deployed could all be measured and tracked.

Many companies would also benefit from specific indicators of knowledge entrepreneurship such as the net income from new knowledge-based ventures and offerings in relation to the value of available intellectual capital. Trends should be monitored and comparisons made between the activities of different groups to identify those who need to learn from others.

Reliance upon numbers, including quantitative measures of knowledge, can lead to a focus upon the consequences of past actions rather than future opportunities. Boards need to ensure they are learning and steering during the processes of planning and implementing.

Pioneers venture into the unknown. At the frontier of exploration there may be little existing knowledge to manage. People may learn by trial and error. The initial challenge may be one of discovery and innovation.

Many companies find their excellence at scientific discovery is not matched by their skill at commercial exploitation. They do not capitalize upon 'being the first'. Boards of many high-tech companies and businesses led by creative entrepreneurs must ensure that insights, opportunities and scientific and technical understanding are more widely shared and that colleagues are equipped to follow up early breakthroughs.

Too often people endure considerable disruption only to find that a new situation is different from what went before rather than better. Learning can help to ensure that growth and evolution as well as change occur. Intelligent monitoring and perceptive and sensitive steering can enable a board to influence and add value. Progress rather than regression should be the desired result.

Many companies require a more entrepreneurial culture and a new philosophy of management to succeed and grow in the global information and knowledge marketplace (Coulson-Thomas, 1997). Their organizations need to metamorphose into communities of knowledge entrepreneurs and become incubators of new enterprises. Members of boards and corporate management teams should review what they can do individually and collectively to support and enable this process.

What each member of the board and management team can do to help

For effective knowledge entrepreneurship the ability to acquire, develop, share and exploit information, knowledge and understanding needs to become a core competence. The following are some basic questions that responsible managers and directors in particular roles should ask if an organization is to become a vibrant community of knowledge entrepreneurs.

Chairman

▶ Does the company operate in a sector in which know-how accounts for an increasing proportion of the value being generated for customers and shareholders? What are the implications for the company, its board and the role of the chairman?

▶ Does the company have an effective board made up of competent directors who understand the requirements for success in the knowledge society and information age?

▶ Would the membership of the board benefit from the addition of one or more knowledge entrepreneurs?

▶ Is the board aware of the concerns that particular groups of stakeholders might have in relation to the acquisition, development, sharing and exploitation of know-how? What could and should be done to establish a better dialogue or improve relationships with these groups?

▶ Does the company have a convincing rationale and clear purpose?

▶ Has the board articulated and shared a distinctive and compelling vision? Is it rooted in the customer and understood by those whose cooperation is needed to make it a reality?

▶ Is there an explicit strategy for the acquisition, development, sharing and exploitation of information, knowledge and understanding? Who among the members of the board has specific responsibility for this?

▶ Who ensures that workgroups have the knowledge-based support tools they need to do their jobs?

▶ Is the board itself properly supported with the information, knowledge and tools it needs to be effective?

▶ Do members of the board exude role model behaviour in relation to learning and the sharing of information and understanding?

▶ Does the board collectively undertake a periodic review of its effectiveness, what it has learnt and its development needs?

▶ Do you undertake a similar assessment of the individual members of the board?

▶ Are the intellectual assets of the organization safeguarded as effectively as its financial and physical assets?

▶ What action has the board taken to ensure that the culture, policies, processes and practices of the organization enable the effective acquisition, development, sharing and exploitation of know-how? Is performance in these areas monitored? What more needs to be done by you and the board?

Managing director

▶ Is the company operating in a sector in which know-how accounts for an increasing proportion of the value being generated for customers? What are the implications for the role of the chief executive?

▶ Have the vision, mission, goals and objectives of the company been effectively communicated and shared? Have the various elements of capability needed to achieve them been assembled?

▶ Are people equipped to communicate quickly what is special and distinctive about the company and what it does? Do their efforts result in a satisfactory level of understanding?

▶ Do members of the management team exude role model behaviour in relation to learning and the sharing of information, knowledge and understanding? Do they sustain the required levels of motivation, commitment and innovation?

▶ What explicit steps are being taken to create and support a community of knowledge entrepreneurs?

▶ Are the corporate culture and the attitudes, values and perspectives of the people of the organization appropriate for successful operation in the information age and knowledge economy?

▶ Are people involved, committed, inspired and innovative? Are they supported with the tools they require to achieve their objectives?

▶ What more does the company need to do to help people to become successful knowledge entrepreneurs?

▶ In particular, what action needs to be taken to break down barriers and overcome obstacles to the acquisition, development, sharing and exploitation of know-how?

▶ Is there effective two-way communication between the corporate centre and business units, and horizontal communication across functional, process and unit boundaries?

▶ Is the organization moving up or sliding down the information, knowledge and understanding value chain within its sector of operation?

▶ Is priority given to the company's customers and the acquisition, development and application of the know-how needed to continue to deliver more value to them?

▶ Have the key processes for the acquisition, development, sharing and exploitation of know-how been identified?

▶ Do information, knowledge and understanding flow effectively up, across and down the organization and around its networks of relationships?

▶ Are there open opportunities for different individuals, work-groups, business units, venture teams and business partners to feed their issues and concerns 'into the system' and register their views?

▶ Are feedback loops built into the company's operating, learning and entrepreneurial processes? Are they regularly reviewed and refined?

Sales and marketing director

▶ Is the company operating in a sector in which know-how accounts for an increasing proportion of the value being generated for customers?

▶ Do colleagues within the company understand the basis of competition? For example, is it competing on response, delivery or learning time?

▶ How important is know-how as a source of competitive advantage?

▶ What new sales and marketing opportunities, additional channels, and job support tool possibilities are being created by the emergence of the information age and knowledge economy?

▶ In particular, do members of the sales force have the tools they need to communicate complex messages, build more intimate relationships with customers, prepare and submit proposals, launch new products and win more business?

▶ Do the company's processes, procedures and practices focus upon the customer?

▶ How accessible are the organization and its people from a customer perspective? Are online links made available?

▶ Is the company's know-how being effectively used to lock customers in and build strategic relationships with them?

▶ What information on the organization is available? Is it appropriate and up to date? Does it communicate its core capabilities and what is special and distinctive about it?

▶ Are the company's credentials available in formats that enable individuals to negotiate their own paths through what is available according to their personal interests and inclinations?

▶ Are communications with the customer one- or two-way? Is sufficient effort devoted to establishing and sustaining relationships with them?

▶ Are appropriate arrangements and processes in place to learn with and from the customer?

▶ Does the company help its customers and prospects to buy?

▶ Are they provided with tools to help them to understand what can be done, review their requirements, discover new options and assess the operational and commercial implications of different alternatives?

Financial director

▶ Is the company operating in a sector in which know-how accounts for an increasing proportion of the value being generated for customers? Is the proportion calculated and tracked?

▶ Does the company assess and track the proportion of its value added that is accounted for by the use and application of know-how? If not, how might this be done?

▶ Is an appropriate share of corporate resources being devoted to enabling, thinking and learning, and the processes, technologies and tools required to support the acquisition, development, sharing and exploitation of know-how?

▶ Is performance measured in terms of its impact upon the customer?

▶ What measures are in place in relation to learning, innovation, and the acquisition, development and sharing of information, knowledge and understanding?

▶ Are appropriate arrangements in place to monitor and measure the know-how created by the company, value and revalue its intellectual property, and assess and track the net income derived from their exploitation?

▶ Does summary information relating to the value of intellectual property appear in the company's annual report and accounts?

▶ Is the company's accounting treatment of intellectual capital appropriate and fair?

▶ What arrangements are in place to identify, package, badge, protect and exploit intellectual capital?

▶ Are costs and revenues, and risks and rewards fairly shared between the collaborative partners involved?

▶ What provision is there to reward fairly individuals who have made a significant contribution to the company's intellectual capital?

Personnel director

▶ Is the company operating in a sector in which know-how accounts for an increasing proportion of the value being generated for customers? What are the implications for personnel policies?

▶ Are people encouraged to take responsibility for their own learning and development?

▶ Does the company encourage them to be true to themselves? Are people allowed to work and learn in whatever ways best enable them to harness their full potential?

▶ Have the competencies required by knowledge entrepreneurs been defined?

▶ What arrangements are in place to acquire and develop them?

▶ Are people equipped to cope? Have relevant information, knowledge, job-related tools, techniques and support networks been made available? Are they used?

▶ Is reward strategy consistent with corporate goals and objectives, and particularly the generation of value for customers?

▶ Is the acquisition of specific competencies and learning rewarded?

▶ What provision is there to reward fairly individuals who have made a significant contribution to the company's intellectual capital?

▶ Are ladders of progression in place for those who aspire to become experts within certain fields?

▶ Are learning and working integrated? Are learning loops built into business, management, support, learning and entrepreneurial processes?

▶ Are processes and procedures in place to monitor and measure the extent of learning and information and knowledge sharing that are occurring, and the use of support tools?

▶ What is being done to develop and retain those who possess scarce information-handling and knowledge development and exploitation skills?

▶ Does the company enter into either revenue and profit-sharing or licensing arrangements with past and current employees with entrepreneurial ideas?

Information technology director

▶ Do the company's people and business partners have effective access to appropriate support tools, information and communications technologies, and relevant sources of know-how?

▶ In particular, are those who need to work together networked up to the level of functionality they require?

▶ What arrangements are made to vary the support provided according to how those involved would prefer to work and learn?

▶ Are networks in place to enable information, knowledge and understanding to be shared with customers, suppliers and business partners?

▶ At the same time, are sensitive information, competitively critical know-how and intellectual property properly protected?

▶ When technologies are upgraded or otherwise changed, are steps taken to safeguard and archive any know-how that has been captured, including on unwanted hard drives?

▶ Are appropriate learning technologies in place to support learning and shared learning?

Research and development director

▶ Do members of the company's research and development community have effective access to appropriate sources of know-how?

▶ Are arrangements, technologies and tools in place to enable know-how to be shared between and across research centres and with colleagues in customer, supplier and business partner organizations?

▶ Does the support that is provided reflect the assignments researchers are engaged in, and how they would prefer to work, collaborate and learn?

▶ Are researchers who need to work together, or otherwise collaborate, linked up to the level of functionality they require?

▶ How imaginative, creative, innovative and entrepreneurial is the research team?

▶ Is research output measured and tracked? What contribution is it making to the flow of new know-how, intellectual capital, products and revenue streams?

▶ How do the returns that are achieved compare with the costs involved?

▶ Are members of the research community actively encouraged and enabled to produce findings that can form the basis of new and additional intellectual capital?

▶ How does the research community ensure that both existing and new know-how are fully exploited?

▶ Would the greater involvement of knowledge entrepreneurs help?

▶ Are researchers allowed to share in the financial returns that result from the exploitation of their work?

▶ Do the most creative and productive members of the research team receive appropriate reward and recognition?

Facilities and infrastructure director

▶ Does the physical layout of corporate premises encourage

both reflection and interaction, and the sharing of information, knowledge and understanding?

▶ Does it encourage learning, shared learning and entrepreneurship? Are there quiet areas for reflection?

▶ Is a variety of different spaces and working and learning environments available to suit the various projects and tasks that need to be undertaken?

▶ What facilities are provided to support new ventures?

▶ Do people need to adjust how they would like to operate to fit in with whatever space and facilities are available, or is the infrastructure sufficiently flexible to support how people would prefer to operate?

▶ How satisfactory are working environments and associated facilities and support such as learning resource centres and incubators of new ventures?

▶ Do they support innovation and entrepreneurship?

▶ Do their design, architecture and facilities accommodate the mix of individual and group working required and the support tools and technologies that are needed?

▶ What arrangements are made to vary the support provided according to how those involved would prefer to work and learn as tasks and priorities change?

▶ What infrastructure and facilities support is provided to mobile workers, 'hot-deskers', nomads who move between locations, those who work from home on a full- or part-time basis, and other categories of flexible worker?

▶ Is help provided to customers, suppliers and business partners?

▶ How are the requirements of users articulated, assessed and addressed?

CHECKLIST

▶ Does the board fully understand the requirements of key groups of stakeholders?

▶ How many of these requirements relate to the more timely delivery of different or better information and knowledge?

▶ How supportive are the board and corporate culture and management practices of knowledge creation, sharing and exploitation?

▶ To what extent is knowledge being effectively communicated and either created or destroyed?

▶ What are individual members of the board doing to help?

▶ Identify the factors that most help or hinder knowledge entrepreneurship?

▶ In the areas in which you operate how important is speed in relation to the cost, quality or perceived value of information and knowledge?

▶ How much extra would customers, clients and users be prepared to pay for earlier availability or delivery?

▶ What is being lost, sidelined or delayed as a result of an emphasis on, preoccupation with or obsession with speed?

▶ To what extent are timescales speeding up?

▶ Considering your own situation, do you react quickly and spontaneously, or would you prefer to make more considered responses?

▶ Do you feel under pressure of time, and what are the main symptoms, consequences and implications of this?

▶ Have you prioritized the various items in your in-tray?

▶ Who would notice or be affected if the lower-priority items were dropped?

▶ What priority do you put upon obtaining extra time as opposed to becoming more healthy or accumulating additional wealth?

▶ What would you do that you do not do now if you were given, or could free up, more time?

▶ What is holding you back from making the effort to do so?

▶ Applying similar questions to the experiences of others, what could be done to help them that might form the basis of a commercial service?

6

Creating enterprise cultures

BECOMING A PLAYER

Knowledge workers, companies, communities and countries increasingly face a stark choice. They can either participate in the global information and knowledge economy or be sidelined. Employees, suppliers, associates and business partners of particular companies also run the risk of being overlooked or bypassed. To become key players they need to connect, participate and collaborate.

Within supply chains companies that do not put the necessary communications and network infrastructures in place to exchange documents, enable online transactions and support virtual teams may be excluded from future involvement. If they cannot be quickly reached they may as well not exist.

Challenges for some represent opportunities for others. Smart operators seize the moment to move from the periphery to the centre. The entrepreneurial can break in, catch up and overtake competitors that might be endowed with greater physical and financial resources. Individuals can make a mark by plugging into live Internet discussion forums and exchanging views with great minds from around the world.

In the knowledge marketplace intellectual positioning can be more important than physical location. Many knowledge entrepreneurs find they can trade globally from almost any point on earth. Freedom of expression and protection of intellectual property may be more important than the presence of docks and highways.

The source of a contribution may be less important than its relevance to the current stage of a debate. Individual authorities and small enterprises can participate as well as giant corporations. They may well be at an advantage. While their peers in large organizations await clearance they can respond more quickly when they have relevant and interesting points to make.

Trade once followed the flag. Now it reflects flows of information, knowledge and understanding. Provide complementary businesses in different countries with a means of communicating with each other and the transmission of information may soon be followed by the discussion of mutually beneficial ventures or electronic commerce.

Where data flow today, ideas may be exchanged tomorrow. New services and jobs may follow soon after. Businesses and societies that fall behind at creating, sharing and exploiting know-how will no longer be able to compete for anything other than 'commodity' opportunities. The relative standards of living of their people will decline compared with those better equipped for knowledge entrepreneurship.

The challenge facing many boards and corporate management teams is to make their organizations more effective at acquiring, developing, sharing and applying information, knowledge and understanding. It is one that should excite and motivate all those involved. The pay-offs from success can be enormous.

The scale of the change required in many corporate contexts is nothing less than a total transformation from a centralized bureaucracy to an incubator of new enterprises with a portfolio of distinct activities. The prospects are alluring. In most companies there is a potential to impact upon almost every aspect of operation and benefit all stakeholders. People need to understand the pay-offs as well as what they need to do.

With appropriate public policy support, local communities and clusters of enterprises have the opportunity to become international centres of information and knowledge entrepreneurship. Community and corporate cultures, working and learning environments and support facilities need to offer the balance and quality of life needed to attract mobile investments and jobs, retain the talents of the brightest and best, and stimulate imagination, initiative and innovation.

Exercise 6a: Compatibility analysis

Many people dwell on issues that are in dispute, rather than focus upon areas of agreement. This approach can lead to suspicion, defensive behaviour and conflict. Instead, the parties to a negotiation or relationship should endeavour to build upon what they have in common with each other.

In the case of your company, its people and its business partners, what are the main points of difference and dissonance? What are the major interests that the various parties have in common? What concerns or objectives do you and other individuals involved share with your employing organizations?

Separate the areas of disagreement from the compatible and mutual interests. How important and critical are each group to the various parties? What could be done to build upon the areas of joint interest and address common concerns? Could people sideline and park some areas of dissension by simply agreeing to disagree on these points, rather than pursue arguments that detract from more positive developments?

WORKING WITH EMPLOYERS

Relationships between individual knowledge workers and business organizations are also about to be transformed. Increasingly, creative and entrepreneurial spirits will work with companies rather than for them. Mutually beneficial partnerships will result. But first the expectations, attitudes and behaviours of the negotiating parties and collaborating interests will need to change (Coulson-Thomas, 1999b).

Let's look at the issues and opportunities that arise from an individual perspective. Have you ever thought of how you might work with one or more larger companies as a business partner? Whether you are an independent entrepreneur or an employee, you have an unprecedented range of choice in relation to how, when, where, for whom and with whom to work. No previous generation has had so many options.

People are also finding it possible to make a business out of a personal leisure interest. In future more of us will be able to live life on our own terms. Intelligent agents will undertake bespoke searches for goods, services, opportunities and possible collaborators on our behalf. Individuals will no longer approach organizations looking for work or seek to become dependent employees. Instead, they will treat corporations and colleagues as actual or potential business partners.

There will no longer be such a stark divide between start-up enterprises and established businesses. Both will attract people with ideas for new knowledge-based offerings and services. Entrepreneurship, either alone or as an intrapreneur with corporate support, will be for the many rather than the few (Coulson-Thomas, 1999b).

As suggested in the last chapter, corporate organizations will become incubators and enablers of new enterprises. Individuals and teams from within companies and from outside will come forward with new business ideas and ask for venture capital support, access to central services, and development and marketing assistance. A growing number of employees will also emulate potential external partners and seek a share of the rewards of success.

Exercise 6b: Greenhouse analysis

Organizations should endeavour to create conditions in which innovation, creativity and enterprise can flourish. Freedom of enquiry and diversity of thought and approach need to be encouraged, but if a hundred or a thousand flowers are to bloom a company must be equipped and ready to deal with the consequences.

In the corporate greenhouse of your organization, what changes need to be made to the culture and working and learning environment to enable new ideas to germinate? What facilities and support tools are required to stimulate subsequent growth? Are there sufficient stakes in place to cope with the number of shoots that may emerge? If thinning becomes necessary, who will do this? Will the plants that are produced be sufficiently hardy to survive outside in the marketplace?

ORGANIZING FOR ENTREPRENEURSHIP

Attitudes towards entrepreneurship within larger organizations must change. Restructuring, retrenchment and re-engineering have largely run their course. They were essentially negative activities, concerned with survival not growth. The mood in boardrooms is swinging against downsizing in favour of creating greater value for customers and generating additional income streams (Coulson-Thomas, 2001).

People are fed up with defensive cost cutting and being asked to do more with less. Many would like to change direction, reduce their dependency upon others, and lead more balanced lives. Employees used to seek security and a regular income. They undertook repetitive tasks, implemented standard procedures and followed prescribed rules.

Today people aspire to more than material rewards. They also want to build, develop, innovate and discover. They desire more balanced lives. They seek inner fulfilment as well as the external trappings of financial success (Coulson-Thomas, 1999b).

We have seen in previous chapters that customers too are restless. They demand distinctive and bespoke responses that reflect their individual concerns and priorities. People in client-facing roles are expected to behave more imaginatively when creating offerings to meet particular requirements. And appropriate job support tools can make it easier for them to tailor existing offerings and create new ones.

Market leadership now goes to those who innovate or assemble a novel combination of elements that represents greater value for consumers. Rather than refer to manuals, mechanically apply a methodology or provide standard offerings, people have to make choices and take risks. They are required to consider alternatives and manage resources and expectations. In short, they must think and act like entrepreneurs.

Many existing employees are struggling to make the transition from corporate dependent to intrapreneur and business partner. More companies are likely to recognize they need external help and that many local independent operators of small businesses may have the attitudes, skills and experience they require.

Of course 'independents' are used to the freedom of operating alone. A clash of cultures could – but might not – arise as more big company bosses come to understand the requirements for contemporary market success.

Giving individuals the discretion to do what they feel is most appropriate for each customer enables them to play a much more creative role. Their 'solutions' might contain unusual elements, unique features, novel approaches or new knowledge, which could be licensed to others. Opportunities abound for 'information entrepreneurship' and for service, lifestyle, healthcare and educational innovation.

The rapid adoption of e-business has eroded many barriers to entry. The imaginative can offer new ways of working, learning and earning that better match the preferences of those involved and greatly increase the prospect of them achieving both commercial success and personal fulfilment. This desired combination is most likely where personal and corporate aspirations are explicit, aligned and focused upon winning new business, establishing partnerships and benefiting customers.

Exercise 6c: Reconciling people and organizations

Within many organizations there is a historic opportunity to align personal and corporate interests as a result of encouraging and supporting enterprise and knowledge entrepreneurship. In relation to organizations with which you are familiar:

- Assess the extent of commitment to the creation of an enterprise culture, for example by examining the proportion of the training budget that is devoted to building entrepreneurial and business development skills.
- Consider whether managers encourage initiative and innovation, for example by inviting people to come forward with ideas for establishing new knowledge-based ventures and creating additional income streams.
- Where people respond, examine the steps that are taken to provide practical support and any start-up capital that may be required by approved ventures.
- Assess whether the corporate culture and available facilities and support tools are conducive to knowledge creation and entrepreneurship.
- In relation to corporate systems, processes and procedures consider whether these are appropriate to the particular needs and requirements of a growing business.
- Consider also how many employees create, discover and pioneer as opposed to imitating and copying others.
- Review how performance is measured, and whether and how the development of new approaches, enterprises, know-how and customer value is identified, assessed and rewarded.
- In particular, consider how much emphasis is placed upon business development activities such as the creation of

---

additional revenues through new offerings and winning incremental business as opposed to reorganization and cost cutting.
- Examine the extent to which people are given the freedom to
determine how they will work, learn and collaborate, and
encouraged to adopt roles that enable them to be true to themselves and operate in ways that allow them to play to their
strengths.
- In all of these areas, consider whether there are deficiencies
and gaps in the enterprise support arrangements and additional
steps that could be taken.
- In relation to the latter, consider whether these might form the
basis of business opportunities in their own right.

UNITY AND DIVERSITY

A more entrepreneurial approach is likely to result in a much greater
diversity of operations, activities and support arrangements in many
companies. For those with a preference for order, or responsibilities for
audit and control, this prospect may seem alarming. Many senior
management teams have been reluctant to try out different models of
operation in order to assess their relative effectiveness.

Attitudes need to change. Too much order, procedure and
predictability can inhibit change, transformation and entrepreneurship:
'Order and formal structure can produce sterile conditions... The
network community may need to maintain a pool of approaches,
modules of processes, learning technologies, creative environments,
tools and techniques which could be drawn upon and used as and when
required to support groups and teams in whatever it is they are wishing
to do' (Coulson-Thomas, 1997).

It may now make sense to adopt very different approaches to work,
learning and entrepreneurship across the same organization, depending
upon the aspirations, tasks and priorities of those concerned and the
people and personalities involved. In the information and knowledge
society, diversity has advantages (Coulson-Thomas, 2000). It may come
to command a premium among investors.

The encouragement of diversity increases the prospect of each
customer being treated in an appropriate, tailored and distinct manner.
More individuals may be encouraged to play to their particular
strengths, and fewer people might be subjected to 'group norms' or

pressured into adopting standard approaches. Support tools should liberate rather than constrain. People need to be encouraged to push back boundaries.

There is now a greater requirement for the considered and imaginative tailoring that can result from the adoption of 'designer quality'. Corporate approaches to quality need to become more subtle, sensitive and adaptive: 'Terms such as "creative quality", "quality and thinking" or "quality and learning" are likely to become more widely used at the expense of "quality assurance" and "quality control". Traditional quality is too rational, too statistical and too engineering oriented in the "softer", sensitive, thinking, feeling world of values and relationships' (Coulson-Thomas, 1997).

Standard performance targets for cases handled or activities undertaken per hour or day prevent many people from providing more personalized treatment. Companies need to understand that different customers can have widely varying attitudes to time. Some will require more attention than others. Knowledge workers need to be given the discretion to allocate different amounts of thinking time, and access and involve alternative networks of support according to particular requirements.

Contemporary technologies and use of the Internet allow suppliers to contact directly individuals with almost every imaginable interest. People can establish and maintain relationships with others around the world who share their passions and preoccupations. They can set out on search-engine-assisted voyages of discovery. Missing pieces of the jigsaw puzzle can be located more quickly than ever before.

Many organizations devote much effort to internal quality standards, inspections and controls. In comparison, they place far too little emphasis upon the quality of relationships, working life and learning; and using job support tools (along the lines of those we will examine in Chapters 9 and 10) to reconcile quality with diversity.

Quality checks can be built into the support tools that people use to design and configure bespoke responses. In the knowledge society, attention needs to shift to the quality of individual imagination, inspiration and motivation in the creation of personal value for each individual customer.

TEN ESSENTIAL FREEDOMS

Naïvety can be dangerous, but excessive control can stunt and eventually suffocate. Support tools should enable and release rather than constrict and restrain. If they are to aspire, reflect, dream, initiate, build and create, people may need to be set free from mundane distractions and petty constraints.

Achieving shared goals needs to become more important than protecting selfish and vested interests, which can become self-defeating within the context of many forms of collaborative relationship. Corporate policies that encourage openness, trust and mutual respect are more likely to encourage effective knowledge entrepreneurship.

If successful transformation from corporate bureaucracy to incubator of enterprise is to be achieved, management approaches must liberate rather than constrain. There are 10 essential freedoms that should be both adopted and actively championed (Coulson-Thomas, 1997):

1. Freedom to dream, aspire, build and create.
2. Freedom to enter into mutually beneficial relationships.
3. Freedom to do what is necessary to deliver value and satisfaction to customers.
4. Freedom as a customer to seek new sources of benefit and value.
5. Freedom to initiate debates, explore, question, challenge, innovate and learn.
6. Freedom to understand one's self, be true to one's self, and develop and build upon natural strengths.
7. Freedom to work at a time, location and mode that best contributes to desired outputs.
8. Freedom to use the most relevant technology, tools and processes depending upon what it is that needs to be done.
9. Freedom to confront reality, identify root causes and tackle obstacles and barriers.
10. Freedom to learn according to one's individual learning potential.

These 10 freedoms should form the basis of a new social contract with key corporate stakeholders. They must become a charter for innovation and enterprise.

The hard protective shells of many companies currently act as barriers to enterprise. Boards and management teams must work to ensure they become frontiers that encourage the migration of people and ideas. They must be turned into open arenas of opportunity if new collaborative activities are to be inspired that will fulfil the aspirations of both individuals and organizations. Out of synergy will come success.

Directors' checklist

Members of corporate boards need to be sensitive to the concerns of investors and other stakeholders. In particular, directors should be alert to any questions they are likely to ask about how effective a company is at acquiring, developing, sharing and exploiting know-how.

Individual directors should also probe and challenge. Certain questions may need to be put if directors are to discharge their moral and legal obligations to ensure a company has the direction and capabilities required both to survive and to thrive in the information age:

▶ How alert and sensitive is the company and its board to what is going on in the business environment and market context within which it is operating?

▶ Has a formal issue monitoring and management process been adopted? Does it operate effectively?

▶ In particular, does it embrace issues relating to the creation, protection and exploitation of knowledge and intellectual capital?

▶ Is the company active in a sector, or sectors, in which know-how in its various forms accounts for an increasing proportion of the value being generated for customers?

▶ Does the company have a distinctive and compelling vision? Is it effectively articulated, communicated and shared? Does it excite and inspire?

▶ Do the company's goals, values, policies, procedures and practices – and its corporate culture – encourage, support and enable imagination, learning, innovation and discovery? Do they energize and stretch the people of the organization?

▶ Does the company know where intellectual leadership lies in critical areas within the markets in which it operates?

▶ Does the company attract and retain the brightest and most creative talents in its field?

▶ Does it know who its 'superstar' performers are in areas vital for competing and winning? What is being done to capture and share the essence of their success?

▶ Have other people been provided with the job support tools they need to improve their performance and emulate the success of superstars?

▶ Are individuals with distinct, high-level and scarce skills and competencies identified? Again, are appropriate steps being taken to attract and retain such people?

▶ Does the company explicitly recognize and reward those who learn, share and excel, and also those who create and/or exploit know-how? Are directors and senior managers role models in this respect?

▶ To what extent is the company a consumer or a producer of information, knowledge and understanding? Is there a know-how 'balance of payments' surplus or deficit?

▶ How are individual business units, workgroups and particular members of staff contributing to the know-how surplus or deficit?

▶ Is there an explicit policy and strategy for the acquisition, development, sharing and exploitation of know-how? Do selection, promotion, reward and remuneration practices reflect and support these activities?

▶ Does the corporate culture encourage people to be both imaginative and entrepreneurial in relation to their use, application and exploitation of know-how and intellectual capital?

▶ What practical arrangements are in place to encourage and support knowledge entrepreneurs?

▶ What proportion of the company's turnover is accounted for by products and services that could be described as 'new' in terms of the timescales of the sectors within which it operates? Are specific innovation targets set and monitored?

▶ What proportion of the cost and the value of the company's products and services is accounted for by the know-how that is embedded within them? How rapidly are the proportions of both rising?

▶ How quickly is the company moving up the value chain in relation to its major competitors?

▶ Does the company know what it knows and does not know? What steps are taken to: capture and share what is known; and turn know-how into intellectual capital?

▶ What arrangements are in place to register and protect the intellectual assets of the company?

▶ Are records maintained of packaged, protected and available intellectual capital and its ownership? Do these make it clear to whom, or from whom, particular intellectual property has been licensed and for what purposes?

▶ Is every opportunity being taken to exploit the company's know-how and achieve a fair return upon its intellectual assets?

▶ What further initiatives are being undertaken or could be explored, for example to license unused know-how and technology to other companies, or seek partners for the joint exploitation of opportunities?

▶ Are employees who create intellectual capital allowed and enabled to participate in any subsequent revenue streams that result from its exploitation?

▶ What mechanisms and processes are in place to encourage and support learning, and the creation, capture, sharing and exploitation of know-how at individual, workgroup, business unit and corporate levels?

▶ Are appropriate technologies and job support tools in place to support the acquisition, building, sharing and exploitation of information, knowledge and understanding?

▶ Have the company and its people joined relevant shared learning networks? Does it have the support of learning, transformation and enterprise partners?

▶ Do the networks and arrangements that are in place enable the company to learn from and with its customers, suppliers and business partners?

▶ How 'clued up' are boardroom colleagues in relation to the above issues? How much importance do they place upon them? Is this enough?

▶ Do directors understand the importance of acquiring, developing, protecting, sharing and exploiting know-how? What could or should you do to increase the current level of understanding?

Setting up an independent corporate learning and/or enterprise centre

Enterprise support units and corporate learning centres, institutes and universities vary greatly in terms of why they are established, the ways in which they are set up and how they operate. If properly conceived, organized, resourced and supported they can make a very significant contribution to the creation and exploitation of know-how.

Setting up a new centre may enable a distinct enterprise culture to be established from scratch. Many different approaches can be found in the marketplace. They reveal much about the commitment of sponsoring organizations to knowledge entrepreneurship. Below are some steps that have been taken by people to create a new institution (Coulson-Thomas, 1999a). They will not all apply in every case, and the order in which they are considered may need to change to reflect the particular situation and circumstances. However, broadly the responsible team will need to:

1. Agree, confirm or revise the rationale, purpose, mission, vision, values and goals of the proposed centre, institute or university. Articulating and discussing them helps to ensure that the interests of the various parties, people and personalities involved are compatible. Setting them out for the record creates a blueprint against which future developments and achievements can be benchmarked.
2. Agree the name, legal status, ownership and branding of the proposed entity. It may also be necessary at this stage to establish a formal structure, *modus operandi* and clear accountabilities. Incorporating a new venture as a separate legal entity

may encourage intellectual and commercial independence, and might help to facilitate collaborative arrangements and joint ventures.

3. Appoint the members of any governing body or advisory board. Either they or the sponsoring team will then elect a chairman and select a chief executive or unit head and possibly other members of the core management team. Certain stakeholders may expect a seat at the top table.

4. Select and appoint professional advisers, for example bankers and lawyers, and educational and business advisers. If the entity is not incorporated separately, services may be provided by central or head office corporate functions, supplemented by appropriate external experts.

5. Agree core policies, broad guidelines and sensitive practical matters such as the ownership of intellectual property, new venture investment policy, executive salary scales, levels of financial contribution, charges to cover inputs of time, and possibly directors' fees.

6. Establish core objectives, key activities and vital few programmes. At this stage it is important to prioritize. For example, if further funding is required early attention may need to be given to income-generating contacts with target sponsors or to identifying possible partner organizations.

7. Assess the availability of relevant internal corporate capability, and identify any additional internal and external resources that might be required to undertake the initial portfolio of activities that have been agreed. Make sure the new unit has the means of handling know-how in a variety of different formats, and the facilities and culture needed to inspire creative thought and imaginative entrepreneurship.

8. Agree an initial development budget and timetable. There may be properties to rationalize, facilities to develop and commission, or support arrangements to be put in place before a centre is likely to be ready to 'open for business'.

9. Identify authorities, entrepreneurs, universities, business schools and strategic, funding and learning partners that might wish to cooperate with the new centre. Key customers might be interested in collaborating. Contacts should be very selective and low-key. Focus upon infilling any gaps that might

emerge. Individual academics, senior practitioners and leading experts could be approached at an early stage. Particular people rather than institutions are often the key to success.

10. Establish a confidentiality framework and agreement prior to approaching and involving external parties. Discretion and caution should be observed. Once alerted to a 'good idea', a potential partner might approach other players, including direct competitors, with a view to establishing and funding an alternative venture. Some academic entrepreneurs are adept at taking over other people's ideas. They will not necessarily feel obliged to observe exclusivity unless legally committed to do so.

11. Prepare and deliver any executive and other presentations that may be needed to explain what is intended and secure the necessary support. Proposals aimed at senior staff and targeted individuals may need to be drafted, and pitches prepared. Various forms of cooperation with other parties might be sought, and collaborative arrangements may have to be explained.

12. Draw up a financial plan and secure whatever commitments might be required to cover initial set-up costs and any additional investment that may be needed to achieve 'critical mass'. Entrepreneurial teams often underestimate their funding requirements. In the case of educational ventures, the cost of validation, learning materials and prospectuses can be substantial.

13. If appropriate, make selective investments in early income generation activities based upon the packaging of existing information, knowledge and experience, in order to establish early contact with potential customers and partners. Revenues created might help to fund future developments.

14. Negotiate and agree terms and arrangements with any initial partner organizations. These might include universities and business schools or business angels and venture capitalists. It often helps to develop a preferred model that can be used as a basis for negotiating with prospective partners. Certain strategically important possibilities could become projects in their own right.

15. Progress the development work that may be required to estab-

lish a network of key clients and strategic partners. The ability to initiate, build and manage relationships with customers and suppliers is a critical success requirement.

16. Draw up account capture and development plans. It may be advisable to start with an entry-level product such as a review or audit before moving on, as a relationship and confidence grows, to a more costly offering such as a collaborative MBA programme or joint venture to develop a range of job support tools.

17. Recruit allies and associates to supplement resources. As a project progresses, and a centre becomes better known, more people may be attracted to its activities. They might wish to offer courses, undertake research or develop a new knowledge-based venture. Individuals and teams might be invited to submit ideas for possible development or compete for funding by writing and presenting a business plan. External specialists could be invited to submit proposals for the use of facilities to develop new offerings.

18. Invite individual authorities with desired expertise to apply for an attachment, sabbatical or 'summer school' appointment. 'Entrepreneurs in residence' could help new venture teams. 'Visiting research fellows' could develop knowledge in particular areas. 'Teaching fellows' could share their experiences and insights. Having to prepare a session sometimes encourages people to structure what they know. 'Experts in residence' or visiting 'superstars' could package their expertise in the form of tools for colleagues to use.

19. Undertake periodic reviews of the extent to which innovation is occurring, and whether knowledge is being created and exploited as well as shared. An independent review may be more objective.

20. Hold regular workshops to establish, map, assess, package and share what is known and identify gaps, knowledge development priorities and exploitation opportunities.

21. Establish any operating standards and procedures that might be required. Without wishing to stifle diversity, basic quality guidelines and common formats for presentation slides, handouts and Web-based material might help to build a new centre's image. Internal and external customers will inevitably make comparisons with the standard of learning materials,

business plans, administration, catering and learning and enterprise support provided by other centres.

22. Launch the new centre. At the right moment, some form of public announcement may be desirable. Information and invitations to launch events could be sent to selected individuals, supplemented by media and promotional activities to achieve publicity and increase awareness. The rationale for action should be carefully considered. An early launch might increase bargaining power with potential partners and 'claim territory'. On the other hand delay may enable the necessary arrangements to be made for visitors to observe learning activities and see venture teams at work.

23. Alternatively, keep the venture under wraps. 'Skunk works' are often hidden for as long as possible. Premature publicity may give rivals time to confuse potential customers and collaborators with 'me-too' imitations. It may be wise to keep the existence of a new centre out of the public domain for as long as possible while building discreet contacts with potential clients, and to postpone a public announcement until certain key prospects have already been signed up as customers.

24. Consider future development opportunities. As a centre gains momentum and builds its credibility and standing, various suggestions may arise for new uses of facilities and additional activities. Plans may need to be established to support induction programmes, graduate trainees or the participation of supply chain partners or alumni. Internal arrangements for charging and recharging may need to be established or reviewed.

25. Review related activities. There may be other programmes, initiatives and ventures that could be brought under the umbrella of a corporate learning and/or enterprise centre. Areas ranging from market research to product development might be relevant. The rapidly growing and global market for education offers exciting opportunities for learning and knowledge entrepreneurship.

26. Examine external approaches and respond to any proposals for collaboration that may be received. Criteria and guidelines for handling them may need to be established. Some centre teams have been surprised at how quickly news of their activities can spread on the grapevine, and how many people are

attracted by the prospect of some form of cooperation, joint appointment or role with a reputable centre. Opportunities for strategically significant collaborations might arise.

27. Consider, initiate and pursue learning and/or enterprise 'partnerships'. Certain opportunities might be so large or complex that they have to be shared. Acting cooperatively may enable a critical scale of operation to be achieved more quickly than might otherwise be the case. Thus 'sponsorship' might be sought for a particular appointment such as an enterprise fellowship or a discrete activity, individual programme or designated facility to enable certain collaborating partners to feel more involved through a more tangible and explicit association.

28. Manage the reactions and responses of others. As a centre widens its network of influence and builds a community of supporters, it becomes more visible as an entity in its own right. This may lead to jealousies, potential conflicts of interest and even acrimonious debates about priorities and disputes over funding or the allocation of resources.

29. Restate goals and celebrate success. A centre's management team should remind protagonists and detractors of the rationale and purpose of what is happening, stress the various direct and spin-off benefits to stakeholders that arise and ensure that sponsors, contributors and successes are duly acknowledged.

Collaboration checklist

Many entrepreneurs and enterprise teams miss opportunities to collaborate on the creation and exploitation of know-how. They devote little effort to establishing and managing joint activities. Working with others might secure additional capabilities, allow a degree of specialization, provide greater geographic coverage or widen the range of experiences available to learners, innovators and intending entrepreneurs. A coincidence of interests, or compatibility of requirements, might lead to the shared funding of certain posts and/or ventures.

However, there is a potential downside. Collaborative relationships can take time to build, and care should be taken to identify appropriate partners and avoid particular parties developing unrealistic expectations. The following are among the questions that should be asked prior to entering into commitments:

▶ Why is the relationship being sought? What is its purpose?
▶ How many parties are there to be?
▶ How compatible are the objectives of the various potential parties? Have they been made explicit and discussed?
▶ Will the parties be able to work together? How well suited to collaboration are their corporate cultures?
▶ Are their requirements and approaches conducive to full participation and effective knowledge entrepreneurship?
▶ What form is the cooperation agreement to take? What is to be covered by it?
▶ Will there be exchanges of learners, entrepreneurs or supporting staff?
▶ Will cooperative research and development activities or the sharing of resources occur? Will joint ventures and common programmes be established?
▶ Which learning and/or enterprise centres and what areas of operation or business units are to be involved?
▶ What information, knowledge and support tools are to be exchanged?
▶ How will the know-how and intellectual property of the parties be protected?
▶ What additional resources, facilities and support tools may be required?
▶ What are the likely barriers to effective collaboration and how might these be overcome?
▶ Will there be a fair allocation of costs in relation to the benefits likely to be enjoyed by the different participating organizations?
▶ Who is going to manage the relationship?
▶ How will performance be monitored and reported upon?
▶ How are exchange candidates and joint venture participants to be selected and assessed?
▶ When will the arrangement start? What should the initial term be?
▶ How will the agreement and collaboration be announced?

▶ At what points will the activities and underlying arrangements be reviewed?

▶ Should there be an agreed procedure for admitting additional parties to the arrangement?

▶ How will the arrangement be terminated?

Ideally the term of an initial agreement or contract should be long enough to allow tangible benefits to arise and secure a return upon the initial investment, but not so long that one or more parties may come to feel 'locked in'. In due course a portfolio of collaborative accords may be established, but many companies opt to tread carefully and enter into relatively modest arrangements at first. More ambitious collaborations can be negotiated once an organization has learnt the ropes.

CHECKLIST

▶ Have any of the organizations of which you are a part developed a 'life of their own' independent of their original purpose and/or the entrepreneurial aspirations of their people?

▶ How highly do these organizations' own internal agendas and objectives rank in relation to those of various stakeholder groups?

▶ Are the interests and concerns of the people of these organizations actively identified, understood, managed and tracked?

▶ What is being done to address people's concerns and further their interests?

▶ What attempts are made to achieve compatibility between individual and organizational objectives and perspectives, and with what success?

▶ What could or should be done to make the organizations that you are associated with more receptive towards individual interests, perspectives and concerns?

▶ How much effort is devoted to exploring alternative ways of operating? Have virtual models of organization been explored?

▶ How open are the organizations in question to joint ventures and partnerships involving current or former members of staff?

▶ Are customers, suppliers, business partners and contractors regarded as part of the organization?

▶ Is individual and collective innovation encouraged, supported and enabled?

▶ What help is provided to those wishing to create new offerings, set up new ventures and generate incremental income streams?

▶ Do allocations of rewards reflect the relative contributions of the people involved?

▶ Are contractual relationships with individuals and external parties mutually beneficial?

▶ What proportion of them could be described as partnerships?

▶ How would you categorize the organizations of which you are a part or with which you associate?

▶ How structured are they? Do they grow organically or operate as flexible networks?

▶ Is their *modus operandi* appropriate for what their leaders, members and clientele are seeking to accomplish?

▶ Are enterprise and entrepreneurship being championed, actively stimulated and effectively supported?

▶ Do people have a stake in what they and their colleagues are achieving? Do they feel a sense of 'ownership'?

▶ In what ways would you like to see these organizations change?

▶ Are you an 'isolated island' or an integrated element of a larger whole?

▶ Are your world and the corporate context compartmentalized or interconnected?

- ▶ Do you form a natural bridge between discrete interests, separate areas and contending views? Could you become one?

- ▶ How aware are you of links and relationships between people, ideas, opportunities, support tools and physical locations?

- ▶ Are you sensitive to links, patterns, relationships and flows?

- ▶ Have you mapped the networks of relationships that you are involved in?

- ▶ Who – if anyone – establishes the goals, values and operating rules of these networks?

- ▶ Can anybody join? What are the requirements for membership and the expectations of continuing members?

- ▶ What would be lost if you ceased to be a member? What other networks should you join?

- ▶ Are there new and alternative support networks that you and others could set up as entrepreneurial ventures?

7

Monitoring trends and the scope for knowledge entrepreneurship

FREEDOM OF OPERATION

The rapid growth in the volume and availability of information and knowledge has created both challenges and opportunities. There is enormous scope for knowledge entrepreneurs to provide services that help people to confront the challenges and address the opportunities. For example, knowledge-based offerings could range from basic personal counselling, through simple job support tools to complex corporate infrastructures.

Individual entrepreneurs and company directors need to be alert to what is happening in the world around them, and in society generally, as well as in the market sectors within which they operate. Political, economic, social and technological developments can all have significant impacts and commercial implications.

To take an example, consider the many knowledge-based services that will be required by older members of ageing societies, and those responsible for their care and welfare. The wires and cabling that allow senior citizens to shop from home can also be used by carers and community wardens to monitor their health and personal security. Advice can be delivered online and visits organized by the exchange of e-mails. Individual citizens can be plugged into appropriate support networks.

Our conception of the world, and of the social and physical infrastructure required to support us, is changing. We no longer need to venture out, travel or visit particular locations to gain access to material in a particular format or certain sources of information. It may now be on tap, accessible when and wherever it may be required. If it cannot yet be downloaded, a CD ROM version may be available through the post.

We have greater freedom than any previous generation in history to decide where, when and how we would like to receive our information in order to understand what we need to do, work with it, learn from it or simply enjoy it. We can also discuss what we find with others. We can swap insights into the relative merits of particular information sources. The ease with which audio material can be illegally downloaded, exchanged and shared has resulted in a significant fall in the sales of music CDs.

People commend certain Web sites just as they might once have recommended a particular restaurant. They tell colleagues and friends. And with good reason. Commercial life is as dependent upon ready access to current information as the body is upon fresh food. Obsolete data can be as dangerous as stale provisions.

Children who cannot text messages to friends are socially excluded. They feel as isolated as a City trader with a blank screen. Not to be accessible or connected is as harmful to contemporary relationships as being incarcerated in a prison or exiled to St Helena might have been in a previous era. It precludes participation in much of what is happening that may directly concern us.

Napoleon used his exile to write his memoirs and influence how he wished to be remembered. Our contemporaries demand more immediate gratification. Today, people on remote islands can buy a satellite dish, modem and terminal and log on.

Information and communications technologies enable us to overcome barriers of organization, distance and time. With accessible information and the ability to connect to the Internet and network with others from the most unlikely of locations every citizen has the potential opportunity to become a knowledge entrepreneur.

Many homes have long been equipped with the media, communications and facilities to support a wide diversity of activities and endeavours. Meanwhile even some workplaces are belatedly becoming more conducive to enterprise. We saw in the last chapter that business decision makers should create corporate cultures, environments and infrastructures that release latent entrepreneurial potential and support and enable the emergence and development of new ventures.

Exercise 7a: Weather watch and weathervane analysis

Trivial ephemera and temporary conditions need to be distinguished from consistent longer-term trends and fundamental discontinuities. Think about either the cultural and operating climate of your organization or the market context in which it operates. Is it getting better or worse? Is it heating up or cooling down? Is the pressure rising or falling? How will you and others cope with any changes that are anticipated?

Repeat the exercise for major customers and attractive prospects. What has been learnt that could be shared with them? Might they be interested in a joint analysis of what needs to be done? How could your organization help them to adapt and respond?

In some corporations people do not seem to know whether they are coming or going. A weathervane may prove more useful than a thermometer or pressure gauge. Which way is the wind blowing? Does it shift around, or is there a prevailing direction? How strong is it? How long is it likely to last? What is coming with the wind and after it, rain or shine? Might damage be done that will need to be repaired?

UNDERSTANDING ISSUES AND IMPLICATIONS

The main constraints to entrepreneurship often lie within us rather than in the social context within which we live and work. We are limited by our imaginations, energies and focus. We need to understand ourselves better in order to determine which of the available possibilities we identify would be right for us (Coulson-Thomas, 1999b). Just because an opportunity exists does not mean it should be grasped. We need to think through the issues and implications.

When so much is happening at once it is easy to overlook or misjudge particular trends and developments. Individual items may not be given sufficient attention to register. While most individuals and organizations regularly decide to ignore opportunities, certain challenges may be unavoidable and their consequences severe.

If the stakes are high, intelligence and judgement will usually be required. As they rise still further, people will increasingly pay for others to screen and sift messages and other 'inputs' on their behalf according to a pre-arranged brief. To fulfil such a monitoring role requires sensitivity to what is occurring in the marketplace and the economic and social environment, an appreciation of how others are coping and responding, and a sense of perspective.

The obvious threat may not pose the greatest danger. Not all competitors may be wiped out overnight. Customer loyalty, brand images and term agreements may prevent a sudden demise. But a failure to respond appropriately might lead to decline and fall. Entrepreneurs need to judge whether or not a fundamental decision is required and how quickly.

Not every person or organization may be equally affected by changes that are occurring. Easier access to information and a greater flow of communications will benefit some more than others. Within a particular group certain individuals might need more help than their colleagues. Also as existing barriers fall so others may be erected as people endeavour to protect privileged positions.

Most individuals' primary concern is the impact of external trends and developments upon themselves. They are self-interested. Their first thoughts are invariably about how developments in the context within which they operate might have implications for them personally.

Entrepreneurs have a different perspective. They look at how others, including those around them, are likely to be affected by what is happening. Certain cherished objectives might be at risk. They consider what help colleagues and prospects might need in order to cope and adjust, and whether there could be an opportunity to offer a commercial service that would provide what is required.

People within companies who aspire to become active contributors rather than passive dependents should consider how corporate know-how and their personal skills, along with those of colleagues, might be better captured, shared, used and exploited for competitive business advantage. Maybe additional services could be offered in the light of what is likely to occur and the assistance and support that customers and prospects might require.

Most companies struggle to address some – if not many – of the requirements for successfully responding to external pressures and openings. Those who have identified that they have a problem represent the best targets. They may already be feeling a degree of insecurity, angst or pain, and may thus be very receptive to offers of help, especially when these demonstrate an understanding of what they are both experiencing and endeavouring to achieve. A sensitive approach that shows a supplier cares can help to forge a closer relationship.

Individuals and organizations that wish to remain relevant need to be alert to significant developments; assess how they and others are likely to be impacted by them; and consider how they, colleagues and prospects should respond. Knowledge entrepreneurs must identify, monitor and manage a range of challenges and opportunities as they arise.

Exercise 7b: People-centred ways of working

People can be put first in reality as well as rhetoric if changes are introduced primarily to enable them to become more fulfilled as well as more productive. This involves putting their issues, concerns and aspirations at the heart of projects to introduce new ways of working and learning and create an enterprise:

- Draw up a list of workgroups and rank these in terms of the potential contribution it is thought they could make to the delivery of value to customers, the creation and exploitation of know-how and/or the achievement of key corporate objectives.
- Examine these groups in terms of the people and personalities involved, and whether or not some of their members are significantly more effective, creative and/or fulfilled than others.
- Consider the factors that distinguish the performance and/or satisfaction 'superstars' or 'high achievers' from their less effective, innovative or fulfilled colleagues.
- Assess also the extent of any latent potential that is not currently being tapped.
- Identify the groups that offer the greatest prospect for increasing both 'impact' and the realization of hidden or latent potential.
- Ask a representative selection of the members of these groups to indicate ways of working and learning that would best allow them to give of their best and be true to themselves.

- Identify areas of concern and future aspirations that need to be addressed while evaluating alternative ways of operating.
- If prompting is required, raise possible 'agenda items' such as the nature and quality of the working environment, preferred work locations for different types of work, or the time of day when people feel most productive or creative.
- Consider also whether there are particular approaches, tools, techniques or methodologies that would benefit them.
- Review their information, knowledge and job support tool requirements.
- Examine whether different processes, facilities or reward mechanisms might be more suited to their requirements.
- Agree, scope and cost the introduction of whatever ways of working and learning would contribute the most to the attainment of customer requirements, corporate objectives and individual aspirations, and attempt to quantify the likely benefits.
- Prioritize the identified opportunities in relation to the size and nature of the gap between benefits and costs.
- Develop the business cases for introducing appropriate responses to the most promising opportunities that have been identified.
- Evaluate whether the approach adopted might form the basis of a performance improvement methodology that could yield benefits for both individuals and organizations.

Issue monitoring and management

Smart people are awake and aware. They keep an eye on factors affecting their current activities and future prospects. Organizations need alert and intelligent systems and procedures for: 1) understanding what is happening within the context or environment in which they operate; 2) assessing what the impacts of the most significant trends and developments are likely to be; and 3) determining what could or should be done in response. The following questions should be posed:

- Are you and your colleagues fully aware of what is happening around you? What steps do you take to identify and track potential threats and significant opportunities?
- Does your organization systematically monitor the impact of external changes upon itself and its customers, suppliers, business partners and own people?
- Does your company understand the major issues, trends and developments affecting each of the markets in which it operates? Is it aware of the likely calendar of any events of particular relevance to its operations, activities and prospects?
- Have you identified the boundaries of current knowledge? Where is the greatest progress being made or where does it need to occur, in terms of the development of new knowledge and improved understanding?
- In which of these areas is your organization active? Where could it make the greatest contribution to the creation and exploitation of new know-how?
- What is happening in the economic, social, political and technological environment that could have a significant impact upon your organization and its key stakeholders?
- In particular, how is the emergence of the 'information age' and 'knowledge society', and the globalization of markets for information, knowledge and understanding, likely to affect it?
- Does your organization have access to the information, knowledge and relationships required effectively to identify, monitor and assess relevant trends and developments?
- What are the possible impacts and future implications for your organization of any identified trends and developments likely to be?
- Have you and/or your colleagues assessed the potential consequences for your organization's operations and people? Have the results of this analysis been shared with those who are most directly concerned?
- How will customers, prospects, suppliers and business partners be affected? What are the implications for their relationships with your organization?
- In relation to customers and prospects, what new needs or additional requirements might be generated? Which of these represent business opportunities?
- What obstacles and barriers are being removed, and what new

ones are being created? What are the implications for future threats and opportunities?

- What does the organization need to do in response at local, unit, national and international levels? Who will monitor and coordinate the various reactions?
- What other people and/or organizations are likely to be similarly affected? Do they have compatible interests, shared concerns and complementary capabilities? What scope is there for collective action?
- Are effective processes in place for involving all relevant parties in the determination and implementation of what needs to be done in response to identified threats and opportunities?
- Does your organization participate in collaborative arrangements for making effective and collective representations at local, regional, national, European and international levels?
- Do outputs from your organization's issue monitoring and management processes feed into its planning and direction-setting processes?

Inputs into an issue monitoring and management process should be practical, succinct and honest. Obstacles, barriers and risks should be reported rather than concealed. Issues should neither be played down nor exaggerated. Everyone involved should be encouraged to 'tell it as it is'.

EFFECTIVE ISSUE MONITORING

People sometimes fear that others will regard them as 'negative' or lacking in motivation and fibre if they report that problem areas exist. Those who raise significant issues must be thanked. They should also be encouraged to suggest what they feel ought to be done about them.

While no important issue should be overlooked, if too many of them are assessed during the course of a review, the more critical ones may not receive the attention they deserve. Some companies limit the number of individual issues that people who participate in annual or quarterly monitoring exercises are allowed to put forward. A total of around five may ensure that each item receives reasonable consideration.

The shorter and more concise the description and analysis of an issue is, the greater likelihood that it will be understood and addressed. Similarly, recommendations that are tight, specific and thought through are more likely to be implemented.

Particular issues might have very different implications at local, unit, national and international levels. Hence, those reporting them should be asked to identify the areas in which, and the levels at which, the impacts are likely to be particularly acute. An issue of special concern for an important group should not be screened out just because it may not be regarded as significant elsewhere.

The objective of an issue monitoring and management exercise should be to improve understanding and enable more effective responses. Its purpose is not to collect information for its own sake or fulfil a reporting requirement. Hence issues should be prioritized according to their potential significance, and described from the perspective of those who will determine what needs to be done and/or take effective action. The focus should be upon those issues that can be effectively managed.

The nature of each issue should be specified and, where possible, its implications quantified in terms of scale and timing. The direct and indirect impact upon a company could be assessed in terms of financial and other costs, or the consequences for the value-creating process or some aspect of corporate policy. For each issue there should be clear recommendations as to the action that should be taken at local, unit and corporate levels. Collaborative responses should be suggested where appropriate.

Exercise 7c: Complexity to simplicity analysis

Human progress is signposted by once complex and time-consuming tasks that have either been automated or transformed from being a burden into a joy. Human nature may have altered little over many thousands of years, but how people allocate their time during the course of a day, or over an annual cycle of events, has changed dramatically in certain respects. There are many opportunities for further innovation:

● Review your own professional or private life and those of others with whom you come into contact and draw up a list of particular activities that are difficult and time consuming, or so complex as to require professional advice and support to undertake them.

- Examine any trends and developments that are likely to exacerbate or ameliorate the issues you have identified.
- Consider how many people are likely to be similarly affected, and whether they can be split into different categories that have particular problems in common.
- Assess the negative impacts or the time and cost implications of the problem areas that you have identified.
- Estimate the strength of feeling of the people who are affected and level of dissatisfaction they are experiencing.
- Consider how much different categories of people might be prepared to pay either to simplify or to tackle each of the problem areas that you have listed.
- Multiply the number of people involved by the amount that each might be prepared to pay to achieve a solution in order to judge the extent of the market for a possible response to each problem area.
- Rank the various problem areas that you have identified in order of market potential.
- Starting with the item at the top of the market potential listing and moving down the ordering of potential opportunities, identify or scope service offerings that would lower anxieties, lessen discomfort, save time, reduce expense or add compensating value.
- Calculate the cost of developing and delivering each possible solution and subtract this from the potential value of each of the opportunities that have been identified.
- Also, assess the likely cost of an individual offering and deduct this from the price that each person would be prepared to pay.
- Rank the opportunities in order of the greatest excess of market potential over development cost, and the largest margin of possible price over estimated cost.
- Subject the hit list of potential business opportunities that has been created to further evaluation such as risk and difficulty analysis or funding requirements.
- Prepare business cases for the possibilities that survive this further scrutiny.

SUPPORTING WEALTH CREATION

To create wealth knowledge entrepreneurs need to know how to access, work with, share and use information; and support and enable the development, application and exploitation of know-how and intellectual capital to provide value for customers and shareholders. The skills and competencies required to do this are not the same as those needed to manage money and machines. Different forms of relationships must be established and sustained.

A distinct perspective is also required. Smart entrepreneurs price their offerings according to the value they help to create, rather than the cost of creating and providing them. Knowledge-based products and services that are relatively cheap to produce can be immensely valuable to a recipient. An intelligence report on a specific topic of concern to targeted prospects may command many times the price of a more general book covering a wider area in less depth.

Information, knowledge and understanding are the building blocks of commerce. They are the triple pillars of contemporary civilization. Their importance, contribution and value should not be underestimated. They are today's equivalent of the bricks, coal and iron that reshaped our physical and social worlds during the industrial revolution.

The relative standing of people who are 'information poor' is likely to continue to decline in comparison with those who are 'information rich'. Once what is known becomes generally available the ability to use it in new and novel ways becomes a critical differentiator.

Ambitious individuals actively seek out organizations, environments and membership networks that facilitate and support the acquisition, development, sharing and exploitation of know-how that will enhance their personal capabilities and market value. Creating an enterprise culture and providing the right environment, facilities and support tools can act as a magnet in attracting intellectually curious and entrepreneurial people. A weather eye should be kept on what other companies are doing in these areas.

The availability, accessibility and use of information, knowledge and relevant support tools are a prime determinant of how much progress is made, where, when and by whom. They enable the general process of wealth creation, as well as opening up specific possibilities for knowledge entrepreneurship.

Some companies track external and tangible developments while overlooking the attitudes and opinions of key stakeholder groups such as existing customers and their own people. The views, perceptions and aspirations of 'superstars' and 'key accounts' should be carefully tracked. Important individuals and groups should be given a 'voice'. An opportunity for them to air their concerns should be built into a monitoring process.

Active monitoring and searching for potential business partners can also yield rich dividends. There are often many opportunities for knowledge entrepreneurs to collaborate with complementary providers.

Physical products and related know-how in various formats are often both compatible and potentially interdependent and mutually reinforcing. A combination may offer significantly more value than either can on its own. Thus investment in a new technology may await the availability of suitable content.

Children request PCs and PlayStations because of the games that can operate on them. Those who are 3G licence holders await the likely availability of further mobile-phone-based services before committing to the infrastructure developments that would enable the handsets to be used. Alert entrepreneurs closely monitor the development and emergence of new technologies that might represent additional channels to market.

Exercise 7d: Organizational support opportunity analysis

Many organizations are ill suited to the business and market context in which they operate. This creates opportunities for entrepreneurs to design more competitive models of operation and develop services that will help others to effect required transitions:

- Consider one or more organizations that you are familiar with and for each identify the various trends and developments that are impacting upon them or are about to affect them.
- Evaluate the implications and likely consequences.
- Assess the qualities, attributes, capabilities and know-how that will be required to respond effectively, either to cope with challenges or to seize opportunities.
- Rank the qualities, attributes, capabilities and areas of know-how that have been identified in order of their assessed significance.
- For each of the factors, assess the gap between where each organization is now and where it would like to be.

- Examine forms of organization and associated ways of working and learning that would best bridge the more significant gaps that have been identified.
- Consider the possibilities for developing information services, training courses, methodologies, techniques and/or job support tools that would also contribute to the achievement of desired outcomes.
- Develop a list of possible offerings that would help, or enable, the organizations examined to achieve the change or transformation that is required.
- Evaluate, and attempt to quantify, the consequences of a failure to adapt, and compare this with the likely cost of developing and providing the offerings required.
- Prioritize the opportunities that have been identified in terms of customer impact, relative profitability and degree of difficulty.
- Select, develop and market the most promising offerings.

The most attractive opportunities to pursue are those that would have the greatest beneficial impacts and also yield relatively high financial returns while being relatively easy to achieve.

CHECKLIST

▶ What are the major issues, trends and developments in the situation or context in which you operate?

▶ Who or what is driving them? Do you understand their root causes?

▶ How are the various developments likely to impact upon you and your colleagues?

▶ Have you ranked them in priority in terms of the degree of likely impact?

▶ Are those around you aware of them?

▶ Will your personal position be strengthened or weakened by what might happen?

▶ What about your colleagues and the organization as a whole? How will they be affected?

▶ What could or should you do in response? What should your colleagues and the organization do?

▶ How could you better position yourself to take advantage of prevailing winds and currents? What could or should your organization do?

▶ Do you and/or your organization have the flexibility and capability to respond effectively?

▶ What control, if any, do you have over the most significant events that are likely to affect you? What influence does your organization have?

▶ Are the main areas in which you are active becoming more complex? In what ways is this trend apparent?

▶ What about the corporate and market context? Is it becoming ever more difficult to operate, compete and win?

▶ How rapidly is the volume of printed and electronic information that you and your colleagues are receiving increasing? For how much longer will you be able to cope?

▶ Are the communications that you and others receive easy to comprehend? What help or guidance is there for those who do not understand?

▶ How willing are those around you to interrupt and ask for clarification when explanations are not clear? Can you identify those who need help?

▶ Do you tend naturally to explore certain aspects of an issue in greater detail, or do you endeavour to form a synthesis or overview?

▶ Are you good at getting to the heart of issues? Could you undertake such a service for others?

▶ Who around you tends to confuse others with jargon? Could you provide a simpler alternative that would improve comprehension?

▶ Are certain people and/or groups making matters more

complex than they need to be in order to justify their roles and existence?

▶ What do you need to do to get at the root causes of the major issues and challenges that you and your colleagues face?

▶ Would the root causes be easier to address at a different level or in another context?

▶ What could be done to address the problem areas you have identified, given the realities of the situation that you and your colleagues find themselves in?

▶ Is your experience atypical or common? How many other people in customer and competitive organizations face similar challenges?

▶ Are there enough of them to support new offerings that might help remove some of the constraints you have identified?

▶ Could you or your organization provide some elements of what is required, which might range from individual counselling to generic support tools?

▶ What alternative form of market arrangements would be simple, transparent and easier to use from a customer perspective?

▶ How many transactions, interactions or relationships are involved? Are there enough of them to justify the cost of developing and providing a better alternative?

▶ What steps need to be taken either to create a new market or to make it easier to undertake a particular activity within an existing one?

▶ Do any of the offerings and/or alternatives you have identified represent a commercial opportunity for either you or your organization?

8

Identifying and assessing specific opportunities

ESTABLISHING SEARCH CRITERIA

People who actively search for possibilities often find there are many arenas of opportunity for knowledge entrepreneurship. Those with an intimate knowledge of particular individuals, workgroups, customers, employers, sectors or communities are likely to encounter many examples of the frustrations discussed in earlier chapters of this book. They may find various occasions when, and areas where, the availability of some form of knowledge-based service or support would help. Establishing search criteria can help to narrow the options.

There are choices to be made between lifestyles, and between income and capital growth. Individuals should consider whether their objective is to secure a flow of assignments that might support operation as a sole practitioner, or to build a business. If the former is true, the intention may be to achieve both commercial success and personal fulfilment. In this case, people can work through a series of steps to understand themselves better, assess what they are good at and most enjoy doing, and identify what support they might need to succeed (Coulson-Thomas, 1999b).

Intending business builders may well be more interested in the likely scale of any opportunities that are identified, the scope for expansion and the size of operation the market might support. The risk averse may prefer to sell less to a much wider range of customers to avoid having too many eggs in a small number of baskets. A business that is not overdependent upon a handful of accounts and the continued presence of its founders will also have a greater sales value.

Many entrepreneurs underestimate their funding requirements. It often takes longer to develop and market an offering, and achieve a critical mass of customers, than was first thought. Looking for opportunities to charge a price premium (Coulson-Thomas, 2002a) and provide a differentiated offering can significantly increase the prospects of commercial success. Exercises and checklists are available for challenging assumptions and crafting alternative options that offer customers and prospects a genuine choice (Coulson-Thomas, 2001).

Within a corporate context effort can be focused where it is likely to have the greatest impact. Critical success factors for competing and winning have been identified (Coulson-Thomas, 2002b). A board, management team and internal entrepreneurs might concentrate upon boosting performance in these areas. For example, helping a central bid team to secure more contracts may contribute much more to future prospects than reducing back-room administrative costs.

At the same time, there may be an external market for a range of central corporate services. For example, one investigation of the Centre for Competitiveness identified 25 different categories of commercial offerings that could be provided by an internal training and development team (Coulson-Thomas, 1999a).

In order to cut costs some companies outsource activities with considerable potential for income generation and thus forgo lucrative opportunities. In some cases, areas have been contracted out that have had better commercial prospects than a mainstream business. A review of the scope for knowledge entrepreneurship should precede any consideration of hiving-off, disposal or buyout options.

While final priority should always be given to possibilities that are rooted in customer requirements, an initial search may be designed to exploit better existing corporate know-how that is special or unique. An investigating entrepreneur or team could start with a systematic examination of the many different categories of intellectual capital (Perrin, 2000) in order to identify overlooked areas with latent potential. Some external involvement in the process may ensure greater objectivity.

Exercise 8a: Asking Father Christmas

Many people who consider a change of direction or search for entrepreneurial opportunities settle for too little, too late. They procrastinate and dither. At heart they lack the courage to take the initiative and reach out towards their dreams.

If Father Christmas could fulfil any wish, what would you most like to do? What entrepreneurial opportunity would you like to have? Who would you want to become? Where and with whom would you prefer to be? What additional qualities, capabilities or attributes would you seek to obtain? What else would you ask for? Could your wish list form the basis of search criteria for identifying and assessing future options?

Learning support as a business opportunity

Forms of learning support that many companies consider a cost can represent significant business opportunities in their own right. Various information- and knowledge-based services, and many training and development activities, can be shared, undertaken collaboratively, and delivered by electronic means. Smart companies earn incremental revenues by offering them to customers and other third parties on a commercial basis. Examples include:

- *Personal improvement services, online gurus and intellectual catalysts.* Fitness instructors advise their clients on how to keep in good physical shape. Ideas laboratories, thinking sessions and creativity coaches may work instead on the mind and stimulate the imagination.
- *Learning support services for busy people.* These can range from guidance, counselling and commissioned research to reviewing, analysing and categorizing learning materials and opportunities, suggesting development options and arranging courses of study.
- *Representation of clients in discussion forums.* Individuals can act as the 'eyes and ears' of people who are unable to attend particular sessions. They can record and report upon key

lessons learnt, and ensure that any particular points of view, or prepared responses, are put across.

- *Customized information searches.* Intelligent search engines may only go so far in seeking out what people really want to know about. Research assistants can follow up lines of enquiry and assess the sourcing and veracity of Web site information.

- *Learning services for particular individuals and groups.* Personal tutors or workgroup advisers can help their clients to develop particular competencies, acquire learning skills or understand specific areas of knowledge, which might be obscure but extremely important to those concerned. Therapists can advise on how to tackle creativity 'blockages' and obstacles to learning.

- *Guidance on the development, selection and implementation of new approaches to individual, group and corporate learning.* People who know how to overcome certain barriers to under-standing successfully may find their expertise is of value to others.

- *Confidential one-to-one counselling.* Senior directors may have difficulty assimilating and comprehending financial informa-tion and quantitative data. There may be long-standing phobias to overcome.

- *Various forms of back-up, stand-in and support services for professionals, knowledge workers and external trainers.* These could include call forwarding and response services, specialist help, and the provision of cover during periods of illness, holidays or times of peak workload. Such assistance can significantly increase the utilization rate of learning resources.

- *Acting as an electronic tutor, coach or counsellor.* People can use a growing range of mobile technologies to contact other students, communicate with shared learning partners and seek help and guidance, as and when required. Access to a confi-dential learning adviser can be immensely valuable.

- *Guidance on such matters as the most appropriate means of assessment, or 'best practice' applications of particular learning technologies, which can be delivered online.* A network, or group, could concentrate upon the needs of a particular sector, for example small and medium-sized enterprises, or people with shared learning requirements and objectives.

- *Provision of a virtual learning centre, with facilities such as learning spaces, discussion forums and computer conferencing that can be booked whenever they are required.* Working with other organizations might enable an entrepreneur to offer a comprehensive 'one-stop-shop' service.

- *Virtual resources, from tutors and tools to classrooms and conferences, that can provide services and capabilities that organizations may be reluctant to acquire or establish themselves.* For example, a particular requirement might not justify a full-time appointment, or it may not be easy to recruit an appropriate individual. A shared resource may be the answer.

- *Various forms of interactive learning environment that can be accessed and experienced online and supported remotely.* These can range from individual learning opportunities and small group conferences, to complex business simulations that might attract the participation of a wide range of teams from many companies and enable them to compete against each other.

- *Online facilities for supporting learning partnerships composed of individuals and organizations that might not otherwise be able to work together in view of barriers of distance and time.* Such collaborations can be global in scope, and could cover the development, marketing, delivery and management of a wide range of learning services.

- *Managing and coordinating the learning of international workgroups and project teams, whose members might operate from a number of locations and/or in different time zones.* A support contract could be awarded to a learning partner.

- *Advice on the use and application of learning technologies, for example how to establish and manage a network of distance learning students, or a 'virtual classroom'.* Fresher students may be unsure of how to participate. Tutors might need help in overcoming the practical problems of operating a virtual campus.

- *The integration of different approaches to learning.* Suppliers of various technologies might not be aware of how two or more of them could operate together. Independent counsel can advise on the extent to which various learning processes, tools and technologies might, or might not, interface and complement each other in a particular context to achieve stated objectives.

- *Development, provision and maintenance of knowledge-based job support tools.* A knowledge framework such as K-frame (www.K-frame.com) can be used to capture best practice and assemble the guidance and tools required by a particular community of people.
- *The independent auditing, assessment, testing and monitoring of development requirements, activities and achievements.* The introduction of a learning management system can enable certain roles to be undertaken 'remotely', and from almost any location.
- *The provision of courses leading to an academic award or form of practitioner certification.* Some universities are prepared to validate qualifications offered by other bodies, including commercial companies. Many information technology suppliers offer assessed courses for those seeking evidence of their user skills.
- *Marketing services related to training and development activities.* Thus the prospects of a proposed course or learning support service could be assessed. Target learners could be identified and surveyed. Competitive intelligence could be undertaken, and sales and marketing campaigns designed and implemented.
- *Learning needs analysis and 'learning outcomes' surveys that can be undertaken, and discussion and focus groups that can be held online.* Requirements can be stimulated, assembled and presented to corporate and educational decision makers. Expressions of interest in particular learning activities and bookings for courses can be undertaken via a Web site.
- *Assessment questionnaires and templates, which can also be made available via e-mail or a corporate intranet or Web site.* Recipients and visitors can opt to download appropriate forms or fill them in on-screen. Once completed they can be sent electronically for analysis. Review results could be returned by secure e-mail.
- *Public relations activities to promote a particular learning centre or the value of certain courses, which can be undertaken by electronic means.* Emerging technologies represent additional channels of communication that can be very effective at reaching tightly defined target groups whose members are widely scattered.

- *Help in challenging complacency, confronting cynicism and overcoming resistance to learning.* Using the Internet to appeal directly to individuals can sometimes circumvent organizational and other barriers. For example, people at whom a proposed learning initiative is aimed might be targeted.

- *Virtual campus stores selling learning-related goods in formats that could range from books, cassettes, videos and compact discs to the membership of shared learning networks.* Packages of processes, technologies and services from fulfilment to accounting can be acquired that cover almost every aspect of setting up an Internet-based learning business.

- *Market trading and brokering services.* These are among the earliest forms of business to be established, and they are particularly suited to electronic operation. A 'learning market' that is accessible over the Internet might attract both buyers and sellers of education, training, learning and development services.

- *Support from individuals and learning centre teams to help others establish and manage a Web site or corporate intranet presence that could be used for learning purposes.* Services could range from the design of a Web page and help line support, to making electronic classroom, library and other services available on a dedicated virtual campus site.

- *Online catalogues, bulletin boards, newsletters and discussion groups, which can be initiated, designed and supported with or without related advertising.* Subscriber and advertisement fees can represent an additional source of income for Web sites that attract a large number of visitors.

- *Issue monitoring and management to assess and track what is happening in the world of corporate learning.* A degree of independence from a particular corporate location and culture can result in greater objectivity. An observer might be more sensitive to trends and developments and how others are likely to react to them.

- *Electronic publishing, which continues to offer many opportunities.* Knowledge entrepreneurs who assemble particular packages of information, knowledge and support services can license them for the internal use of client networks, business or supply chain partners, customers and other external parties.

An individual company's training and development team may be able to offer various combinations of the above list of possible offerings. The likely value of any opportunities should be assessed against other uses of people's time and the resources required to exploit them properly. If there are practical constraints and a management team is keen to avoid distraction from current priorities, an external development partner could be sought to exploit any latent commercial potential that is identified.

SEARCHING FOR PERFORMANCE IMPROVEMENT OPPORTUNITIES

As well as initiating new and external activities, knowledge entrepreneurs can also take steps to increase individual productivity and workgroup performance at existing tasks within organizations. Providing people with knowledge-based support tools that enable them to be more effective and successful can yield very attractive commercial returns and increase job satisfaction. Within a partnering arrangement the different parties involved can share in the rewards that are generated.

Many companies initiate grandiose culture change, re-engineering and knowledge management initiatives to improve corporate profitability but do little to help individuals in key roles improve their performance. A consistent finding of successive research projects undertaken by the Centre for Competitiveness of the University of Luton is that successful companies take practical steps to enable their people to manage change, compete and win (Coulson-Thomas, 2002b).

Struggling companies sometimes devote much time and resource to making a wide range of information and knowledge available on a corporate intranet. 'Winners' are more focused and selective. They recognize that much of the know-how they could capture may not be relevant to current priorities, future aspirations and the critical success factors for building their businesses. Also, the expertise to do something better, new or different may require specific skills and particular tools as well as access to relevant knowledge.

One of the most cost-effective ways of quickly improving individual performance and raising corporate productivity is to provide workgroups with practical knowledge-based tools. People often need help when applying relevant knowledge. The right job support tools can capture and spread best practice and increase understanding each time they are used. They can also incorporate devices such as traffic lighting that can influence or change behaviour.

Within most organizations there are many areas of know-how that can be packaged to increase understanding and make it easier for people to do their jobs. Retailer B&Q's vendors manual captures both information and processes and disseminates them to the company's supply chain.

In the finance and banking sector HSBC has used support tools to package its economics knowledge and help customers implement card programs. Friends Provident uses a sales development support kit to assist staff running local marketing campaigns. Smart companies apply effort where it is likely to yield the greatest returns.

Checklist for assessing knowledge-based opportunities

The nature of any entrepreneurial opportunities for knowledge-based offerings should be carefully assessed:

▶ Have you identified a real opportunity to add value by providing a distinct service to an identifiable group of people who are, or might be, willing to pay for it?

▶ In relation to your potential customers or 'prospects', what information or know-how is required, where, when and by whom? What do they intend to do with it?

▶ What further work needs to be done before the information or know-how in question is likely to be in a form required by end users? Who does or would do this and how much might it cost?

▶ Could you or your company undertake the additional work more cost-effectively than the current arrangements or provide what is required by some other means?

▶ Have the people involved thought about and articulated their requirements for a different service or additional provision? If not, could you help to facilitate the review process?

▶ Are there different and better sources that could be used? Have these already been identified and assessed? If not, could you undertake any search and evaluation that is required?

▶ What is wrong with the existing provision of information or know-how? How could its content, format, access and reliability be improved? Could you review and critique the current situation and practice?

▶ Are the potential beneficiaries currently in receipt of an alternative offer? In what ways would your offering represent an improvement?

▶ Is the information or know-how in question always to hand when it is needed? Could you extend the window of availability? Could on-demand access be provided?

▶ Could the supply of information or know-how be speeded up? Could you provide a job support tool that would make it easier for people to use and apply it?

▶ What steps could be taken to reduce the cost of the current provision? Are there particular services that are 'gold plated' or no longer required?

▶ What changes to the current formats and further analysis would make the information easier to comprehend and assimilate?

▶ Would the users be interested in an offering that was tailored or customized to their individual needs? Is this an activity that you or your company could undertake?

▶ How responsive are existing suppliers to their customers' requests for help and support? Is cover available outside of normal working hours?

▶ Could you provide some form of online help desk service that represents a noticeable improvement on what is currently available?

▶ What else could be done to add value to what is currently provided and differentiate your proposed offering from those of any alternative providers?

▶ What value do the current users place upon the information or know-how in question? Would they be willing and able to pay more for an improved service?

▶ How much extra would the users be prepared to pay for particular enhancements they are seeking? Would they fund the specific changes that need to be made, or would the costs involved have to be recovered from subsequent user fees or new subscribers?

▶ Who else might be interested in the same information or

know-how, or a similar service? Could the provision of what is required generate incremental income?

▶ What other information, know-how or expertise within the organization could be brought together to form a commercial package or job support tool that would meet the needs of other communities of people or workgroups in the external marketplace?

▶ What price levels could be sustained? Could various categories of user be charged at different rates?

▶ How would external customers pay for the provision of the information, know-how or service in question? Could users be charged at the point and time of access, or while the information is being downloaded?

▶ How much would the desired information, know-how or service cost to produce? Could it be provided at a profit? Would the returns compensate for the risks involved?

▶ Will corporate or start-up finance be required to launch the proposed service? How might the users or business partners contribute to this?

▶ Might external sources of finance be interested in the proposition? What forms of security could you or your company provide?

▶ If a commercial opportunity exists, should you or your company exploit this alone, or should you seek a collaborative venture with another entity?

▶ Who might suggest an appropriate arrangement or potential partners?

▶ Could exploitation rights be licensed to other parties?

▶ Is there a particular role that you or your company could provide within an external arrangement, for example acting as a publisher?

▶ Are all the capabilities to do what is required available in-house, or will additional and external support be required?

▶ Is anyone within your company or a potential partner organization interested in collaborating with you to exploit the opportunity on a profit-sharing basis?

▶ Who is going to initiate discussions and establish and manage the relationship? Is this something you could undertake?

IMPROVING SALES PRODUCTIVITY

Sales productivity is of critical importance for many companies. Many sales teams are being pressured to win more orders in a difficult economic environment, sometimes with reduced budgets. With competitors snapping at their heels and customers demanding more bespoke responses, prices and margins are also under threat. The rate of staff turnover in sales forces is often high, and companies in some sectors are becoming more dependent on indirect channels and third parties.

There are other problems that sales managers may need to address, such as a wide gulf in performance between superstars and average performers who struggle to keep up to date or find it difficult to achieve their targets. Those who lack product knowledge may rely increasingly upon colleagues with specialist expertise. There may also be a desire to reduce the time it takes to achieve a sale.

Inducting new sales people can take a lot of time. Eyretel's products record and analyse 'customer interactions'. The company found its growth limited by the speed with which it could recruit and train new sales staff, and ensure existing members of the team understood new offerings. According to Marketing Director Nathan George: 'We had to find a way to get knowledge about our complicated product line to a large number of sales people quickly.'

Many companies lack a reliable and systematic approach to sales. With complex products people find it difficult systematically to gather information about customer requirements and configure solutions. Proposals and other documents are of uneven quality, as desired standards are not built into the sales process. Different staff communicate inconsistent messages. Indirect channels might have to be brought up to speed. Also the emphasis may need to change from selling hard to helping prospects to buy.

Sales managers often find that some sales staff will take risks, cut corners or ignore regulatory requirements, particularly if they are desperate to land an order. They make errors when pricing, or leave out standard clauses from proposals. They may also struggle to explain clearly what is special and distinctive about an offering. Many sales people find it difficult to communicate complex messages and cope with different languages and cultures. In short they may require support when in front of customers and prospects.

Exercise 8b: Gain and loss analysis

Changes are occurring all around us. The following steps could indicate whether or not these are likely to represent challenges or opportunities:

- Identify the more significant contemporary trends and developments.
- Consider who are likely to be 'gainers' and 'losers' as the developments gather momentum.
- Determine how many and what sorts of people are likely to be in both categories.
- Evaluate what it is that these groups might gain or lose respectively.
- Assess whether the possession of advance information or particular know-how would influence the likely outcomes.
- Consider what the people involved might like to continue, preserve or re-create.
- Consider also whether there are alternative options that they might prefer.
- Review the available information on these alternatives and whether those interested in them might require additional help, guidance or support.
- Consider possible offerings that would enable potential 'winners' to take fuller advantage of whatever is likely to occur.
- Assess whether whatever service would help the 'winners' and/or the 'losers' might represent a business opportunity.
- So far as the 'losers' are concerned, examine whether there are significant minorities who feel, or are likely to feel, strongly about what is or might be lost.
- Assess whether any of the groups that might be adversely affected by changes would be sufficiently large and motivated to represent a potential target market for products and services tailored to their particular interests.

Don't overlook the desire of many people to preserve, re-create and relive the past. Nostalgia has led to opportunities for specialist magazines aimed at those with an interest in fields such as antiques, country houses, historical modelling, record collecting, steam railways, vintage aeroplanes, and classic cars and boats. Major bookshops invariably stock published collections of old and local photographs.

JOB SUPPORT TOOLS

The problems just described represent an ideal opportunity for entre-preneurship. Smart companies can address them by providing their sales teams with a laptop-based job support package that gathers together the critical information, knowledge and tools a sales person needs. It could incorporate 'best practice' and the approaches used by 'superstars' as well as the critical success factors for winning business identified by research at the Centre for Competitiveness (Coulson-Thomas, 2002b).

Sales support tools developed by Cotoco for Eyretel and clients such as Bolero, Cisco, Dana and ICB have included slides with voice-overs, interactive presentations that support particular sales methodologies, demonstrations of products in operation, and explanations to help customers understand key points. They have also incorporated configuration tools for developing solutions, pricing engines that calculate their cost, proposal generators, and decision trees to assist account strategy planning. Cost justification tools can calculate the likely returns on the investments involved.

Job support tools can automate routine tasks and provide help for every stage of the sales process from prospecting and qualification to negotiation meetings. Quality and regulatory requirement checks can be built in. A library of detailed background information can help users to answer customers' questions on the spot. Marketing materials such as templates, case studies, testimonials and independent endorsements can be included.

Seamless links can be provided to Web sites and online information and applications. Feedback mechanisms can be used to gather information from the field. Guides for up-selling and cross-selling can extend the comfort zone of sales representatives to further product areas. The specific identification of cross-selling and upgrade opportunities can also be built into a sales support tool.

Sales support tools are particularly suited to the launch of new products. A single repository able to handle material in different formats can hold all the information and knowledge needed. Technical details can be quickly communicated to various groups in multiple locations around the world. Animations and video footage can be used to show offerings in use, and secrecy can be maintained until the moment of release.

The Innovation Group (TIG) has used support tools to launch a new local authority operating system and roll out its project management methodology, and 3Com has employed a similar tool to introduce network products to both direct and indirect channels. We will return to this area and examine some important issues to address when building support tools and lessons to be learnt in the next chapter.

Exercise 8c: Defining a new role

Consider major trends and developments in the business environment in arenas such as the use of the Internet, e-business and mobile technologies and how these might impact upon your customers, your activities and how you operate:

- Set out what they might mean for those whom you currently serve or with whom you need to come into contact.
- List the challenges and opportunities that they face, steps they might be able to take and various forms of support they might need.
- Assess how many other individuals and/or organizations might be in need of similar services.
- Relate what is required to your own experience and skill base, and your company's capabilities and know-how, and search for areas of overlap.
- Look also for launch or entry points: good stepping-off places for assembling what may be needed to provide whatever is required.
- Relate the prospects and opportunities to your own situation, what you know about your own strengths, weaknesses and preferences, and what you would like to do with your life.
- Relate them also to your company's strengths, resources and priorities.
- Consider whether the possibilities you have identified might represent suitable openings for individual and/or corporate entrepreneurship.
- Screen out the personal opportunities that are not really you, as business options do not have to be pursued just because they exist.
- Prioritize the opportunities that remain, using practical criteria such as affordability and other potential barriers to entry, and what you feel you would most enjoy doing.

BENEFITS OF USING SUPPORT TOOLS

Users of support tools report significant increases in productivity and the ease with which best practice can be spread. Some of their experiences are very positive. Quick paybacks of the cost of developing them can be achieved, one project paying for itself through additional orders within the first week of introduction. Returns on investment of 20:1 or more can be obtained.

Such results are much better than those achieved by sales technology in general. Research by the Gartner Group found that 75 per cent of sales application projects have been perceived by their users to have failed to meet expectations 12 months after deployment (Thompson and Eisenfeld, 2000a, 2000b). The Gartner team found sales often dip during a period of up to six months while new technology is being embedded, whereas users of specific sales support tools report rapid adoption and quick improvements in performance.

Tools can enable the consistent application of best sales practice and ensure a high standard of proposals. Marked improvements in product and market knowledge occur. Other benefits include a reduction in errors, higher win rates, greater customer retention, fewer support staff, increased order value and lower sales force churn.

People find it easier to meet submission deadlines, and a shorter sales cycle can bring orders forward. Users can spend more time in front of customers and less on routine administration. Better prospecting and improved qualification can result in a greater focus on the most productive accounts.

The induction of new staff can also be quicker and less expensive. Learning through doing is particularly effective. Building knowledge into tools makes it very easy for people to get complex tasks right first time and every time.

Bolero's tool, according to Director of Consulting Tony Duggan, made its 'sophisticated' electronic trade standards and software 'so easy to understand, and to follow a structured sales process. It usually took me an hour to explain what we do, and even then people had difficulty really understanding it. Using Cotoco's sales tool, I can give someone a far clearer understanding of the essence of what we can do for customers, and in only a few minutes.'

Integrated Communications for Business (ICB) uses its Navigator sales support tool to build product knowledge and communicate with customers. According to Marketing Director Janetta Evans:

The company have all reacted brilliantly to Navigator. We now rely on the simple but effective tool as the knowledge base for the whole company. Navigator will become an intrinsic part of how ICB works. The message, the confidence, the ability to prove what we sell as a deliverable have all been greatly enhanced – this must lead to a great return on investment.

Dana has packaged knowledge about its technology and manufacture of the bearings it produces in the form of a support tool for both internal and market communications. Some companies make their sales support tools available to dealers, business partners and customers. For Avaya, Cotoco produced an INDeX Engineers Toolkit that provides all the documentation and tools required by an engineer in the field.

Using iterative processes in the presence of prospects can help them to meet their needs better. They may discover new options. When operating a tool themselves some customers order more than they would in the presence of a sales representative. They feel in control and are able to explore alternatives in their own time. Automated calculations enable them quickly to assess the consequences of different approaches.

Support tools allow managers to maintain control of quality and avoid risks when delegating responsibilities. They may feel able to encourage more bespoke responses. The automation of routine tasks frees up time for the greater differentiation and tailoring that may enable a price premium to be charged (Coulson-Thomas, 2002a). Often less experienced and less qualified staff can also be used.

Sales support tools can also be used to secure control over an indirect sales process. Standard clauses can be automatically included in proposals. There is less need for separate commercial quality and regulatory checks, or for specialist and local language support. Reliance upon technical specialists can be reduced considerably. Users of Eyretel's tool felt so confident in the presence of customers that the ratio of support to sales staff fell to a third of the previous level.

Exercise 8d: Potential for collective action

Searches for new commercial opportunities can be undertaken in association with customers and business partners. If there are common interests, complementary capabilities and alluring prospects, collective action may prove irresistible.

Directors of significant organizations within a particular area, network or community, and individual entrepreneurs with aspirations to make an impact could consider the following steps:

● Draw up a list of whatever the organization's board would like more of within the area or group concerned, another one containing whatever it wishes to see less of and a third one for whatever it would prefer to remain more or less the same.
● Invite the people of the organization, particularly employees, business partners, local suppliers and key customers – and also representatives of the local community – to do likewise, ie compose lists of whatever they want to see more of, less of and roughly the same amount of.
● Rank the organization's own lists in priority order in terms of the changes its board would most like to bring about and what its directors most want to remain the same.
● Invite the people of the organization and representatives of key stakeholder groups to do likewise, ie produce their particular prioritized lists.
● Arrange an event at which the various lists and rankings can be compared and areas of overlap, compatibility or conflict identified.
● Identify where there appear to be common interests, and prioritize these in order of importance for the various parties concerned.
● Starting with the areas in which there would appear to be the greatest potential for collaboration, ie all the significant players involved in the exercise rank them highly in importance, formulate shared objectives and priorities.
● Taking the item ranked highest first, draw up a list of complementary actions that each of the parties is willing to undertake or support to achieve the desired objectives.
● Identify information, know-how and support requirements and related business opportunities arising from the agreed programme.

The exercise could be repeated in all the markets and various virtual or physical communities in which an organization has a significant presence. For example, members of a supply or value chain could be invited to a conference to identify mutual interests, develop shared objectives, decide priorities, discuss common problems, consider collective responses, allocate responsibilities and agree joint actions.

CHECKLIST

▶ Have the organizations with which you are associated defined clear roles and responsibilities?

▶ Have these and priorities been agreed with the individuals and workgroups involved?

▶ Do they reflect the qualities, strengths and preferences of the people concerned?

▶ Have competencies and knowledge and support requirements also been defined for the roles and priorities that have been agreed?

▶ Are people clear about their own roles and how they relate to those of others?

▶ Have people been equipped with appropriate support tools that share best practice?

▶ How satisfactory and robust are the relationships that are vital for competing and winning? Are they waxing or waning? Is shared learning occurring?

▶ Do all of the parties involved obtain clear benefits? Are rewards for success fairly allocated?

▶ Are there knowledge-based services that would strengthen particular relationships?

▶ Do you review and refine or renegotiate your existing relationships, and actively network and establish new ones?

▶ How effective are you at relationship management? What particular deficiencies should you address?

▶ What professional networks or creative communities do you belong to? Do members assume personal responsibility for remaining current?

▶ Is there a core body of knowledge and/or a central repository of know-how in its various formats? Are there regular meetings and communications?

▶ Are responsibilities to fellow members acknowledged and obligations to the community acted upon? Are information and knowledge being created and shared?

▶ What additional forms of help might be required? Are there enough members to fund the development of particular support tools?

▶ Is the community sensitive to the changing information and support requirements of its members?

▶ Are additional forums for sharing information and exchanging views required?

▶ Are reviews undertaken to identify information and knowledge gaps, and assess the commercial value of the know-how of the community and its members?

▶ What could be done to exploit this know-how better? How could you help?

▶ What would you most like to change in the information, knowledge and support that you receive in your life and work, and what would you like to remain the same?

▶ How would your customers, prospects and colleagues answer the same question?

▶ To what extent is steady progress being made as opposed to change for change's sake? Has understanding of critical areas increased?

▶ Do the people around you automatically assume that change is a good thing?

▶ How easy is it for individuals to speak up against change? To what extent can they influence the information, knowledge and support they receive?

▶ What is constant in the context within which you operate? Have you identified a 'comfort zone' of continuity factors?

▶ What are the anchor points? What is the social cement that holds people together?

▶ Do those with whom you work have compatible values and views? Is there a common understanding of what needs to be done? Are information and knowledge shared?

▶ Who is responsible for maintaining the factors that perpetuate and strengthen the relationships that are most important to you?

▶ Is the boundary of knowledge getting closer or moving further away? Are gaps in understanding emerging?

▶ Is regression occurring? Are critical areas of knowledge and expertise being lost as people leave, reorganizations occur, equipment is scrapped and files are destroyed?

▶ What needs to be done to capture and share valuable insights and understanding that might otherwise be lost?

▶ What has been dropped or discarded that you would like to bring back? Is there particular information and knowledge that people miss?

▶ Are there certain aspects of the past that interest you and which could be re-enacted or recreated?

▶ Are there values and beliefs you would like to see rekindled, or practices that should be reintroduced?

▶ How many other people share your views of what is important?

▶ What do you feel especially passionate about? What would you most like to know, learn about or see happen?

▶ Are there particular interests or small groups of enthusiasts who might be set alight with the same vision?

▶ Is there a knowledge-based offering that would meet the information and communication needs of this community?

9

Creating information- and knowledge-based offerings

PACKAGING WHAT YOU KNOW

Many experts struggle to explain the nature of their expertise, what they do and how they can help others. They are not understood and they do not stand out. As a first step towards creating knowledge-based offerings, people and organizations need to package their know-how so that others can appreciate their particular capabilities.

Potential clients often find it very difficult to determine the point at which external expertise is required and to assess the qualities and calibre of those who might be able to help. Individual knowledge workers and professional firms can spend a lot of time endeavouring to understand whether or not problems people bring to them might form the basis of an assignment and client relationship in an area within which they specialize.

Most experts would prefer to spend their time applying their skills to challenges that justify high charge-out rates. Practice development, dealing with initial enquiries, qualifying opportunities and capturing basic information about prospects can all represent non-chargeable time.

So how can knowledge entrepreneurs help? The risk management practices of AIG Europe, Clifford Chance, Dames & Moore, Deloitte & Touche, Hill and Knowlton and Kroll Associates tackled this problem by assembling their core expertise in the form of a self-diagnostic toolkit that people could use to carry out an initial risk assessment. The resulting PROMPT-RPS tool provided an overview understanding of the major areas of corporate risk, and enabled users to capture basic information about their situation and identify where they required specialist help.

A tool such as PROMPT-RPS can be distributed via a Web site or by direct mailing a CD ROM to a target group. Its focus can be upon a problem that recipients are either known or likely to have. Self-assessment checklists can be included for completion by either the recipient or colleagues to whom they are e-mailed. Explanations can be provided where appropriate. Once an initial review has been completed the results can be e-mailed to the expert sources of advice the tool suggests for tackling whatever problems have been identified.

The recipient of a completed review can quickly check that an enquirer has followed a suggested process. If this has happened, any subsequent relationship can be built upon the overview obtained and the understanding gained during the self-assessment process. The expert will not need to spend time collecting basic information and may be able to avoid an iterative process to determine whether or not there is an issue to address and in what area.

Exercise 9a: Storm analysis

Intending entrepreneurs need to assess the resilience of the roots and foundations of their lives, and the extent to which they will be able to withstand current pressures and future challenges. Once a new venture is under way they may find themselves buffeted in all directions by contending forces. They need to identify areas of weakness and take steps to strengthen their defences.

Dark enterprise clouds can range from lost orders and staff defections, through fraud, deception and legal challenge, to the threat of bankruptcy or liquidation. If a storm were to rage through your life, what would be left standing and what would be swept or blown away? Would the trappings or the fundamentals be lost? What is most exposed and what is most secure? What if anything could be recovered?

If the going really got tough how many of those around you would remain by your side? Who would cut and run? Who or what is dispensable, and who or what could you least afford to lose? Are the latter at risk? Overall, how well placed or vulnerable are you? What needs to be done to strengthen your position?

BUILDING JOB SUPPORT TOOLS

In the last chapter we examined how some companies have used knowledge-based job support tools to achieve more sales. Let us now turn to some of the practical considerations involved in building such tools, and important lessons that emerge from the experiences of early pioneers.

Some companies struggle to explain what they do. Multimedia capabilities can improve comprehension and understanding. They usually enhance the portrayal of corporate credentials and capabilities, while animations can bring technology to life. They also ensure sales people focus on value and benefits to the customer, and do not devote too much time to extolling the features of their own company's offerings.

Dana Glacier Vandervell Bearings, a leading supplier of engine bearings, found it very difficult to explain to customers and internal staff the sophisticated technology behind what appeared to be relatively simple products. The dependence of the properties of bearings upon the structure and composition of the materials of which they are made was particularly hard to visualize.

The solution adopted by Dana GVB was to capture, structure and package product information and technological expertise on to a CD that provided audio-visual presentations to explain the essential characteristics of bearing materials within the overall design of an engine. Explanations and visual demonstrations of the company's unique technology and advanced manufacturing techniques were also given.

CD ROMs are ideal for disseminating job support tools. There is usually space to include a search and information management facility and a presentation wizard to allow tailoring of presentations using pre-approved standard modules. A company may choose to include a photographic library, interactive training modules, and self-assessment tests that identify knowledge gaps and advise on further study. Competitor analysis and response strategies, and industry and market knowledge can also be added.

Effective job support tools use whatever formats, from text and graphics to animations, visual images and video and audio clips, that best help understanding. When tools are assembled using a knowledge framework such as K-frame (www.K-frame.com), search and fuzzy search facilities can cover a wide range of formats. Complex material can be more easily communicated, and fewer visits may be required to achieve a sale.

Dana GVB used animations with voice-overs to show what is required in particular circumstances. Customers were found to understand quickly the chemical and engineering technologies involved. The tool was also used to induct new employees. Staff and users could appreciate what the company did without needing to visit its factory.

Foreign language versions of support tools can be relatively easy to produce. There are French and English language editions of Eyretel's sales support tool, while 10 different language versions have been issued of a tool developed for Bolero, including Chinese, Japanese, Korean and Arabic.

Employees' checklist

Smart entrepreneurs work with the people involved in the processes they are seeking to improve. Such individuals and groups should be encouraged to pose questions that will help them to determine the support they require and take more control of their immediate work situation. There are various matters that all employees who wish to remain employable should actively reflect upon:

▶ Is the organization that employs you operating in a sector in which information, knowledge and understanding are accounting for an increasing proportion of the value being generated for customers? What are the implications for your future prospects?

▶ What responsibility are you willing to assume for the development of your own knowledge, understanding and competence? In these areas, are you by nature an active initiator and leader, or a passive reactor and follower?

▶ Are you prepared to take the initiative in demanding and/or developing know-how and support tools that would enable you and your colleagues to do a better job? Do you track the support provided to other individuals and groups undertaking similar work?

▶ Do you regularly review what you have learnt in relation to what you need to know in order to be effective in your current role? Do you know: 1) what you know and can do; and 2) what you do not know and cannot do?

▶ What activities do you undertake to remain competent, current and employable? Do you belong to information-, knowledge- and tool-sharing networks relating to your current role and future aspirations?

▶ What does your employer do to help? Is appropriate coun- selling, mentoring or other development and job support provided? If not, what steps do you propose to take to secure the assistance that you feel you need?

▶ Do you consciously think about and periodically assess how effective you are at acquiring, sharing and using relevant infor- mation, knowledge and support tools? In what areas could you do better?

▶ Do you have access to the information, knowledge and support tools you need to be effective in your role? Where deficiencies exist, have you formulated and articulated your requirements? Do you make your colleagues aware of what is needed?

▶ Are you a producer or consumer of information, knowledge and understanding? Do you contribute to the knowledge base of your employer, or live off it?

▶ Are your particular contributions recognized and rewarded? Who else might be interested in what you are producing? Could it form the basis of one or more distinct offerings?

▶ At heart are you an individualist or a team player? Would you prefer to 'do your own thing' or work collaboratively with others?

▶ If you had an idea for a new business would you seek to involve your current employer and/or work colleagues? Do you have anyone else to whom in the first instance you would turn?

▶ Do you obtain the greatest satisfaction from producing rather than exploiting original ideas, or do you find implementing or commercializing them more fulfilling?

▶ Which would you prefer: to receive a royalty or licence fee from someone else who uses your intellectual capital, or to build a profitable income stream as a result of exploiting it yourself?

▶ What are the main obstacles and barriers to your becoming a more effective creator and/or user of knowledge and/or a more successful entrepreneur? What are you doing, or intending to do, about them?

▶ What have you done to encourage your employer to: 1) develop a culture that actively encourages the creation and exploitation of know-how and information and knowledge entrepreneurship; and 2) establish whatever arrangements are required to support these activities?

LESSONS THAT CAN BE LEARNT

When support tools provide the easiest way to accomplish desired outcomes, take-up is encouraged and tangible changes in behaviour can be achieved. Users have found that the way they communicate with a prospect can in itself become a differentiator. A systematic and customer-focused approach enhances a supplier's reputation and helps to build customer relationships.

There are also some potential dangers. Without a proper roll-out plan, the full potential of a proposed solution may not be achieved. Just putting a CD ROM into the post and assuming its eventual use is unlikely to succeed. People need to understand the significance of what is being provided.

The value of a tool reflects the quality of its individual elements. A component such as a pricing engine will only be as good as the assumptions upon which it is based. Data sets such as a schedule of prices may need to be regularly updated in order to remain current.

Avoid tools that deskill. Cisco's IP Telephony Sales Tool up-skills people working in its direct and indirect sales channels. As users work through prospect qualification and response decision tools, windows open up to explain why certain courses of action are advocated. Users learn from each use.

There may be a degree of scepticism to overcome. Some companies are initially cautious because past and unrelated investments in sales technology, e-learning and knowledge management have delivered questionable results. Such outcomes are not surprising. These other initiatives have usually been excessively general, and they fail to provide people with the practical support tools they need to do a better job.

Ill-considered sales technology in general can be harmful, although the Gartner research team did find that new and less experienced sales staff do in some cases benefit enormously (Thompson and Eisenfeld, 2000a, 2000b). The key to success lies not in trying to shave a few per cent off administrative time, but instead in focusing upon and transforming what happens in front of the customer.

Within any community of knowledge workers, some are likely to be more effective than others. Every opportunity should be taken to review existing approaches during the development phase, and capture effective short cuts and how high achievers operate. Improvements based upon best practice and the insights of superstars are much more likely to get better results than just automating current practices.

The greatest benefits from job support tools are usually achieved with relatively homogeneous groups of people undertaking similar tasks. Companies should avoid investing in fixed and inflexible tools in areas that may be subject to rapid change, unless arrangements are made for continuing review and regular updating. Performance improvements will need to cover the costs involved. This is most likely in areas such as sales that contribute directly to the 'bottom line'.

Companies interested in exploring the possibilities for providing workgroups with new or improved job support tools should seek a demonstration of the possibilities. If better understanding of complex material is required, a tool should use visual means of helping comprehension such as animations and diagrams. One or more workshops should be held to examine the applicability of job support tools to the particular context and to the people, problems and products involved.

Once support requirements have been agreed rapid and tangible progress can usually be made. Even complex tools can often be developed and tested within a few weeks of a go-ahead being given. However, the introduction of a new tool will need to be carefully planned if people are to obtain the maximum of benefit from it. Backup needs to be arranged. The shelf-life of a job support tool can be greatly increased with an ongoing maintenance program.

Job support tools can represent a much more cost-effective way of improving understanding and increasing workgroup performance than traditional training and development activities. Rates of return on investment will depend upon the number of people involved. A medium-sized company found the cost of creating an effective tool to be similar to that of sending its sales team on a one-day commercial training course. For a major corporation the cost per sales representative may be no more than providing each of them with a bottle of wine.

Exercise 9b: Incremental opportunity analysis

Within many situations and contexts there is enormous scope for performance improvement. In areas or organizations that you are familiar with there may be many opportunities to achieve far more than is currently being accomplished:

● Ask people about the recent occasions on which they have been most disappointed with what has been achieved or delivered.

● Ask them also to identify areas in which they believe there is latent potential to accomplish so much more.

● Draw up a list of instances or areas in which more than one person has either expressed disappointment or felt more could be done.

● Rank the items according to the number of times each was cited.

● Investigate why people feel the perceived underachievement occurred.

● Enquire as to whether more might have been delivered had additional time, know-how or support been made available.

● Find out what those who were involved felt was missing that could have been provided.

● Consider whether sufficient options for undertaking the activities in question had been identified and explored by those involved.

● Look for evidence that might explain why further work was not done, for example whether those concerned were under time pressure to switch effort to other priorities.

● Assess what is required to realize the latent potential that appears to exist.

● Examine whether relevant information, knowledge and experience are still available.

● Assess the practicality of assembling the people and resources needed and the likely cost-effectiveness of doing what is required to realize the opportunity.

DIFFERENTIATION

However effective they might be, new offerings need to be noticed to score. Because of the growing speed with which competitive insights, product improvements and breakthroughs in thinking can be captured, copied and shared, windows of opportunity are becoming more limited. Processes for developing new knowledge-based products and differentiating them from other alternatives must be speeded up.

Imitation and 'me-too' approaches are no longer sufficient. Companies that practise 'catch-up', 'benchmarking' or 'copy your neighbour' management may not have a distinctive or compelling rationale for continued operation. Maybe if they ceased to exist, very little would be lost. Customers could simply transfer their business to another supplier of a very similar product or service.

A new offering that is distinctive if not unique is more likely to stand out, register and achieve an impact. Differentiation has become a major challenge of the age. People must know what competitors are doing and what is available from other suppliers in order to be different. Effective entrepreneurs need to be both engaged and detached at the same time. They must challenge prevailing assumptions and come up with new and better alternatives. Guidance for doing this is available (Coulson-Thomas, 2001).

Opportunities to be distinctive are often found in the 'gaps' or 'spaces' that may lie between subjects, markets, technologies, skill sets or the existing players within a particular marketplace. Often such areas appear to represent a barren desert so far as information and know-how are concerned. They remain unexplored: hence the value of people who can operate at the frontiers of knowledge and in unknown territory, and assemble, deduce or construct what is relevant for creating new offerings.

A wide range of possibilities can represent a challenge rather than an opportunity for those who lack the means of evaluating them. No generation in history has had so many options for consuming, working or learning at times and places and in a mode of their choice. Indeed the barriers between these and other activities are becoming blurred. There are many potential combinations of the various possibilities.

There are indeed often so many options that most people and institutions may only be aware of a small fraction of the full range that is available. Hence, they need help in identifying, assessing and selecting the most promising prospects. Companies that do not know what they do not know are vulnerable. Knowledge entrepreneurs can help their people to recognize blind spots, highlight overlooked information and supply missing expertise.

Exercise 9c: Information and knowledge sifting services

Opportunities abound for identifying and satisfying personal and organizational requirements for information, knowledge and greater understanding. Some entrepreneurs find them under their noses. In relation to areas and situations that you are familiar with:

- Consider whether there are people who would benefit from the provision of some form of filter that would sift through incoming calls, e-mails and documents and identify, select, summarize and present only that which is relevant.
- Consider also whether such a service could be proactive in terms of setting out at defined intervals, or even on a continuous basis, to monitor, screen, access and test relevant sources of information, knowledge and news, with a view to presenting what has been found in a pre-defined and agreed format.
- Assess the extent to which others also share the needs that have been identified and whether these might form the basis of a subscription service.
- Identify flows of information, news and messages that could be screened to categorize and prioritize the contents and filter out less relevant material.
- Consider filters that would identify material that might waste time, cause offence, infringe legal or regulatory requirements, or indicate a conscious attempt to steal intellectual property.
- Identify opportunities to provide people with an independent review, categorization and filtering service that would free them from spending time working through irrelevant material.

CHECKLIST

▶ When did you last list the factors and forces that are most likely to test you?

▶ Have you identified a range of options for handling each of the major issues and challenges that you face?

▶ How practical and realistic are they in relation to your current situation and circumstances?

▶ Which of the options would preclude others? Could elements of one or more of them be combined?

▶ Do any of the options have the potential to become a 'big idea' that could achieve a breakthrough or become the basis of a commercial offering?

▶ Have those around you identified the options that are available? Do they understand them?

▶ Are they under pressure to select the first acceptable option?

▶ To whom could you go, or refer, to assess whether there are further and better options?

▶ On what basis do you and your colleagues select between options? What criteria do you employ? Do you use some means of formal assessment or rely upon instinct or 'feel'?

▶ Would you benefit from having more time to explore other possibilities, or work up additional alternatives?

▶ What additional value might be added if certain deadlines were extended, additional information obtained or other people involved?

▶ Are there others with whom you could work or collaborate in order to achieve an outcome that would be more distinctive?

▶ What proportion of the value of the products and services that you and your colleagues provide is accounted for by know-how in its various forms?

▶ Is this proportion increasing or decreasing?

▶ Have you identified the main sources of information, knowledge and support tools that are relevant to your current and planned future activities?

► How accessible are they? Do you have the access that you require?

► Is what is available in a format that enables it to be easily used?

► Do you and your colleagues suffer from information overload? If so, what do you intend to do about this?

► Are there gaps in what is available that might constitute an opportunity to provide an information- or knowledge-based service? Could this form the basis of a business?

► Do those with whom you work readily share information, knowledge and understanding?

► Is know-how systematically captured, shared, valued and protected?

► Are working conditions and environments conducive to the development or acquisition and exploitation of new knowledge and understanding?

► Do they enable intellectual capital to be created, packaged, managed and exploited?

► What part can you play in this process? How could these arrangements be used to develop and exploit your own ideas?

10

Becoming a knowledge entrepreneur

ENTREPRENEURIAL QUALITIES

All entrepreneurs require certain qualities, attributes and competencies to succeed. For example, they have to be able to identify commercial opportunities to add value by meeting requirements of customers that are not being addressed by existing provision. They must be focused and disciplined to assemble what is required, and tenacious in response to various setbacks and disappointments that invariably arise. In competitive markets and difficult times they will need to be tough, pragmatic and resilient.

Particular opportunities may favour certain people and personalities. Intending entrepreneurs need sufficient self-awareness to operate in situations where they can play to their strengths and be true to themselves, and complement their qualities with colleagues who compensate for their deficiencies (Coulson-Thomas, 1999b). They will require a clear sense of direction and an ability to motivate if they are to inspire others.

Aspiring entrepreneurs' checklist

Before actively setting out to become a knowledge entrepreneur there are certain basic questions that you should address:

▶ Are you in control of your life? Do you have a sense of mission and purpose? Or are you happy to be a piece on someone else's chessboard?

▶ How strongly do you want to become an entrepreneur? Have you thought through the implications and requirements for success?

▶ Are you robust and determined? Do you have the energy and drive to sustain the growth of a business?

▶ How supportive are members of your immediate family and other people who are close to you? What is their honest assessment of your prospects?

▶ Where does your drive come from? Are you inwardly motivated and self-directed, or do you depend upon others for direction and motivation?

▶ Do you cope on your own? Are you self-contained and at ease with yourself, or does your sense of self-worth depend upon the assessments of other people?

▶ By nature, do you unthinkingly accept and accommodate, or are you a radical or revolutionary who challenges and questions the status quo?

▶ Are you alert and sensitive to what is happening in the world around you? Do you notice unsolved problems, gaps in the existing provision of goods and services, and needs that are not met?

▶ At heart, are you a leader or a follower? Are you active or passive? Do you initiate or copy? Could you innovate, pioneer and discover?

▶ Would you rather be an employee or the owner of a business? Do you seek or shun responsibility and accountability? Are you a risk taker or risk averse?

▶ Are you imaginative, innovative and creative? Do you instinctively search for new and better ways of doing things?

▶ Are you an 'ideas person' or someone who likes to 'make things happen'? Are you content to make suggestions and come up with new concepts, or do you also like to implement them?

▶ Do you have a strong desire for personal recognition and achievement? Do you want to change things and to have an impact?

▶ How sound is your judgement of requirements, situations, people and opportunities? Are you perceived as shrewd, or do you get taken in?

▶ Do you actively network with potential customers and maintain contact with possible business partners? Have you stayed in touch with former employers?

▶ How acute are your antennae? Are you aware of contemporary trends, alert to threats and sensitive to risks?

▶ Would you stake your own money and that of others upon a venture that was dependent upon your personal judgement?

▶ Do you have your feet on the ground? Are you realistic and imperturbable?

▶ Are you dogged, persistent, resilient and determined? When the 'going gets tough', is your first instinct to 'cut and run', or do you hold true to the vision and stay the course?

▶ At the same time, are you flexible and adaptable? When a particular course of action does not work, do you look for alternative ways of achieving your objectives?

▶ Have you the tenacity to succeed, and the will to compete and win? Ultimately, do you deliver? Do other people regard you as a 'talker' or a 'doer'?

▶ When the time is right do you 'have a go'? Do you wait for a consensus to form or are you prepared to give a lead and act?

▶ Have you missed attractive possibilities? Do you delay and dither, or take action while windows of opportunity still exist?

▶ Are you selective? Do you prioritize and focus? Do you tackle the most important matters first, or do you procrastinate when there are difficult decisions to be taken?

▶ Do you engender trust? Can other people rely upon your word? Do they like and respect you? Can you establish and sustain longer-term relationships?

▶ Are you a good listener? Do you take advice from others where appropriate?

▶ How self-aware are you? Do you recognize your own limitations? How willing are you to share opportunities with people who have complementary skills and qualities?

> ▶ Are you a leader? Do you involve, inspire and motivate colleagues and partners? Can you get other people to play your game?

Some organizations may feel they already employ information managers, librarians, information technology specialists and other staff with specific knowledge management responsibilities, and hence have covered what is required to exploit their know-how. Why do they now need knowledge entrepreneurs? Aren't the qualities and skills required already in place to do what is required for greater effectiveness?

On the first of these questions, we saw in earlier chapters that far too many people are passively reacting to incoming messages, rather than actively setting out to identify, assemble and work with the particular advice and data they need. Very often they are receiving much more information than they can comfortably handle, and they lack the time to assimilate properly and understand complex messages. Important workgroups also lack knowledge-based support tools that would make them more successful.

The outcome of widespread overload is confusion, insecurity and procrastination. Rather than take decisive action, managers call for yet more proposals. In uncertain economic circumstances many boards are like chapels of rest. Directors wait for 'something to turn up', 'confidence to return' or 'things to become clear'. In essence, too many people are hiding behind the lack of relevant information, rather than proactively gathering the knowledge and building the understanding they need to move ahead.

In addition, too high a proportion of people in knowledge management roles are engaged in custodial activities. They administer a stock of know-how and a corporate intranet. They are not actively identifying and supporting operational needs, or managing a portfolio of relationships between people and flows of new information, switching off some and turning on others as requirements change.

THE KNOWLEDGE ENTREPRENEUR

To assess the adequacy of existing skills we need to understand the particular qualities needed by information and knowledge entrepreneurs (Coulson-Thomas, 2000). The core requirements were listed in Chapter 1.

Knowledge entrepreneurs have to know enough about systems to be able to use appropriate technologies to identify, access and exploit relevant sources of know-how. However, technical understanding on its own is not enough. Communication and relationship-building skills are also needed to interact with information providers and assemble the experience and skills required to assemble a support package with market value.

Some 'techies' are 'in their own space'. Information and communications technologies can attract people who prefer to interact with a VDU screen rather than with other human beings. Yet the individual customers or buyers whose needs are to be addressed may demand empathy and concern. To relate to them and obtain a rounded view of their requirements, entrepreneurs must possess both human awareness and sensitivity to the concerns of their colleagues and clients.

Some operators function almost as an extension of the information provision and sharing process (Coulson-Thomas, 2000). Many current technologies have become so user friendly that increasingly managers and professionals can manage what they need themselves via a desktop PC. They can undertake their own searches and order their own software upgrades. Entrepreneurs must do more than act as a link in a chain or a stage in a process. They should create additional or improved chains and new processes.

Knowledge entrepreneurs must shape the future. They should aim to provide better ways of addressing clear and pressing needs (Coulson-Thomas, 2001). They also need business acumen to contribute an additional dimension. Because something is technically possible does not mean that it represents a commercial opportunity. Large numbers of investors during the era of the 'dot com' bubble made mistaken assumptions.

Many knowledge entrepreneurs will have access to the same technology as their colleagues. However, their motivations are likely to be very different. They look beyond individual tasks and particular assignments at what is driving them and whether specific responses might form the basis of a generic product or commercial service.

Entrepreneurs may also need to keep one step ahead to command attention. This might require the curiosity to undertake more intelligent searches and the ability to assess better the significance and value of what they uncover. Many more people can access information than assess it or use it effectively.

Searching for relevant information can be a creative rather than a mechanical process. It may require the investigative skills of a detective or private investigator to open up new lines of enquiry as others run into blind alleys or dead ends.

There may be opportunities to act as an analyst and confidant when particular decisions are likely to have significant if not traumatic consequences. How many senior executives are fully aware of the veracity and quality of the evidence they consider? Understanding where information has come from, underlying assumptions, and how it has been compiled can prevent a venture, new enterprise or course of action being built upon foundations of sand.

Of course knowledge entrepreneurs are not identikit clones. Many different approaches and lifestyles can lead to achieving commercial success and satisfying personal requirements. One individual may set out to become an international authority within a specialist area, while another might opt instead to provide a broader range of services, perhaps based upon bringing together particular combinations of experience, know-how and skill.

Knowledge entrepreneurs need to look outwards as well as inwards. They must focus upon future flows and relationships, and avoid an excessive preoccupation with what is already known. Networks of relationships and partnerships need to be established with people and organizations that can provide complementary information, more detailed knowledge and relevant support tools. Independent and corporate entrepreneurs must know how to form, build and manage networks, project teams, Internet communities and virtual organizations.

Exercise 10a: Visioning

Prior to embarking upon a first knowledge-based venture it may be advisable to undertake a visioning exercise. Aspiring knowledge entrepreneurs need to understand their own personal drives, be sure of the direction in which they are headed and retain a sharp picture of their intended destination to enter into an effective dialogue with potential backers, clients and collaborators. People require well-defined and unambiguous objectives in order to know when and how to conclude negotiations, or whether to break them off in favour of other alternatives.

Consider the following questions. What are you seeking to achieve or aspiring to become? Are you driven by an overriding aim or explicit purpose in life? Do you have a clear vision of where you would like to be? Is it capable of achievement? Do the people who are closest to you share it? Could it form the basis of a new business or collaborative arrangement with your current employer?

CROSSING THE RUBICON

However qualified enterprise candidates might be, their potential will only be realized if they decide to research and exploit a particular opportunity. This is the key first step in becoming a knowledge entrepreneur. As we have seen, there are many possibilities for entrepreneurship. Chapter 1 contains a long list of areas in which new information- and knowledge-based ventures could be established.

Budding entrepreneurs might also discover various commercial possibilities within an existing employer. Chapter 8 identifies many learning support activities that could form the basis of new services and offerings.

There are also the many negative consequences of information overload considered in Chapter 4 and the stakeholder requirements in Chapter 5 to address. The productivity of many workgroups, and the performance of most organizations, would be massively improved if people were provided with, and allowed to concentrate upon, the know-how and tools they need to do a better job.

The skills of consultants who are practised at identifying and analysing particular problem areas and suggesting potential solutions can be very relevant to knowledge entrepreneurship. Opportunities also have to be explored and assessed. Prior to implementation they need to be scoped and their benefits articulated if adoption is to occur. Decision makers may also request some form of cost justification.

Smart consultants – like effective knowledge entrepreneurs – look for opportunities to minimize pain and maximize gain. Building upon the examples of job support toolkits examined in Chapter 8 let us consider another example of how knowledge-based tools can transform an important activity. In many sectors the relentless pace of innovation is such that companies need to introduce additional offerings to survive. Competitive pressures require them to speed up and reduce the cost of new product launches.

THE CHALLENGE OF LAUNCHING NEW PRODUCTS

Informing different groups about a new product represents a daunting challenge. New – and possibly complex – material has to be communicated to a variety of audiences with distinct information requirements. In particular:

- Sales staff and indirect sales channels must be able to sell new products.
- Service engineers may have to be equipped to service additional offerings.
- Contact centre and other support staff may need to be prepared to answer questions competently about a further product or service.
- Corporate communicators will need to know enough to be able to talk intelligently to the media, analysts, key customers and other publics.
- Technical staff may require a significantly higher level of technical detail than their colleagues.
- Customers may request or expect implementation guides that will help them to gain the maximum benefit from the product.
- Existing users of previous or related products could be informed of upgrade or trade-in and exchange opportunities.

Communication with all of these groups may need to occur against the background of tight deadlines. People may also wish either to see or to visualize a new product in operation. Without some form of demonstration they may not fully appreciate its advantages and benefits, yet this may be difficult or physically impossible to organize in the time remaining and cost available.

As a launch date approaches, new product managers face considerable pressure to 'get everything done'. A major challenge is to coordinate the largely simultaneous communication of consistent messages to multiple and disparate audiences, some of which may be potentially diverse in terms of their roles, languages and geography.

Budget limitations and resource constraints in relation to the number of different groups that may need to know about a new product can be compounded by a variety of other factors. For example, an instantaneous launch rather than a phased roll-out may be required. Messages may have to be communicated globally. A new product might also incorporate features that are difficult to understand.

In some sectors, there may be regulatory constraints and legal requirements to observe, and these may vary from one territory to another. Furthermore, they may have to be implemented by staff unused to them. There might be commercial, quality or technical risks associated with the new product that need to be addressed or minimized.

There might also be a competitive requirement to keep the existence, nature or name of a new product secret until the moment of launch, and yet thereafter interested customers and prospects may expect a whole sales channel to be competent to explain and/or demonstrate it. Such a capability has to be created quickly and simultaneously in widely scattered locations.

Exercise 10b: Identifying value-based opportunities

The values implicit or explicit in some offerings represent an important element of their acceptance and appeal. Many people find themselves assaulted on all sides by alien values. The media, advertisements, brands, products and services can all assume and embody certain values that are not shared by many of those who come into contact with them.

Contemporary societies are increasingly composed of a diversity of interests, religions and cultures. Significant and alienated minorities may find their particular concerns, values and requirements for information and knowledge are not recognized by major providers. This creates opportunities for astute and more sensitive entrepreneurs to introduce alternatives that reflect or embody different qualities or principles:

- Draw up a list of knowledge-based products and services with which you are familiar or have a personal interest.
- Identify the major values that are implicit or explicit within them.
- Produce a product value matrix with columns for each of the significant values that you have identified.
- Consider the values that are important to you and list these.
- List also the values that are important to distinct and minority groups or market segments.
- Compare your own values with those of the groups or market segments you have identified, and assess whether you empathize with them and understand their information and knowledge requirements.

- Consider how each of the knowledge-based products and services you have selected might be modified in order to match, reflect or address their values.
- Consider also whether alternative approaches would better achieve the purposes for which these products and services ostensibly exist in relation to the groups and market segments you have identified.
- Assess the cost of making whatever changes would best embrace under-represented or excluded values, and unmet requirements.
- Estimate how many people might be interested in an alternative offering, and how much they would be prepared to pay to secure a product or service that was more in line with their values and better attuned to their distinct requirements.
- Subtract from the likely revenues the anticipated costs of making the changes that would be needed, and creating and launching an alternative offering.
- Delete any likely loss-making ventures and rank the remaining opportunities in terms of their relative profitability.
- Develop business cases for the more promising opportunities and seek the resources and capabilities you will require to commercialize them.

CREATING A NEW PRODUCT LAUNCH SUPPORT TOOL

Having assessed a serious and significant problem, and the requirements of those affected, the budding knowledge entrepreneur must now create a solution. One option might be to capture all the relevant information and knowledge related to launching new products within a single repository that can handle material in many different formats. Incorporating a search facility would enable people to find what they need for a particular purpose very quickly.

The know-how that is captured could be used to produce a communication tool for each of the groups that need to be informed about the latest offering and equipped to understand and explain, sell, buy or support it. Elements of the content might be common to certain audiences, thus spreading any costs of producing animations, graphics and other audio or visual material. The result could be much more cost-effective and quicker to implement than printing several separately designed items.

A family of multimedia communication tools could be produced comprising one or more of: a sales support tool; an indirect sales channel version for dealers, distributors and agents; a service or engineering support toolkit; marketing and/or internal communications tools; an investor relations briefing for analysts and financial institutions; and customer information manuals and interactive training. Each tool could incorporate appropriate quality and other checks.

Putting the contents into formats that make it easy for recipients to comprehend and learn could facilitate assimilation. Interactive tools could also be included to help people understand. All the derived tools aimed at staff and business partners could contain relevant on-the-job training and appropriate competence assessments.

As we saw in the last chapter, tools could be provided to operate over the Internet, a corporate intranet or extranet, and on CD formats. A device such as traffic lighting could be used to build checks and controls into work practices. Automation of routine aspects of key tasks could again include configuration, pricing and issuing proposals.

All the information and knowledge required could also once again be held within a single scalable searchable repository to facilitate access and reuse, for example to launch related and other products. A proven and award-winning framework such as K-frame (www.K-frame.com) could be licensed and used to manage any material that is stored and produce the job support tools required.

ADVANTAGES OF A PRODUCT LAUNCH SUPPORT TOOL

Stressing clear 'benefits' is the key to selling many knowledge-based services. The approach just outlined has many advantages, and addresses the problems identified above. It ensures consistent messages, which may help to build a brand image and can enable simultaneous and bespoke communication to a diversity of audiences in multiple locations and languages. The result is likely to be more rapid and widespread awareness of a new product, and increased understanding of its value and benefits.

There are likely to be other gains along the lines of those alluded to in Chapter 8. Job support tools can help people implement change. They can reduce commercial, technical, regulatory and quality risks. Fewer errors may be made. Animations may make it easy to understand how a product works, while video footage can show it in operation. People can see a new offering as well as being told about it.

The suggested approach might differentiate a company and enhance its reputation with the various external groups it needs to communicate with. It can provide a base for future relationships with them, eg a product launch tool could be augmented to cater for both existing and further new offerings and become a general sales support tool. Feedback mechanisms could be included to initiate a dialogue. A clear demonstration of a product's value, advantages and superiority over competitive alternatives might allow a premium price to be charged.

Support from an experienced partner can ease the workload of implementation and take the pressure off a new product manager during the launch phase. Existing and proven technologies can be used to speed up delivery and cut training times. Reusing and sharing elements of content across the various audiences reduces development effort and cost.

Much of the time that users might otherwise spend looking for relevant information can be saved because it is now all available in one place, within a repository that is easy to update and maintain. The cost of producing, storing and distributing supporting documentation may be significantly reduced. Issuing updates and follow-up communication is also relatively straightforward, while working electronically reduces investment in paper that may become out of date. There may be less to pulp.

Overall, substantial savings can be achieved by taking an integrated approach to launching new products to diverse audiences. Some or all of the effort and resource involved might also be regarded as an investment rather than a cost. A central repository can add significantly to an individual or organization's intellectual capital, because know-how can be more easily reused, re-versioned and exploited.

USING EXAMPLES OF BEST PRACTICE

Aspiring knowledge entrepreneurs often find that prospects are reluctant to stick their necks out and become initial or early adopters. Even though there may be a clear 'first mover' advantage, it may be necessary to provide examples of how other people and organizations have addressed similar problems. Hence, when undertaking the monitoring and search activities advocated in Chapters 7 and 8 respectively it is important to be alert to what others are doing.

In relation to the area of opportunity just considered, 3Com has brought together – and within a single repository – everything needed to introduce an entire range of networks products to market. Bolero used a support tool to launch a new technology across the world. The tool made it easier for prospects to understand what the company's proposition did, and countered a previous and prevailing sense that it was complicated and the assumption that it would be difficult to adopt. The essence of what was on offer could now be communicated in less than three minutes.

Cisco gathered together and packaged all the information, distilled knowledge and interactive tools its sales and indirect sales channel needed, including a market communication CD to explain the value and benefits of the corporation's technology. This consolidated approach has been well received, as previously people sometimes found it very difficult to locate and manage inputs from disparate sources.

Avaya – formerly Lucent – introduced a CD ROM-based after-sales engineers toolkit to help people service and support its growing product range. A dramatic reduction in cost was achieved, compared with printing and distributing the manual that preceded it. Comprehensive information was now available when needed. The company duplicated far more copies of the CD than the number of engineers employed, because people quickly recognized its value and it was adopted in many other areas of the business. The toolkit won an eBusiness Innovations Award.

As with the tools considered in the last chapter, once the concept of a new product launch toolkit is agreed a comprehensive support package can be produced in a matter of weeks, allowing a relatively quick response to a 'go decision'. A solid base can then be established for subsequent initiatives and future corporate communications.

Achieving an impact and making a difference are among the joys of becoming a knowledge entrepreneur. New product launch experience further confirms that presenting information in appropriate formats can greatly enhance understanding and the speed with which people can assimilate fresh knowledge and apply it. Again, significant productivity improvements can be achieved by supplying people with job-focused and knowledge-based support tools.

CHECKLIST

▶ Are there commercial opportunities either to improve productivity and performance or to generate additional revenues either within or with your current organization?

▶ Does the organization have a clear, distinctive and compelling vision?

▶ Has the vision been communicated and shared? Is it supportive of knowledge entrepreneurship?

▶ Are the values and conduct of corporate leaders compatible with it? How committed are they to its achievement? What, if anything, do they do to encourage enterprise and support entrepreneurship?

▶ Is the vision understood by your colleagues within the organization, and also by its various external stakeholders?

▶ What does the vision mean to them? How important or significant is it? Is the vision exciting and challenging? Does it inspire and motivate? Is it a catalyst of entrepreneurship?

▶ Do you have a clear, distinctive and compelling vision of what you would like to do with your life?

▶ How does your current organization's vision relate to your individual goals, personal view of where you would like to be, and entrepreneurial aspirations?

▶ Is your current organization aware of your personal aspirations, and do your seniors and peers recognize, address and support them?

▶ What is being done to help you develop the experience, skills and relationships you will need to become an effective knowledge entrepreneur?

▶ Has your current organization articulated a clear set of values? Are these monitored and adhered to? Are they supportive of enterprise and entrepreneurship?

▶ Are corporate values reflected in management practice, the attitudes and behaviours of members of staff, how people are treated and the conduct of relationships?

▶ Have you drawn up a statement of personal values? How compatible is it with current corporate values?

▶ Do you share the prevailing values of those with whom you work? Are there groups, communities or disaffected minorities with whom you feel more comfortable?

▶ How important are your personal values when you take decisions concerning whether or not to enter into certain relationships?

▶ Are guidance and counselling available to those who encounter conflicts of interest, and ethical and moral dilemmas?

▶ Could and should you open up and collaborate with your current organization, or would you stand a better chance of becoming a knowledge entrepreneur if you sought external support and branched out on your own?

11

Getting started

ROUTES TO ENTREPRENEURSHIP

There are unprecedented possibilities for imaginative entrepreneurs to create knowledge-based offerings, increase workgroup productivity and generally improve the quality of our lives by finding new ways of acquiring, developing, packaging, sharing, applying and exploiting know-how. The extent of the opportunities is clear. The immediate challenge for many individuals and organizations is to take the first steps on the road to building successful information- and knowledge-based ventures.

In the last chapter we considered some of the qualities needed and the requirements for becoming a knowledge entrepreneur, and in Chapter 6 we examined what companies must do to create enterprise cultures that are conducive to entrepreneurship. In the contemporary knowledge society, organizations are increasingly communities and frameworks within which people with shared aspirations, common goals and compatible values can work together to assemble and use the information, knowledge, skills and tools required to create value and achieve mutually beneficial outcomes.

A key question for many individuals who believe they have 'what it takes' is whether to branch out on their own or collaborate with an existing or past employer. Have you ever thought about how you might work with one or more larger companies as a business partner? Similarly, boards must decide the action they need to take to stimulate and support new knowledge-based ventures. Can an existing organization inspire and spawn new enterprises, or should a new greenfield operation be established, perhaps using the learning and enterprise centre checklist in Chapter 6?

Exercise 11a: Voyage analysis

Before knowledge entrepreneurs leave port they should ensure they have everything that is likely to be required for the first leg of whatever enterprise journey they intend to make. Stumbling over an initial step can harm inner confidence and external credibility.

Is everything that you may need on board? What else should you take? Which items do you require now, and what can be picked up later en route? Have you identified likely suppliers of stores and possible ports of call? How long have you got before people might jump ship if the going gets hard?

Situations and circumstances in competitive knowledge economies can change as suddenly and unpredictably as the wind. Will your planned provisions keep, or might they deteriorate and become stale during the early stages of your journey? When the tides and other conditions are expected to be most favourable, will you be ready to set sail? Are there still loose ends? Will you be free to go forth?

TURNING A HOBBY INTO A BUSINESS

An initial step for an aspiring entrepreneur is to answer some basic questions. Is your intention solely to make as much money as possible, or would you also like to enjoy your work? If the latter is true, what would you really like to do and what are you especially good at? How many other people are actually being paid to live aspects of the life you desire? Who else would be able and prepared to fund these activities if they could be turned into some form of service for others? How might this be done?

Having a passion for a particular activity can make it easier to shape the future (Coulson-Thomas, 2001). Many successful entrepreneurs are driven. They believe in and love what they do. A much enjoyed activity, pastime or lifestyle can sometimes become a springboard to a profitable venture. For example, being paid to deliver yachts enables some people to sail 'for free'. Smart knowledge entrepreneurs seek the intellectual equivalent of being under way for groups they prefer to associate with.

An increasing number of individuals find it is possible to turn a personal leisure interest into a business. The trick is to establish a way of moving forward that will minimize distractions; allow concentration upon innovation, differentiation and securing customers; and maximize the chances of creativity, personal fulfilment and commercial success. The precise path chosen will depend upon the activity in question, but ideally it should be in harmony with a person's inner self.

There are many examples of hobbies that have become money-making ventures. Craft fairs display the work of individual enthusiasts. The more ambitious assemble self-build homes, or fit out boats if they have an interest in the inland waterways. Couples make their dream of living in the countryside come true by working as professionals from home, operating country house hotels or running rural inns. Knowledge entrepreneurs can select areas of know-how and expertise that fascinate them, and provide support services for people and personalities they would love to work with.

People who have had their fill of daily commuting run a wide range of ventures from spare rooms and garden sheds based upon activities they really enjoy. In the case of knowledge-based ventures, the infrastructure required for effective operation now comes at a price individuals can afford. Owners of older buildings convert lofts or outbuildings. 'Home offices' are now a standard feature of many newly built estates.

Once a business concept has been formulated and potential customers have been identified, the next steps are especially daunting for many would-be entrepreneurs. Securing initial funding, finding suitable premises, recruiting support staff and 'doing the books' can all be time consuming and frustrating for people who are both better at and would prefer to do other things. This is where collaboration with an established company can help.

Many intending entrepreneurs do not think of taking new business ideas to an existing employer or a local company that operates in a related field and has complementary interests. They worry about losing control or fear that a big corporation might either 'steal' their ideas or not be interested in a proposed venture. The 'not invented here' syndrome may apply, but in competitive markets in which continuous innovation is a critical success requirement companies need to be open to ideas from any source.

SELECTING CORPORATE PARTNERS

If significant start-up capital and support are required to establish either a lifestyle business or a blatantly commercial venture, it may be worth looking for one or more potential collaborators. However, independent entrepreneurs should choose corporate patrons, partners and sponsors with care. A significantly higher prospect of success may have to be balanced against the risk of a loss of control and a lower equity stake.

Some potential partners might show more interest than others. A proposed activity might be of strategic or peripheral interest. The support likely to be provided may vary greatly in quality and relevance. Suitors should look for evidence of serious commitment to new ventures. For example, how much of the training budget is devoted to building entrepreneurial skills and supporting business development?

They should also consider whether a corporate culture and working environment encourages initiative, innovation and enterprise or stifles them. Contracts, facilities, processes, systems and support tools should allow and enable questioning, resourceful and inventive individuals and their business partners to explore and create.

The rewards for successful innovation and entrepreneurship should be fairly allocated in proportion to the respective contributions of those involved. Separate incorporation of new ventures allows more people to become directors, and may facilitate buy-ins and the external involvement of business angels and venture capitalists. From a corporate perspective a share of returns is preferable to 100 per cent of a lost opportunity should those involved leave to set up in business on their own account.

As an alternative to independent operation, intending entrepreneurs can either join or work with flexible organizations that are tolerant of diversity, allow people to be true to themselves and enable them to play to their distinct strengths (Coulson-Thomas, 2002b). Enterprise flourishes where people are enabled to work, learn and collaborate in ways that best enable them to harness their particular talents, and assemble new venture teams composed of individuals with compatible aspirations and complementary skills.

Confident individuals join organizations that promote enterprise, invite collaboration and support intrapreneurship. As we saw in

Chapter 6, they prefer to work with people who view them as potential business partners and who will suggest ideas for new ventures, add value and generate incremental revenues. An established business with an existing customer base and efficient route to market that lacks new products can represent a promising partner for an entrepreneur with limited resources whose forte is crafting new offerings that address identified opportunities.

Exercise 11b: Lift-off analysis

Some knowledge-based ventures are easier to get airborne than others. Many aspiring entrepreneurs remain desk bound and stay grounded. For one reason or another, even though the conditions may seem favourable, their ventures do not fly.

Yet, in various walks of life, there are others who have managed to transcend the limitations of their circumstances. They succeed in making their childhood dreams a reality. People who have still not achieved their ambitions should identify what is holding them back and work out how to secure additional lift. They should actively investigate how to take off and stay aloft.

How close are you and your entrepreneurial colleagues to getting airborne? Is there any unnecessary or dead weight that you could jettison? Have all the restraining ropes been cut and the chocks taken away? Is someone holding back the throttle? What else do you need, and who or what would help? Have you thought of a winch, tow or catapult? How might you get some extra power or increased lift?

CREATING A WELCOMING CORPORATE ENVIRONMENT

Smart companies put arrangements in place to assess the proposals of aspiring entrepreneurs and provide concept development support and venture capital. Where this is not being done there may be opportunities for others to help. Practical advice on securing family support, assembling a venture team and winning business could be provided, along with counselling on overcoming the inhibitions, pitfalls and constraints likely to be encountered and getting started (Coulson-Thomas, 1999b).

As we saw in Chapter 6, companies need to become enterprise colonies that tap, build and release the entrepreneurial potential within their people and collaborating external networks and communities (Coulson-Thomas, 1999b). As mentioned above, ambitious individuals want to work with organizations rather than for them.

Far-sighted companies will approach independent entrepreneurs when lining up the external support required by new venture teams. Their internal procedures, processes, support tools and contractual arrangements will reflect the distinct and diverse needs of growing businesses. Their reward mechanisms will allow those responsible to participate in the resulting financial returns.

Share-ownership, option or profit-sharing schemes may need to be established, to satisfy the increasing desire of many people to build capital. Energetic and talented individuals who create knowledge rather than merely consume it, and who can innovate and develop tailored solutions, are seeking a greater share of the value that their energies and imaginations create.

Investors should avoid companies that do not champion enterprise and entrepreneurship, because their most capable people and their most valuable customers will simply walk, and they will not attract the external partners they require. Major corporations cannot afford to be excluded from successful new ventures established by independent entrepreneurs and past employees. Could you collaborate with a current or former customer or employer?

The interests of customers, independent entrepreneurs, companies and investors are rapidly converging. We are at a turning point in the relationship between people and organizations, and between micro-businesses and larger companies. We have a historic opportunity to reconcile and align individual and corporate goals. Go for it.

Exercise 11c: Tug-of-war analysis

Entrepreneurs can sometimes find themselves being pulled simultaneously in a number of different ways. The trick in such circumstances is to stay on track. While entrepreneurs should remain alert to threats and opportunities, they should keep at least one eye firmly on the desired direction of travel. Handling the balance of contending forces can be likened to playing a multiple game of tug-of-war:

- Before the start of a game it is usually advisable to assess the battleground and identify any apparent features that are likely to either assist or impede progress.
- Some preparatory work may need to be undertaken, for example to remove an obstacle to fair play.
- An assessment should be made of the qualities and likely tenacity of the opponents who will be endeavouring to pull in the opposite direction.
- A team needs to be selected from colleagues who are prepared to roll up their sleeves and give full commitment to 'doing the business'.
- Some thought should be given to tactics and the relative positioning of each member of the team.
- It may be advisable to put the most determined players in front where they can act as positive role models and visibly inspire others who are more likely to lose heart.
- Supporters in the wings should be sought who can shout encouragement, analyse what is happening to both the competing teams, and offer tactical advice.
- At the end of each tussle an assessment should be made of critical success factors for winning the game, the major reasons for success or failure, any impediments to better results, and any changes that would improve performance.
- Consider the extent to which any of the 'helps' and 'hinders' that have been identified might also apply to others and, if so, explore the possibilities for joint action to reinforce or tackle them respectively.
- Assess whether there might also be opportunities to introduce commercial products and services that people could use to overcome particular 'hinders' and strengthen any helpful factors.
- Review any other ways in which what has been learnt might be exploited, for example to mentor, coach or counsel other teams.
- Explore ways of getting paid for organizing, playing and/or supporting a game that you and your colleagues enjoy.

CREATING COMMUNITIES OF ENTREPRENEURS

Throughout history many of the greatest cities on earth have been vibrant communities of traders and entrepreneurs. Energetic individuals, smart companies and many other bodies must actively work together to create more enterprising societies if we are to take full advantage of the potential for knowledge entrepreneurship (Coulson-Thomas, 2000).

People and organizations should assess the implications, for both themselves and their customers or clients, of the emergence of a global information and knowledge economy, and consider and determine the role they would like to play in it. Some will opt to become players, others enablers, sponsors and supporters. New rules, skills and support tools are required.

Corporate, public and voluntary sector decision makers must create environments and cultures that are more conducive to enterprise. They must establish and guarantee the necessary freedoms, and provide infrastructures and support tools that enable knowledge entrepreneurship. They should also endeavour to become role models in relation to the acquisition, development, sharing and exploitation of know-how.

Directors and senior managers should assess and track the extent to which the various problem areas and requirements highlighted in Chapters 4 and 5 respectively are present and recognized within their organizations, and being effectively addressed. For example, they should identify situations and circumstances in which information, knowledge and understanding are being lost and take action to stem any further leakage.

People and organizations should map the areas of knowledge relevant to their activities, and the connections and networks of relationships they need to remain competitive. Collaborators, supply chain partners and members of virtual communities should establish and agree principles and rules covering how information, knowledge and understanding are to be categorized, captured, accessed and shared, and, where appropriate, recognized and protected.

The scope for knowledge entrepreneurship should be monitored as advocated in Chapter 7. Many organizations need to devote greater effort to the identification, evaluation and protection of intellectual capital. Arrangements should also be put in place to ensure that when it is exploited all those who have played a part in its creation are fairly rewarded.

When future investment decisions are made the emphasis is likely to switch from physical assets such as machinery and buildings to processes, networks, practices and tools for acquiring, developing, sharing and applying information, knowledge and understanding. Accounting, management and reporting practice will likewise need to devote more attention to the creation and exploitation of know-how.

ORGANIZING FOR LEARNING AND ENTREPRENEURSHIP

A designated person at board level should be made personally accountable for corporate effectiveness at acquiring, developing, sharing and exploiting know-how. Individual mangers should be similarly held to account in relation to the people for whom they are responsible.

Learning and knowledge creation needs to occur along the lines suggested in Chapter 3. The motivations, connections, learning partnerships and shared learning arrangements required to ensure that learning becomes a dynamic activity should be put in place at corporate, managerial and individual levels. Sufficient learning and shared learning should occur to ensure that the know-how needed to achieve desired goals is developed, regularly reviewed and remains current and relevant.

Selection and promotion decisions, career progression opportunities, and reward and remuneration should reflect individual and group contributions to the acquisition, development, sharing and exploitation of information, knowledge and understanding. These activities and learning among employees, contractors, collaborating and supply chain partners, and network community members will need to be monitored and tracked in order to identify 'learning gaps' and distinguish between people who are contributing to know-how and those who are living off an existing knowledge base.

Learning partnerships will become more significant. Organizations need to work with educators, trainers and professional bodies to develop the competencies required to create and exploit know-how. Specific courses, competency assessments and development support may also be needed. Entrepreneurship programmes should reflect the particular requirements of knowledge entrepreneurs. School, college and university curricula should give more weight to knowledge creation and exploitation.

Professional and representative institutes and associations must prepare their members for operation in the information economy and knowledge society, and provide whatever support is necessary to enable them to cope and excel. Academic research and professional investigation should focus more upon practical problems of knowledge entrepreneurship, such as managing network organizations, leading virtual teams and recognizing and rewarding collaborative contributions.

Exercise 11d: Self-assessment for changing direction

Many entrepreneurs have derived successful businesses from activities they enjoy. People who are both busy and unfulfilled should take time out to review the situation they find themselves in and consider alternative lifestyle options. There are various aspects to consider and different areas to explore when assessing whether or not a new direction in life might be appropriate:

- A first step is to commit to a frank and honest assessment of the extent to which a current situation is compatible with personal life goals.
- Consider what will probably happen and/or change as a result of continuing as before and simply 'going with the flow'.
- Assess whether any movement is likely to be towards or away from personal aspirations.
- Identify early ambitions that remain unfulfilled and/or any significant gaps between initial intentions and contemporary reality.
- Specify whether either more of or less of certain aspects of the current situation would be preferred.
- Profile any dimensions of the 'inner person' that remain unfulfilled or areas of latent potential that have not been tapped.
- List and assess any obstacles and barriers to the achievement of more of whatever is desired.
- Determine 'who' or 'what' is standing in the way of greater personal fulfilment.
- Examine whether there are entrepreneurial or alternative lifestyle opportunities in the current situation.
- Assess how much freedom of action there is to explore and exploit the possibilities that have been identified.
- Consider what would be requested if Father Christmas undertook to satisfy expressed desires and was able to 'deliver'.

- Explore alternative courses of action, particular roles and different lifestyles that might provide more of whatever is sought or remains unfulfilled.
- Review what it would take to succeed in these endeavours, and the prospects of a satisfactory outcome.
- Assess also the practicalities of undertaking the required steps, and the changes of situation and circumstances that might result.
- Reflect upon what would be lost and gained in comparison with continuing on an existing course.
- Identify the downside potential and what might be needed to ameliorate any disadvantages and compensate for the areas of greatest deficiency.
- Search for possible sources of encouragement and practical help.
- Sound out the possibilities for gaining support from colleagues, a current employer and/or members of the immediate family.
- Consider who else might 'share the vision' and review the prospects for mutually beneficial collaboration.
- Prepare an action plan for breaking out of a current situation and moving in a new direction, and when the moment is opportune be prepared to act.

PUBLIC POLICY REQUIREMENTS

Governments too have a part to play in encouraging knowledge entrepreneurship (Coulson-Thomas, 2000). Their indicators and statistics should track the emergence of both global and national information and knowledge markets, and the nature and extent of the roles that their national enterprises and institutions play within them. SWOT analyses could be undertaken to determine how well placed these organizations are to exploit emerging areas of opportunity.

The acid test for members of the business community is whether or not a government's proposals help them to compete and win. Libertarian approaches to establish national equivalents of the fundamental freedoms advocated for companies in Chapter 6, light regulation, low taxes and a flexible labour market are particularly conducive to enterprise and entrepreneurship. World-class universities and an effective legal framework for protecting intellectual property can also greatly help.

Countries with high taxes, over-regulation, excessive red tape and rigid labour markets are likely to slip down competitiveness league tables. Government departments should identify whatever barriers to knowledge entrepreneurship, freedom of enquiry and the safeguarding of know-how exist within the areas for which they are responsible and take appropriate steps to overcome them. Getting the basic structure right should precede quibbles over the detail of the furnishings.

Governments are sometimes tempted to provide eye-catching incentives and tax breaks to stimulate certain activities. These can introduce market distortions and be expensive to administer. Many enterprise support measures are overly complex and costly to implement. Entrepreneurs are provided with heavy diving boots that hold them down, when what they need is light flippers and plimsolls to help them rise up and get ahead.

Too often specific and headline-grabbing measures are 'possibilities', schemes that may or may not be relevant or applicable to a particular knowledge-based venture or business. In comparison, the burdens of higher employment costs and restrictive red tape are real. They bite, and they impact negatively upon every business. And as we have seen there are opportunities for creating new knowledge-based ventures, initiatives and tools in companies of all sizes and in all sectors.

Rhetoric about encouraging an enterprise culture does not 'pay the rent'. The devil is often in the detail or hidden away. Stealth taxes are especially pernicious when their implications are not immediately understood by those affected. For example, the ending of double tax relief on dividends and the resulting loss of pension fund income means people need to make extra provision for old age. This, coupled with the additional savings required by ageing societies, reduces the amount available for investing in new entrepreneurial ventures.

The business community itself should concentrate upon innovating and competing rather than securing special assistance, lobbying for favours or creating new forms of protection. There is much that needs to be done within the existing regulatory frameworks of many countries to create more open and flexible markets, before effort is devoted to ever more marginal areas. For example, across the EU there are still many anti-competitive practices, barriers to entry and obstacles to takeovers to be addressed.

Special measures and incentives are often 'red herrings'. The potential benefits of knowledge entrepreneurship are so alluring and exciting that societies cannot afford such distractions. Governments should concentrate upon providing a low tax and light regulation business environment that will allow businesses of all sizes to thrive and prosper. In the global knowledge economy, the focus should be unashamedly upon international competitiveness.

Many knowledge-based businesses can operate as a virtual network from just about anywhere that offers the required legal protection (Coulson-Thomas, 2002b). Hence, countries will increasingly compete for 'physical-location-free' ventures. Winners are likely to be communities that champion inspired individuality, academic excellence, knowledge creation and enterprise.

Relatively open markets, particularly in telecommunications, information and knowledge industries, and an individualistic and diverse culture are particularly conducive to entrepreneurship. Widespread familiarity with a major business, scientific and technical language such as English also attracts inward investment.

In many countries governments need to ignore special pleading, parochialism, introverted nationalism and narrow self-interest in favour of 'opening up', encouraging wider participation and collaboration, and promoting the common good. They may need to 'let go' in order to release latent entrepreneurial potential and realize the contributions that knowledge entrepreneurs could make.

If public and corporate decision makers have the courage to allow more people to aspire and achieve, additional knowledge will light up many areas of darkness and remove much uncertainty. Entrepreneurs will create new options and choices. Our lives will become immeasurably richer and more satisfying.

Winning business checklist

A key priority for knowledge entrepreneurs is to sign up new customers. There may also be opportunities to help other companies secure more accounts. As we saw in Chapters 9 and 10, knowledge-based support tools can be used to increase sales and launch new products.

In many commercial organizations there is enormous potential to improve processes and practices for winning business in competitive situations. The following questions could be considered from the perspective of either an entrepreneur's own company or the business of a customer:

▶ Does the company examine and monitor trends and developments relating to purchasing practice and competitive bidding? What are their impacts likely to be?

▶ Over the next few years, is the proportion of new business opportunities facing the company that is put out to competitive tender likely to increase or decrease? What is being done about this?

▶ Is there a formal, documented, understood and practised corporate process for winning business? How effective is it? When was the last time that this process was subjected to an independent review? What happened as a result?

▶ Do processes and practices for winning business reflect the critical success factors identified by the winning business research and best practice programme (see the Appendix to this chapter)?

▶ Is the company's approach to winning business focused and proactive, or is it undisciplined and reactive? Do sales and marketing staff and key players target the people and organizations they would like to do business with and take the initiative in approaching them?

▶ Do they pursue and initiate relationships with potential customers and collaborators that have clear ambitions and bright prospects? Are clear objectives set ahead of contacts and negotiations?

▶ How selective is the company in terms of the opportunities that it pursues? Do its people qualify prospects and concentrate effort on the opportunities that satisfy its criteria for being potentially both important and winnable?

▶ Do the company's people allocate sufficient effort in the early stages of the winning business process when there may be the best opportunity to establish a leading position? Do they aim to secure and maintain an early advantage?

▶ Are they excessively preoccupied with the internal production of proposals and presentations, or are they focused upon the value and benefits that prospects are seeking and how their buying decisions are likely to be made?

▶ Do people identify the evaluation criteria that prospects are likely to use? Are bids and pitches structured around them?

▶ Do they effectively communicate what is relevant, special and distinctive about corporate capability, and position the company as a desirable business partner that others would want to associate with?

▶ Do communications focus upon what prospects are seeking to achieve? Are support tools used to help them understand complex issues and buy?

▶ During negotiations, is an effort made to establish a rapport and 'cultural fit'. Are senior managers involved? Is there a willingness to offer guarantees and form partnering relationships?

▶ How effective is competitor intelligence? Are the company's people plugged into appropriate information flows? Are they active members of relevant networks and accessible by electronic means?

▶ Motivation is vital. Do members of the sales and marketing team make excuses and rationalize failure, or do they exude a will to compete and win?

▶ Do those who are responsible for winning new business review and learn from both their successes and their failures? Are debrief meetings held?

▶ Are significant prospects asked about how and why final purchase decisions, whether positive or negative, were reached? Are they questioned about how the procurement might have been more effective from their perspective?

▶ Are the knowledge and experience obtained from new business and account reviews captured and shared? In what ways could the dissemination process be improved?

▶ Is experience shared with other organizations? Does the company take regular advantage of the benchmarking services offered by the winning business research and best practice programme (see the Appendix to this chapter)?

▶ What is the company planning to do, or what could it do, to reduce its dependence upon competitive tender opportunities? What alternative business development strategies are being pursued or would be appropriate?

Knowledge entrepreneurs need to keep their feet on the ground. Winning business is not an area to be 'ticked off' once they become preoccupied with other issues such as premises and hiring additional staff. Customers can both define and fund the development of a business. Ways of securing and building relationships with them should be continually reviewed and refined.

CHECKLIST

▶ Do you feel liberated or trapped by your current situation, role or lifestyle? Who needs to let go and what must end if you are to be liberated?

▶ Are you in the driving seat? How much control do you have over the most important aspects of your life?

▶ How satisfied are you with your lot? Are there areas in which you feel unfulfilled?

▶ What could or should you do to secure more control over your life and achieve greater personal fulfilment?

▶ Are the various elements of your life in harmony? Have you struck a satisfactory balance between the demands of work, leisure activities and family commitments?

▶ Have you identified the root causes of any disharmony, stress and lack of equilibrium? What would you prefer to have more or less of?

▶ Would your colleagues and friends like to see more or less of you? Do the members of your family want or deserve greater attention and demand quality time?

▶ Are you aware of their requirements and aspirations? How compatible are they with yours, and do these people feature in your future plans?

▶ Who among those you associate with are supportive of your aspirations? What if anything is helping you to move closer to your life goals and personal objectives?

▶ Who is frustrating you or holding you back? What is constraining you or getting in the way?

▶ How formidable are the obstacles and barriers that you face? How strong are the bonds that constrict you?

▶ Have you identified and prioritized the various 'helps' and 'hinders'? Looking ahead, which of these factors are likely to become more significant?

▶ What could and should you do to obtain more leverage and secure greater advantage from the 'helps' and reduce or counter the negative impacts of the 'hinders'?

▶ How much discretion do you have to tackle the obstacles, barriers and inhibitors that are either holding you back or frustrating your progress?

▶ Who or what might help you to escape or progress? What additional support do you require to advance more quickly in desired directions?

▶ Whose agreement do you need to remove constraints and/or put positive enablers in place? How might you acquire or negotiate access to whatever is required?

▶ Who might be potential allies, sponsors or supporters, and how should they be approached and engaged?

▶ Also, who is likely to oppose what is desired, and how might opposers be neutralized?

▶ Do other people face the same or similar obstacles and barriers? Could you cooperate or collaborate with them?

▶ Is there a service that you could provide to help these people overcome one or more of the obstacles or barriers that they face?

▶ What practical action might government take either to address the various negative factors that have been identified or to encourage and support the positive ones?

Appendix to Chapter 11

The winning business research and best practice programme of the Centre for Competitiveness is identifying the critical success factors for winning and retaining customers in competitive markets. Over 2,500 companies and professional practices have participated. The approaches and practices of 'winners' are compared with those of 'losers' to reveal why some companies are so much more successful than others at bidding and building customer relationships.

Outputs include 'critical success factors' reports, 'best practice' case studies, practical bidding tools and techniques, key business development skills, in-house training, winning business audits and reviews and a benchmarking service that provides companies and professional firms with bespoke reports that compare their approaches, strategies and tactics with those of their competitors and peers.

Published best practice reports that are currently available include:

- *Winning Major Bids: The critical success factors,* which examines the processes and practices for winning business in competitive situations of 293 companies;
- *Bidding for Business in Construction, IT & Telecoms, Engineering and Manufacturing,* three best practice resource packs that include reports on critical success factors for winning business in particular sectors;
- *Bidding for Business: The skills agenda,* which covers the top 20 skills required;
- *The Contract Bid Manager's Toolkit,* containing 30 practical tools for winning contracts through successful bidding;
- *Winning New Business: The critical success factors,* reports covering the seven professions of management consultancy; advertising; accountancy; PR and marketing consultancy; engineering consultancy; IT consultancy; and law;
- *Developing Strategic Customers and Key Accounts: The critical success factors,* which examines the experiences and key customer relationship practices of 194 companies;
- *The Close to the Customer* series of 28 management briefings on particular customer relationship management issues and best practice in different business sectors;
- *Developing a Corporate Learning Strategy,* which examines training and development, learning and knowledge creation plans, priorities and practices;
- *Effective Purchasing: The critical success factors,* a review of the procurement strategies and practices of 296 European companies;
- *Managing Intellectual Capital to Grow Shareholder Value,* a comparative examination of how 'leader' and 'laggard' companies manage 20 different categories of intellectual property;
- *Pricing for Profit: The critical success factors,* a report that reveals how 'leader' companies achieve the benefits of effective pricing.

All of these reports and the *Close to the Customer* series of briefings on customer relationship management are published by Policy Publications Ltd, Bedford. Full details, including free brochures about each report and related benchmarking services, can be obtained from Policy Publications (tel: +44 (0)1234 328448; fax: +44 (0)1234 357231; e-mail: policypubs@kbnet.co.uk) or www.ntwkfirm.com/bookshop.

Further information about the winning business research and best practice programme can be obtained from its leader, Professor Colin Coulson-Thomas (tel: +44 (0)1733 361149; fax: +44 (0)1733 361459; e-mail: colinct@tiscali.co.uk).

References

Bartram, P (1996) *The Competitive Network*, Policy Publications, Bedford

Coulson-Thomas, C (1993a) *Creating Excellence in the Boardroom*, McGraw-Hill, London

Coulson-Thomas, C (1993b) *Developing Directors: Building an effective boardroom team*, McGraw-Hill, London

Coulson-Thomas, C (ed) (1994) *Business Process Re-engineering: Myth and reality*, Kogan Page, London

Coulson-Thomas, C (principal author) (1995) *The Responsive Organisation: Re-engineering new patterns of work*, Policy Publications, Bedford

Coulson-Thomas, C (1997) *The Future of the Organization: Achieving excellence through business transformation*, Kogan Page, London

Coulson-Thomas, C (1999a) *Developing a Corporate Learning Strategy: The key knowledge management challenge for the HR function*, Policy Publications, Bedford

Coulson-Thomas, C (1999b) *Individuals and Enterprise: Creating entrepreneurs for the new millennium through personal transformation*, Blackhall Publishing, Dublin

Coulson-Thomas, C (2000) *The Information Entrepreneur: Changing requirements for corporate and individual success*, 3Com Active Business Unit, Winnersh

Coulson-Thomas, C (2001) *Shaping Things to Come: Strategies for creating alternative enterprises*, Blackhall Publishing, Dublin

Coulson-Thomas, C (2002a) *Pricing for Profit: The critical success factors*, Policy Publications, Bedford

Coulson-Thomas, C (2002b) *Transforming the Company: Manage change, compete and win*, Kogan Page, London

FitzGerald, P (2000) *Effective Purchasing: The critical success factors*, Policy Publications, Bedford

Hurcomb, J (1998) *Developing Strategic Customers and Key Accounts: The critical success factors*, Policy Publications, Bedford

Kennedy, C and O'Connor, M (1997) *Winning Major Bids: The critical success factors*, Policy Publications, Bedford

Perrin, S (2000) *Managing Intellectual Capital to Grow Shareholder Value*, Policy Publications, Bedford

Thompson, E and Eisenfeld, B (2000a) *Top 10 Management Failings in Sales Technology Rollouts*, Research Note, 3 November, Gartner Group, Egham, Surrey

Thompson, E and Eisenfeld, B (2000b) *Top 10 Technology Failings in Sales Technology Rollouts*, Research Note, 21 November, Gartner Group, Egham, Surrey

Further reading

Argyris, C (1994) *On Organizational Learning*, Blackwell, Oxford

Aubrey, R and Cohan, P (1995) *Working Wisdom: Timeless skills and vanguard strategies for learning organizations*, Jossey Bass, San Francisco, CA

Beaver, G (2002) *Small Business, Entrepreneurship and Enterprise Development*, Financial Times Prentice Hall, Harlow

Bokin, J (1999) *Smart Business: How knowledge communities can revolutionize your company*, Free Press, New York

Breu, K (2002) *Developing a High Performance Workforce: Practical strategies for exploiting knowledge in the intelligent enterprise*, Financial Times Prentice Hall/Cranfield University School of Management, London

Bukowitz, W and Williams, R (1999) *The Knowledge Management Fieldbook*, Pearson Education, Harlow

Burgoyne, J, Pedler, M and Boydell, T (1994) *Towards the Learning Company: Concepts and practices*, McGraw-Hill, Maidenhead

Burton Jones, A (1999) *Knowledge Capitalism, Business, Work and Learning in the New Economy*, Oxford University Press, Oxford

Carter, S (ed) (2000) *Enterprise and Small Business: Principles, practice and policy*, Pearson Education, Harlow

Chase, R (1998) *Creating a Knowledge Management Business Strategy: Delivering bottom line results*, Management Trends International, Lavendon

Coulson-Thomas, C (1999) *Developing a Corporate Learning Strategy: The key knowledge management challenge for the HR function*, Policy Publications, Bedford

Coulson-Thomas, C (1999) *Individuals and Enterprise: Creating entrepreneurs for the new millennium through personal transformation*, Blackhall Publishing, Dublin

Coulson-Thomas, C (2000) *The Information Entrepreneur: Changing requirements for corporate and individual success*, 3Com Active Business Unit, Winnersh

Coulson-Thomas, C (2001) *Shaping Things to Come: Strategies for creating alternative enterprises*, Blackhall Publishing, Dublin

Coulson-Thomas, C (2002) *Transforming the Company: Manage change, compete and win*, Kogan Page, London

Davenport, T and Prusak, L (1998) *Working Knowledge: How organisations manage what they know*, Harvard Business School Press, Boston, MA

Davis, S and Botkin, J (1994) *The Monster under the Bed: How business is mastering the opportunity of knowledge for profit*, Simon & Schuster, London

Deakins, D (2002) *Entrepreneurship and Small Firms*, McGraw-Hill Education, Maidenhead

Dixon, N (2000) *Common Knowledge: How companies thrive by sharing what they know*, Harvard Business School Press, Boston, MA

Evans, C (2000) *Developing a Knowledge Creating Culture*, Roffey Park Institute, Horsham

Gamble, P and Blackwell, J (2001) *Knowledge Management: A state of the art guide*, Kogan Page, London

Garvey, B and Williamson, B (2002) *Beyond Knowledge Management: Dialogue creativity and the corporate curriculum*, Financial Times Prentice Hall, Harlow

Guns, B and Anundsen, K (1996) *Faster Learning Organization: Gain and sustain the competitive edge*, Pfeiffer, San Diego, CA

Hisrich, R and Peters, M (1998) *Entrepreneurship*, Irwin/McGraw-Hill, Boston, MA

Huseman, R and Goodman, J (1999) *Leading with Knowledge: The nature of competition in the 21st century*, Sage, Thousand Oaks, CA

Klein, D (1998) *The Strategic Management of Intellectual Capital*, Butterworth Heinemann, Boston, MA

Koulopoulos, T and Frappaolo, C (1999) *Smart Things to Know About Knowledge Management*, Capstone, Oxford

McGill, M and Slocum, J (1994) *The Smarter Organization: How to build a business that learns and adapts to marketplace needs*, John Wiley, New York

Perrin, S (2000) *Managing Intellectual Capital to Grow Shareholder Value*, Policy Publications, Bedford

Pfeffer, J and Sutton, R (1999) *The Knowing Doing Gap: How smart companies turn knowledge into action*, Harvard Business School Press, Boston, MA

Probst, G, Raub, S and Romhardt, K (2000) *Managing Knowledge: Building blocks for success*, John Wiley, Chichester

Sabroski, S (2002) *Supersearchers Make It on their Own: Top independent information professionals share their secrets for starting and running a research business*, CyberAge Books, Medford, NJ

Sanchez, R (ed) (2001) *Knowledge Management and Organizational Competence*, Oxford University Press, Oxford

Skyrme, D (1999) *Knowledge Networking: Creating the collaborative enterprise*, Butterworth Heinemann, Oxford

Skyrme, D (2001) *Capitalizing on Knowledge: From e business to k business*, Butterworth Heinemann, Oxford

Stewart, T (1997) *Intellectual Capital: The new wealth of organisations*, Nicholas Brealey, London

Stewart, T (2001) *The Wealth of Knowledge: Intellectual capital and the twenty first century organization*, Nicholas Brealey, London

Sveiby, K (1997) *The New Organizational Wealth: Managing and measuring knowledge based assets*, Berrett Koehler, San Francisco, CA

Tobin, D (1996) *Transformational Learning: Renewing your company through knowledge and skills*, John Wiley, New York

Weitzen, S (1991) *Infopreneurs: Turning data into dollars*, John Wiley, New York

Zack, M (ed) (1999) *Knowledge and Strategy*, Butterworth Heinemann, Boston, MA

Index

ageing societies   147–48, 221
aims, purpose and scope of book   18–23
  checklist of questions to address
    22–23

balance   37–38, 88, 93–94
Bartram, P 100, 229
best practice   165
  examples   206–09
  research/reports   226–28
business process re-engineering (BPR)
  110

change, threat of   27
checklists
  aspiring entrepreneurs   196–98
  assessing knowledge-based
    opportunities   170–72
  becoming a knowledge entrepreneur
    208–09
  collaboration   142–44
  contemporary information problems
    95–96
  creating enterprise cultures   144–46
  directors'   134–37
  employees'   186–88
  identifying and assessing specific
    opportunities   180–82

information- and knowledge-based
  offerings   193–94
  managers'   90–92
  managing knowledge and intellectual
    capital   40–42
  monitoring trends and scope for
    entrepreneurship   159–61
  questions to address   22–23
  requirements of different stakeholders
    123–24
  strategic opportunity   14–17
  winning business   222–24
commodity knowledge   49
compatability analysis   127
Competitiveness, Centre for (University of
    Luton)   21, 45, 163, 169, 226 see
    also Web sites
competitor intelligence   10
complexity to simplicity analysis
  155–56
consumer research   10
contemporary information problems
  76–96
  barriers to entry   89–92
    managers' checklist   90–92
    uncertainty   90
  changing organizations and emerging
    issues   92–96

balance 93–94
    holistic perspective 94
    information explosion 93
    overvaluing knowledge per se 93
checklist 95–96
impact and reaction analysis (exercise)
    80
information overload 76–78
likes and dislikes 77–78
missed opportunities 87–88
    lack of balance 88
    rationalization v inspiration 87
    re-engineering 87–88
single solutions, the search for 80–83
    confronting reality 82–83
    core competencies 81
taking approaches too far 83–86
    bespoke responses 84
    generalists v specialists 83
    multi-skilling 83
    obstacles and barriers analysis 85–86
    re-engineering 85
winners/losers 76–78
winning and losing 78–80
core competencies 28, 81
corporate environment, the 214–16
    customers and investors 215
    independent entrepreneurs 215
    share ownership, option or profit-
        sharing 215
    tug-of-war analysis (exercise) 215–16
corporate learning and knowledge
    creation 43–75
    checklist 68–69
    freedom analysis (exercise) 47–48
    intellectual capital, protecting 65–66
    knowledge and learning 48–52
        analysis paralysis 49
        commodity knowledge 49
        reflection v daydreaming 49
        using knowledge entrepreneurs
            49–50
    knowledge as flow v stock 46–48
        information- and knowledge-sharing
            46–47
        shared learning, importance of 46
    knowledge creation 43–45
        as end-to-end process 45
        fundamental questions 44
    knowledge creation as corporate
        priority 52–64
        corporate learning/enterprise centre,
            establishing a 56–64 see also
            main entry
        expenditure 55
        findings of corporate learning
            investigation 54

learning partners/learning catalysts
    53
knowledge entrepreneurs, skills and
    uses of 66–75
learning as a business opportunity
    (exercise) 51
people, process and organization
    (appendix/checklist) 70–75
    process accountability 75
    process context 74–75
    process control 74
    process documentation 71
    process management 71–72
    process operation and support
        72–73
    process ownership and status
        70–71
    process review and revision 73
    process vision 70
work experience analysis (exercise)
    45
corporate learning/enterprise centre,
    establishing a 56–64, 137–42
    academic quality 60–61
    background 56
    collaborative arrangements 63–64
    constitution 57–58
    corporate context 57
    customers 62–63
    enterprise support 61
    learning assessment 63
    performance assessment 64
    programmes 61–62
    resources 58–59
    role and purpose 57
    staffing 59–60
corporate partners, selecting 213–14
    lift-off analysis (exercise) 214
Cotoco Ltd 21, 175, 177, 178 see also
    Web sites
    INDeX Engineers Toolkit 178
creating information- and knowledge-
    based offerings see information-
    and knowledge-based offerings
customers see stakeholders,
    requirements of different

Developing a Corporate Learning
    Strategy 54, 55

eBusiness Innovations Awards 21 see
    also Web sites
Eisenfeld, B 177, 189, 230
electronic publishing 7, 168
electronic tutoring/counselling 165
enterprise cultures, creating 125–46
    becoming a player 125–27

checklist   144–46
collaboration checklist   142
compatability analysis (exercise)   127
directors' checklist   134–37
greenhouse analysis (exercise)   128
organizing for entrepreneurship
   128–31
reconciling people and organizations
   (exercise)   130–31
setting up independent corporate
   learning/enterprise centre   137–42
ten essential freedoms   132–33
unity and diversity   131–32
working with employers   127–28
entrepreneurs, communities of   217–18
entrepreneurship, routes to   210–11
   voyage analysis (exercise)   211
entrepreneurship in the knowledge
   economy   1–23
   abundant and accessible information
      1–3
   help, the need for   12–13
   implications, impacts and consequences
      3–6
   job support tools   18
   knowledge entrepreneur, the   13–18
      see also main entry
      skills and qualities of   13–14
   knowledge-based opportunities   6–11
      gap analysis (exercise)   11
      information- and knowledge-based
         businesses – examples   6–11
   looking beneath the surface (exercise)
      17–18
   strategic opportunity checklist   14–17
exercises
   balance between action and reaction
      37–38
   breakout analysis   103
   compatability analysis   127
   complexity to simplicity analysis
      155–56
   confronting reality   82–83
   defining a new role   176
   establishing fundamentals of success
      30–31
   freedom analysis   47–48
   gain and loss analysis   174
   gap analysis   11
   greenhouse analysis   128
   identifying value-based opportunities
      203–04
   impact and reaction analysis   80
   incremental opportunity analysis   190
   information and knowledge
      entrepreneurship   192
   learning as a business opportunity   51

lift-off analysis   214
likes and dislikes   77–78
looking beneath the surface   17–18
'more of' and 'less of' analysis   99
obstacles and barriers analysis   85–86
organizational support opportunity
   analysis   158–59
people-centred ways of working
   151–52
potential for collective action   178–80
reconciling people and organizations
   130–31
self-assessment for changing direction
   219–20
time analysis   108–09
tug-of-war analysis   215–16
visioning   200–01
volcano analysis   26
voyage analysis   211
weather-watch and weathervane
   analysis   149
work experience analysis   45
Eyretel   36, 173, 175, 178, 186

Fitzgerald, P   98, 230
freedom analysis   47–48
Freedom of Information Act   1
freedoms, essential   132–33
further reading   231–33

gain and loss analysis   174
gap analysis   11
Gartner Group research   177, 189
getting started   210–28
   checklist   225–26
   communities of entrepreneurs, creating
      217–18
   corporate environment, the   214–16
   corporate partners, selecting
      213–14
   entrepreneurship, routes to   210–11
      see also main entry
   hobby into business   211–13
   learning and entrepreneurship
      218–20 see also main entry
   public policy requirements   220–22
      see also main entry
   winning business checklist   222–24
greenhouse analysis   128

hobby into business   211–13
holistic perspective   26, 94, 106, 113
homes/offices as information/knowledge
   resource centres   9
Hurcomb, J   100, 105, 230

impact and reaction analysis   80

incremental opportunity analysis 190
in-depth expertise 4
information
    availability of 3
    direct access to 3
    disadvantages 2
    education, effect on 5
    free 3
    overload 2
Information Entrepreneur, The 32
information- and knowledge-based
    businesses 6–11
information- and knowledge-based
    offerings 183–94
    building job support tools 185–86
    checklist 193–94
    differentiation 191–92
    employees' checklist 186–88
    incremental opportunity analysis
        (exercise) 190
    information and knowledge
        entrepreneurship (exercise) 192
    lessons that can be learnt 188–90
    packaging what you know 183–85
information- and knowledge-sharing
    46–47
Innovation Group, The (TIG) 175
Integrated Communications for Business
    (ICB) 175, 177
intellectual capital 163 *see also*
    managing knowledge and intellectual
    capital protecting 65–66
interactive learning 166
International Labour Organization (ILO)
    19
Internet 1, 7, 12, 20, 32, 36, 125, 168,
    176, 200, 205
investors 101–03
investors' checklist 33–35
issue monitoring/management 10,
    168

job support tools 5, 32, 51, 55, 83, 99,
    104, 132–33, 157, 175–76, 185–86,
    188–90, 205–06
    3Com 175
    Avaya 207
    benefits of using 177–78
    Bolero 175, 177, 186
    Cisco 175, 188
    Dana GVB 175, 178, 185–86
    knowledge-based 167
    Navigator sales support 177, 186
    product launch 204–06

Kennedy, C 87, 105, 230
knowledge economy 1–23

knowledge entrepreneur, the 13–18, 83,
    105, 106, 113, 195–209
    advantages of a product launch support
        tool 205–06
    aspiring entrepreneurs' checklist
        196–98
    best practice, using examples of
        206–09
    checklist 208–09
    creating a new product launch support
        tool 204–05
    entrepreneurial qualities 195–98
    identifying value-based opportunities
        (exercise) 203–04
    new products, launching 202–03
    product launch support tools 204–06
        K-frame 205
    qualities and skills of 198–200
        addressing needs 199
        focus on future 200
        motivations 199
        shaping the future 199
    researching/exploiting opportunities
        201
    skills and uses of 66–75
    using 49–50
    visioning (exercise) 200–01
knowledge frameworks 5, 7–8, 21,
    36–37, 167
    K-frame 5, 7–8, 21, 36, 37, 205 *see
    also* Web sites
knowledge management 4 *see also*
    managing knowledge and intellectual
    capital
knowledge map 26
knowledge-related counselling/support
    8

leaders/laggards 31–33
learning, interactive 166
learning and entrepreneurship 218–20
    academic research/professional
        investigation 218
    learning partnerships 218
    self-assessment for changing direction
        (exercise) 219–20
learning as a business opportunity
    (exercise) 51
learning needs analysis/learning outcomes
    167
learning partners/learning catalysts 53
learning support 164–69
    assessment questionnaires 167
    auditing/assessment, testing/monitoring
        167
    courses and qualifications 167
    customized searches 165

electronic publishing   168
electronic tutor/counsellor   165
guide on assessment/best practice   165
integrating learning approaches   166
interactive learning   166
issue monitoring/management   168
knowledge framework   167
knowledge-based job support tools
     167
learning needs analysis/learning
     outcomes   167
learning technologies   166
market trading/brokering services   168
one-to-one counselling   165
online catalogues/newsletters/discussion
     groups   168
personal tutors/workgroup advisers
     165
public relations activities   167
stand-in/support services   165
virtual campus stores   168
virtual learning provision   166
learning technologies   166
location-independent work   5

*Managing Intellectual Capital to Grow
     Shareholder Value*   31, 32, 35
managing knowledge and intellectual
     capital   24–42
   balance between action and reaction
      (exercise)   37–38
   checklist   40–42
   establishing fundamentals of success
      (exercise)   30–31
   knowledge exploitation   31–35
      intellectual capital   32–33
      investors' checklist   33–35
      leaders/laggards   31–33
   knowledge frameworks   35–38
      compatability with Internet/mobile
         technologies   36
      K-frame   36, 37 *see also* Web sites
   knowledge management   24–26
      knowledge map   26
   loss of knowledge   26–31
      change, threat of   27
      core competencies   28
      multi-skilling   27–28
      outsourcing   28
      re-engineering/dumbsizing   27
      technology/upgrades   29
   premium knowledge   38–40
   volcano analysis (exercise)   26
medicine, evidence-based   5
monitoring trends and scope for
     knowledge entrepreneurship
     147–61

ageing societies   147–48
   checklist   159–61
   current information, access to   148
   effective issue monitoring   154–56
      complexity to simplicity analysis
         (exercise) 155–56
   freedom of operation   147–49
   issues and implications, understanding
      149–54
      issue monitoring and management
         152–54
      people-centred ways of working
         (exercise)   151–52
   wealth creation, supporting   157–69
      organizational support opportunity
         analysis (exercise)   158–59
   weather-watch and weathervane
      analysis (exercise)   149
multi-skilling   27–28, 83

O'Connor, M   87, 105, 230
obstacles and barriers analysis   85–86
online information services   7
online markets   10
opinion surveys/lobby campaigns   10
opportunities – identifying and assessing
     specific   162–82
   assessing knowledge-based
      opportunities – checklist   170–72
   benefits of using support tools
      177–82
   checklist   180–82
   defining a new role (exercise)   176
   job support tools   175–76
   learning support as business
      opportunity   164–69 *see also*
         learning support
   performance improvement
      opportunities, searching for   169–72
   potential for collective action (exercise)
      178–80
   sales productivity, improving   173–75
      gain and loss analysis (exercise)
         174
search criteria, establishing   162–69
   asking Father Christmas (exercise)
      164
      central corporate services   163
      funding requirements   163
      intellectual capital   163
organizational support opportunity
     analysis   158–59
outsourcing   28

Perrin, S   21, 31, 32, 35, 39, 104, 105,
     109, 112, 163, 230
process management   71–72, 83

process/organization checklist   70–75
   accountability   75
   context   74–75
   control   74
   documentation   71
   management   71–72
   operation and support   72–73
   ownership and status   70–71
   review and revision   73
   vision   70
project management   9
promotional campaigns   10
public policy requirements   220–22
   ageing societies   221
   employment costs   221
   EU restrictions   221
   incentives and tax breaks   221
   physical-location-free ventures   222
   stealth taxes   221
   use of English language   222
public relations   10
public services, online delivery of   5

re-engineering   4, 27, 55, 85, 87–88, 94
reconciling people and organizations
   130–31
references   229–30

stakeholders, requirements of different
   97–124
   boards, contribution of   103–06
      commodity product status   105
      effectiveness   103–04
      holistic perspective   106
      physical assets/hard issues, bias
         towards   104
   breakout analysis (exercise)   103
   checklist   123–24
   customers   97–99
   inevitable progress – the myth
      107–09
      time analysis (exercise)   108–09
   investors   101–03
   leadership for learning   112–24
      board meetings as learning events
         112
      learning and review processes   113
   'more of' and 'less of' analysis
      (exercise)   99
   questions to be asked by
      board/management   114–22
      chairman   114–15
      facilities and infrastructure director
         121–22
      financial director   118–19
      information technology director
         120

managing director   115–17
personnel director   119–20
research and development director
   121
sales and marketing director
   117–18
suppliers and business partners
   99–101
supportive approaches to management
   109–12
   business process re-engineering (BPR)
      110
   forging new relationships   111
   key areas of knowledge/
      understanding   111–12
   superstars   110–11
   total quality management (TQM)
      110
strategic opportunity checklist
   14–17
success, establishing fundamentals of
   (exercise)   30–31
support activities   9
support tools   see job support tools
SWOT analyses   220

Thompson, E   177, 189, 230
time analysis   108–09
total quality management (TQM)   110
tug-of-war analysis   215–16

University of Luton Centre for
   Competitiveness   21 see also Web
   sites

virtual campus stores   168
virtual communities   10–11
virtual learning provision   166
visioning   200–01
volcano analysis   26
voyage analysis   211

weather-watch and weathervane analysis
   149
Web sites
   Cotoco Ltd: www.cotoco.com   21
   eBusiness Innovations Awards:
      www.ecommerce-awards.com
      21
   knowledge management framework:
      www.K-frame.com   21
   University of Luton Centre for
      Competitiveness:
      www.luton.ac.uk/cfc   21
   www.ntwkfirm.com   21, 227
winning business research   226–28
work experience analysis   45